A RHETORIC OF THE *DECAMERON*

D1594587

Both a passionate denunciation of masculinist readings of the *Decameron* and a meticulous critique of previous feminist analyses, Marilyn Migiel's *A Rhetoric of the Decameron* offers a sophisticated re-examination of the representations of women, men, gender identity, sexuality, love, hate, morality, and truth in Boccaccio's masterpiece. The *Decameron* stages an ongoing, dynamic, and spirited debate about issues as urgent now as in the fourteenth century – a debate that can only be understood if the *Decameron*'s rhetorical objectives and strategies are completely reconceived.

Addressing herself equally to those who argue for a proto-feminist Boccaccio – a quasi-liberal champion of women's autonomy – and to those who argue for a positivistically secure, historical Boccaccio who could not possibly anticipate the concerns of the twenty-first century, Migiel challenges readers to pay attention to Boccaccio's language, to his pronouns, his passives, his patterns of repetition, and his figurative language. She argues that human experience, particularly in the sexual realm, is articulated differently by the *Decameron*'s male and female narrators, and refutes the notion that the *Decameron* offers an undifferentiated celebration of Eros. Ultimately, Migiel contends, the stories of the *Decameron* suggest that as women become more empowered, the limitations on them, including the threat of violence, become more insistent.

(Toronto Italian Studies)

MARILYN MIGIEL is an associate professor in the Department of Romance Studies at Cornell University.

A RHETORIC
OF THE
Decameron

Marilyn Migiel

UNIVERSITY OF TORONTO PRESS
Toronto Buffalo London

© University of Toronto Press Incorporated 2003
Toronto Buffalo London
Printed in Canada

ISBN 0-8020-8819-8 (cloth)
ISBN 0-8020-8594-6 (paper)

Printed on acid-free paper

Toronto Italian Studies

National Library of Canada Cataloguing in Publication

Migiel, Marilyn, 1954–
A rhetoric of the Decameron / Marilyn Migiel.

(Toronto Italian studies)
Includes bibliographical references and index.
ISBN 0-8020-8819-8 (bound)   ISBN 0-8020-8594-6 (pbk.)

1. Boccaccio, Giovanni, 1313–1375. Decamerone.   I. Title.   II. Series.

PQ4287.M54 2003   853'.1   C2003-903297-3

This book has been published with the assistance of a grant from the
Hull Memorial Publication Fund of Cornell University.

University of Toronto Press acknowledges the financial assistance to its publishing program of the Canada Council for the Arts and the Ontario Arts Council.

University of Toronto Press acknowledges the financial support for its
publishing activities of the Government of Canada through the
Book Publishing Industry Development Program (BPIDP).

For my students of the *Decameron*

Contents

Acknowledgments

My greatest debt is to the students who, since the late 1980s, read, discussed, debated, and wrote about the *Decameron* with me, and therefore it is to them that I have dedicated this book. They appeared not only as graduate and undergraduate students in upper-level seminars on the *Decameron*, in independent studies, and in reading groups, but also as students in freshman writing courses, Cornell Summer College courses for high-school juniors, and the occasional Telluride Association Summer Program afternoon seminar. Special recognition goes to the youngest students – mainly freshmen in my Freshman Writing Seminar entitled 'The Craft of Storytelling' – who were most open to thinking about the *Decameron* in new ways and who came to the *Decameron* with questions and responses that encouraged new ideas and critical reflection on my part. I have always set great store by the animated debates we had and the joy we found in looking for new ways to write about the *Decameron*.

If I owe a debt to my students, and particularly to the students in my writing courses, then I also owe a debt to the colleagues who love writing, who love literature, and who inspired my ongoing work with the J.S. Knight Institute for Writing in the Disciplines. These colleagues made my ongoing collaboration with students a real possibility: Mary Gaylord, who encouraged me to participate in a faculty seminar on teaching writing in the early 1990s; Jim Slevin of Georgetown University, who directed that seminar; Katy Gottschalk, director of the Freshman Writing Program; and Jonathan Monroe, director of the J.S. Knight Institute for Writing in the Disciplines.

To my colleagues Bill Kennedy, John Najemy, and Kathleen Long I extend thanks for their long-time support and for their intelligent, cordial, and discriminating readings. Alice Colby-Hall, who values teaching and writing about medieval texts, has always been exemplary for her astuteness, her precision, and her ability to assess evidence; she has been an invaluable model in this respect. Beverly Ballaro – briefly a Cornell colleague, now a writer and editor in the 'real world' – has always been inspirational to me for her ability to see through to the quick of a matter. Dolora Wojciehowski offered expert and nuanced readings of portions of this manuscript. Giancarlo Lombardi, Gina Psaki, Disa Gambera, Alan Smith, Suzanne Hagedorn, Carlo Zei, Lynn Laufenberg, Mary DeCoste, Natasha Chang, and Irene Eibenstein-Alvisi deserve thanks not only for the feedback they provided when they were graduate students at Cornell but for the insights they provided as full-fledged members of the profession. To Giancarlo I extend special thanks for his friendship, his warm encouragement, and ongoing dialogue. I warmly thank Italianist colleagues (many of them also members of the American Boccaccio Association) who responded to my work both at conference and lecture presentations: Penny Marcus, Vicky Kirkham, Michael Sherberg, Christopher Kleinhenz, Stefania Lucamante, Eugenio Giusti, and Stefano Cracolici. Discussions with some fellow colleagues (Leslie Zarker Morgan, John McLucas, Ann Marie Rasmussen, and Barbara Spackman) span a period that goes back to our days at Yale; these exchanges have been vital for me. I thank Eve Salisbury and Georgiana Donavin for the opportunity to present at the Medieval Institute in Kalamazoo the early version of chapter 7, 'Domestic Violence in the *Decameron*,' and for their apt editorial interventions, which helped shape that portion of the book.

I gratefully acknowledge permission to reproduce in this book portions of it that were previously published elsewhere. Part of chapter 2 originally appeared as 'How (thanks to a woman) Andreuccio da Perugia became such a loser, and how (also thanks to a woman) reading could have become a more complicated affair,' *Romance Languages Annual* 10 (1999): 302–7. Part of chapter 6 originally appeared as 'Encrypted Messages: Men, Women, and Figurative Language in *Decameron* 5.4,' *Philological Quarterly* 77 (1998): 1–13. Chapter 7 originally appeared as 'Domestic Violence in the *Decameron*,' in Eve Salisbury, Georgiana Donavin, and Merrall Pryce, eds, *Domestic Violence in Medieval Texts* (Gainesville: University Press of Florida, 2002), 164–79; it is reprinted here with permission of the University Press of Florida.

Boccaccio knew that, in the risky business of living, one always needs friends to make it through. Janie Sue Brooks – observer of the world,

writer, teacher, thinker, ruthless reviser of prose, and above all, friend –
often provided me with a much-needed perspective on life events.

I suppose Boccaccio didn't quite have to deal with the risky business
of publishing as it exists in the twenty-first century, but if he had had to,
he certainly would have known that one always needs an editor to make
it through. Ron Schoeffel of the University of Toronto Press has been
the wise and judicious presence that ultimately made this book possible.

Note on Citations of the *Decameron*

In citing the Italian text of the *Decameron*, I have relied on Giovanni Boccaccio, *Decameron*, ed. Vittore Branca (Milan: Mondadori, 1985). Italian passages from the *Decameron* are identified not by page number but by Day, novella, and section (i.e., *comma*). Thus '2.9.67' should be understood as '*Decameron*, Day 2, novella 9, comma (or section) 67.'

For the English translation, I have relied on Giovanni Boccaccio, *The Decameron*, trans. Mark Musa and Peter Bondanella (New York: Mentor, 1982). The citations of this English translation are by page number.

A RHETORIC OF THE *DECAMERON*

Introduction

A Rhetoric of the *Decameron* (and why women should read it)

I have written this study of Boccaccio's *Decameron* because it made real many of the questions I have been asking over and over, and in a variety of contexts, for the last decade. In the *Decameron* (written ca. 1349–51), seven women and three men struggle to claim authority for competing narratives about institutions and individuals. Contemporaneously, Author and readers (male Author and imagined female readers) struggle to find the place or places from which they may hear, re-articulate, and respond to the one hundred stories told by these seven women and three men.[1] The *Decameron* is concerned with power and knowledge, with reading and narrating. It ponders the possibility of human action in a changing social, ethical, and moral landscape. It explores gender, and yes, in accord with its reputation, it is also most concerned with sexuality. It asks questions like, What sort of storytellers and readers are we? Who gets to decide what the master narratives and readings are? What are the proper roles for men and women in these social and cultural investments? These feel like life and death matters to the ten narrators portrayed in the *Decameron*. Indeed, storytelling *is* a matter of survival for them: they tell stories while they are momentarily safe from the Black Death that rages in their native city of Florence.[2]

Questions like these reverberate in our own communities every time that we come up against the mysterious workings of matter and the amazing and terrifying power of representations to alter lives. How to sustain life as we know it, or as we wish it to be? Pushed to the edge, what sort of life do we wish to preserve? And given that this discussion happens, at least presumably, among members of different sexes and sexual preference, different races, different ethnic groups, different classes, how can we come to a mutually satisfying set of narratives about ourselves, one that guarantees justice and fosters individual pursuit of happiness? These are heavy questions, and the *Decameron*, in its light-hearted way, has a good deal to tell us about how we might answer them.

My book addresses the branch of these questions that regards woman. When I read the *Decameron*, I see as cardinal the strategies used to control discourses about women, their agency, and their sexuality – and I am, to tell the truth, deeply disturbed to see how deep-rooted these strategies remain to this very day. By this, I do not mean that the *Decameron* is a 'bad' work, that Giovanni Boccaccio should be censured as a misogynist writer, or that we could not also find within the *Decameron* a variety of discourses about gender and sexuality that would be liberating for women. Fundamentally, I read the *Decameron* not as a work that dictates which sort of narratives will be best for women, but rather as a work that invites us to reflect on how narratives can be used for good or ill. These two reading stances imply two different types of rhetorics. In the former, the prime focus of a rhetorical inquiry would Author-centred: we would ask questions such as 'Of what does the Author wish to persuade us?' The latter way of reading, to which I subscribe, places much more responsibility on the reader, whose active engagement with the text is required to produce meaning.

If the reader is to assume this responsibility, she must also be aware of how the Author of the *Decameron* seeks to position her as he addresses himself to women readers, specifically to women in love. He offers his book as consolation – or so he claims in his preface to his book. What this means has been a subject of debate. As far as we know, medieval and early modern women were not usually the owners, copiers, and readers of the *Decameron*. As Victoria Kirkham notes, 'History ... informs us that the *Decameron*'s most avid early readers belonged to the very group whom [Boccaccio] is least concerned about reaching: powerful men of business. Marginal account records in the oldest manuscripts attest to the profession of their owners, who bore such distinguished names as Buondelmonti, Acciaiuoli, Bonaccorsi, Cavalcanti, and Verazzano.'[3] Indeed, it appears Boccaccio might not have meant women to read his book at all. In 1373 (granted, Boccaccio's assessment of women seems not to have improved after several decades of contact with Petrarch and humanism), Boccaccio wrote to Maghinardo Cavalcanti:

> I cannot praise your having allowed the honorable ladies of your household to read my trifles, rather I beg you to give me your word you will not do so again. You know how much they contain that is less than decent and

offensive to propriety, how much sting from the unwelcome Venus, how many incitements to vice even for those of iron will; and even if they do not drive to indecent behavior illustrious women, most especially those with brows marked by holy chastity, nevertheless illicit burnings slip in with silent step and not infrequently penetrate and irritate unchaste souls with the obscene wasting of concupiscence, a thing to be avoided at all costs ... Readers will suppose me a smutty panderer, an incestuous old man, an impure person, a foul-mouthed scandalmonger, avid to bruit about people's wickedness. I will not always find someone to stand up and excuse me by saying, 'He wrote this in his youth, compelled by the authority of one more powerful.'[4]

This communication, as Kirkham points out, 'complicates matters.'[5] Were there fourteenth-century women readers of the *Decameron?* Maybe, maybe not. Kirkham puts aside the question of historical readership to show, very expertly, that Boccaccio represented his audience of lovelorn ladies by drawing on Ovidian and other literary representations of women poised for a downfall on account of their lustfulness. In so doing, Kirkham deflates the 'admirably chivalrous gesture' of the *Decameron*'s preface.[6]

So far, this seems quite reasonable. The Author of the *Decameron* is representing his female audience according to paradigms offered him by literary antecedents, much as later he will model his description of the Black Death of 1348 on the account of a sixth-century plague in Paulus Diaconus (720–99?), *Historia Langobardorum* (*The History of the Langobards*). It is the next step in Kirkham's argument that makes me pause. She takes the Author's representation of women as lustful to mean that female readers are being adequately warned: When you read the *Decameron*, choose well whom you wish to imitate! Don't choose Ghismonda (4.1), Elena (8.7), Alatiel (2.7), or Madonna Filippa (6.7). Choose instead to be one of the 'model wives, the paragon being patient, obedient Griselda (X 10).'[7] It seems from this that it would suffice for the female reader to choose licit love, sanctioned by marriage, over extra-marital dalliances. While I would agree with Kirkham that the *Decameron* does in many cases illustrate the deleterious consequences of illicit love, I am not entirely sure that it makes an unqualified case for embracing licit love, sanctioned by marriage, over illicit alliances, and I am even less sure that we should accept Griselda as an exemplar for imitation in our own lives. As a result, I would be hard pressed to say that there is any clear guidance from the book; rather, I would urge us to examine more closely the ways in which the stories of the *Decameron* lead us to see how difficult it is to take one side or the other.

What does this mean with specific reference to the Author–reader relationship? Many readers have accepted without much ado the Author's claim that his book is addressed to a female audience sorely in need of his consolatory services. Were we to stop focusing on the womanly defects that Giovanni Boccaccio created in his fictional Author's audience, however, we might see the dubious benefits that accrue to the Author. If that Author were to address himself to an audience that were more critical, more discriminating, he would find himself in a tight squeeze.

Not only does the Author of the *Decameron* write for a female public that is presumably more accepting of his proffered gift, he will later respond to male critics on Day 4 of the *Decameron*, the better to limit the kinds of criticism imagined to be permissible. Some readers of the Introduction to Day 4, seeing the mention of male readers who scoff contemptuously at an Author who writes for women's pleasure and benefit, have taken this as proof that the first three days of the *Decameron* were distributed for comment before the entire work was completed. There is, however, not a shred of historical evidence to back this up. In my opinion, these constructed male critics serve quite a different function. The very fact that they are *male* implies that criticisms of the Author are not rising from female quarters; the presence of critics who stormily contest the Author's decision to try to please and console women readers in fact bolsters the Author's claim, yet to be proven, that he does in fact write to please and console women.

In framing the audience as he does, does not the Author of the *Decameron* – and behind him, Giovanni Boccaccio – lay a snare for the reader? No reader's subject position is a particularly good one. Either we take up the position of the fictive welcoming audience as he defines it (passive, lovelorn females) or we accept a variety of other subject positions that are also less than desirable. We could take up the position of active industrious females – but then why would we be reading this book? We could be voyeurs with respect to the female audience – but then one has the sense of being engaged in illicit activity, and a male engaged in illicit activity at that. We could be critical of the Author – but we are then manoeuvered, via his defence in the Introduction to Day 4, into looking as if we are dismissive of women. Thus, the Author manages to channel the reader into identifying with a non-existent audience (i.e., the women the Author spuriously claims as his audience) or identifying with an audience for whom the Author claims never to have intended to write (men).

Given this constant displacement of the reader, it isn't so terribly easy to read the *Decameron* at all – let alone with a specific ideological orientation in mind. The experience of feminist readers confirms this. [8] About ten to twelve years ago, mostly at Italianist conferences held in the United States, readers of explicitly feminist disposition turned a quizzical eye on Boccaccio's *Decameron*. Was it possible to talk about Boccaccio as a 'proto-feminist,' given that Boccaccio addresses the *Decameron* to women and his characters do not always embrace traditional ideals of female virtue? What evidence was there that the *Decameron* was pro-woman? Should we classify Boccaccio instead as a misogynist, given the pronounced anti-woman sentiment of certain novellas in the *Decameron* and of his last fictional work, the *Corbaccio?*[9] As a result of the fervour surrounding these questions, Gina Psaki and Thomas Stillinger compiled a volume entitled *Boccaccio and Feminist Criticism*, to which I contributed an essay entitled 'The Untidy Business of Gender Studies: Or, Why It's Almost Useless to Ask if the *Decameron* Is Feminist.'[10] By now, however, many of the voices from the early 1990s seem to have receded. Perhaps it is that readers have finally seen the uselessness of arguing about whether Boccaccio was a feminist or not. In any case, it doesn't appear that our understanding of gendered viewpoints in the *Decameron* has made much headway.

What keeps us from making progress in feminist readings of this work? How might feminist readers benefit from thinking about the *Decameron*'s rhetoric? And how can a feminist reading open up for us the reading experience of works like the *Decameron* in the way that other reading practices have not yet been able to do? In order to begin to answer some of these questions, we need to consider why feminist readings of the *Decameron* have not yet come to be recognized as germane.

During the time that I was writing this book on Boccaccio and feminist criticism that follows, the illustrious Italian scholar Vittore Branca, widely acclaimed both in Italy and in the United States as the 'dean' of Boccaccio studies, advanced a critique of feminist revisionism in the United States. His views appeared in a newspaper article entitled 'Isolate dal femminismo' ('Women Isolated by Feminism') and published in *Il Sole – 24 ore* (roughly the equivalent of the *Wall Street Journal*) on 17 November 1996. The journalistic forum brought key issues to the fore. Putting it more candidly: Branca probably would not have published a good portion of 'Isolate dal femminismo' in a scholarly journal, the language of scholarliness being enough to mute and redirect what the dean of Boccaccio studies really thinks about feminism, and in particular about feminist readings of Boccaccio. So we should be grateful to *Il Sole – 24 ore* for publishing this article under the rubric 'Dalla parte delle donne' ('Her Side'), and grateful to Branca for his directness. Misogyny has been most powerful when it has remained a tacit and unidentifiable given. Here, at least, we can see exposed in print the incriminating arguments of the opposition.

Unbeknownst to Branca, his article reveals how limited is his knowledge and experience of feminism. This in itself doesn't warrant much further commentary, except to say that, clearly, ignorance of feminist activism and thinking isn't a barrier to its opponents. In fact, nescience can help shore up a view unsympathetic to feminism.

Having men speak for women on these issues seems out of place – but ever so Boccaccian. In fact, Branca mimes several basic strategies of the Boccaccian Author in relation to his female audience. He addresses a group of women who are isolated and ghettoized (or as the *Decameron* would have it, restricted and contained), and he offers them advice on how to transcend the negative effects of their isolation; this allows him to orchestrate the definition of what frees, what fetters. Like the Author of the *Decameron*, Branca actually creates female addressees whom he can exalt and comfort – all the better to narrow women's sphere of activity, all the better to exercise control.

Branca's clash with feminist revisionism takes place within the U.S. academy, more specifically, it seems, during a visit to Los Angeles. Branca is just off the plane, apparently invited to teach a course on Boccaccio, as we shall surmise a bit later. Greeting him is Luigi Ballerini, chair of the UCLA Italian department. Ballerini is in the midst of briefing Branca on the state of things departmental when suddenly he explodes:

'E ti romperanno le scatole queste scatenate di femministe, per le quali una metodologia critica è il femminismo, per le quali non importa che si scriva o si dipinga bene ma che sia una donna a scrivere e a dipingere. Mi hanno ridotto a una sedia: non sono *chairman* ma *chair* nel Dipartimento, per un pretenzioso e scemo rispetto alle donne. Per la stessa ragione Dio non è più Dio, ma la divinità: e così via. Sai che se tu dirai *history* ti contesteranno imponendoti di cambiare la parola in *herstory*.'

'And you'll find out how much of a pain in the neck these wild feminists are. For them, feminism is actually a critical methodology; for them it doesn't matter whether one writes or paints well but whether it's a woman writing and painting. They have reduced me to a seat – in the Department, I'm no longer "chairman" but "chair," out of a pretentious and empty respect for women. For the same reason, God is no longer God, but the divinity. And so on and so forth. You know if you say "history," they'll object, requiring you to change the term to "herstory."'[11]

Luigi Ballerini, as Branca has introduced him, is genuinely impressive ('fra i più autentici'), a combination of poet-writer-critic, and, as evidenced by his leadership in the arena of neo-avant-garde poetry, truly radical and militant. Should we think that Ballerini has lost his youthful forcefulness, Branca assures us otherwise. Ballerini's academic robes have not vanquished his ardour; he still deals in irony and self-irony, presumed confirmation that he has maintained his critical spirit. How terrible this feminism must be if even the radical Ballerini cannot tolerate its excesses! And how could the reader expect him to, when he has been denied his humanity, reduced from chairman to mere chair, reified object. Worse, the opening phrase suggests, there is the spectre of loss of flesh. 'E ti romperanno le scatole' (literally, 'they'll break your boxes'), Ballerini says, rendering the more vulgar 'E ti romperanno i coglioni' ('And they'll break your balls') with a polite substitute. How real is the threat? We do not know for certain. But since Ballerini's commentary on these uncontrollable feminists begins with the conjunctive 'and,' one is encouraged to imagine that this is but a snippet of Ballerini's diatribe, and that Branca is gracefully presenting the minimalist version of the awful physical and psychic mutilation to which man has been subjected.

Branca reports that he laughed, thinking this portrayal of events a mere fiction. He refers to the story as a 'battuta saporosa che mi sapeva tutta di scanzonata invenzione balleriniana' ('deliciously witty story that had the flavour of one of Ballerini's light-hearted inventions'). But the story is stark truth, Branca discovers three days later, and it is no laughing matter. Docents and untutored students alike are mouthing the terms *herstory* and *herstoric*. The toothsome tidbit wrests the smile from Branca's face.

Branca does not engage the 'authoritative woman historian' ('autorevole storica') after her 'learned lecture' ('dotta conferenza'). Or, as he might have it in his defence, she does not engage with him. Both of them can remain unscathed until Branca is hailed, very courteously ('molto cortesemente') by a group of well-mannered female students ('alcune gentili allieve'). They ask, Why did Branca not use *herstory* instead of *history*? And why, in his discussion of critical perspectives on Boccaccio, did he not consider Boccaccio's feminism or anti-feminism, or assess Boccaccio's portrayal of women's condition?

The query is one that Branca cannot dismiss. He has portrayed the first part of the question as authenticated by the authoritative woman historian. He has portrayed the vessels of the entire request as far from wild and bacchic; indeed, they might well fit in with the well-mannered and gentle ladies of Boccaccio's own time. But lest we fear Branca bested by a group of gentle women in the City of Angels, we should look at the response that follows. Branca – blessed with a surname that means, among other things, 'jaw,' 'claw,' and 'clutches' – will live to smile at his victory.

Describing his response, Branca says that 'fortunately' ('per fortuna') he was 'not contemptuous, but amused' ('non disdegnato, ma divertito'). Perhaps it was the fortune of his name that brought the smile back to his jaw. He deflects the first part of the question, about feminist terminology, by adopting the topos of humility. Citing his limited knowledge of English, he claims that he fears his command of such terms would be necessarily imperfect, a 'neologismo improprio' or 'improper creation.' He has thus liberated himself from having to move on their terms. They do it so much better than he does.

In his response to the second part of the question, Branca saves men and their cultural products from being rendered mere matter. At the same time, like the Boccaccio of the *De mulieribus claris* (*On Illustrious Women* [1362]), he raises woman to the level of man, where she too, if she knows what is best for her, will flee corporeality. He says:

> [T]rattare del femminismo e dei problemi femminili nel Boccaccio non sarebbe stato fare metodologia o critica, come mi sentivo il dovere di fare in un corso universitario, ma una passiva descrizione di materia, di 'contenuti' si diceva una volta. Sarebbe stato come trattare dei cibi o delle piante o delle vesti o delle navi citate dal Boccaccio. Non dunque metodologia o critica ma sia pur utili inventaristica o archiviazione: anche se certo il Boccaccio fu il primo grande rivendicatore dei diritti della donna come persona umana, uguali a quelli degli uomini, specialmente nella *Fiammetta*, nel *Decameron*, nel *De mulieribus claris* (la prima opera sulle donne illustri dopo tutte quelle sugli uomini illustri).

To discuss feminism and women's issues in Boccaccio would not have involved a methodological or critical investigation, which I felt duty-bound to carry out in a university course. Rather, it would have been a passive description of matter, of 'content' as we used to say. It would have been like discussing foods, or plants, or clothes, or ships cited by Boccaccio. Therefore it was not a methodology or a mode of criticism, though it might be useful as inventory-taking or archival sorting. Of course, Boccaccio was the first great vindicator of the rights of woman as a human being, rights equal to those of men; this we see especially in the *Fiammetta*, in the *Decameron*, in the *De mulieribus claris* (the first work on illustrious women, after so many works on illustrious men).

If readers adopt feminist paradigms, Branca argues, they will reify the text, seeing it as the repository of objects to be inventoried and archived, numbered and catalogued. (Unfortunately, Branca seems to have missed out on the positive contributions of cultural studies in precisely such archival spaces.) According to Branca, the feminist reading is restricted to a passive description of matter; it does not actively analyse the inspirational form of the text. Does Branca see that he is tacitly reproducing the very equations that feminists have questioned, that is, woman as matter, corporeality, passivity, and formlessness, man and his cultural products as spirit, mind, activity, and form? It seems not. But no matter, for Branca it's better to rise above that critique.

Branca proposes an alternative. He tells the young women to stop fighting over such trivial matters as names. Rather, they should organize a protest about something significant, for example, about the need for maternity leave for women faculty and for others. Branca speaks with great urgency, quoting directly what he had said. The presence of direct discourse encourages us to think that his response is not only to the young women, whose questions were never reported directly, but also to Ballerini, whose explosion about wild feminists had been reported word for word. Fear not, *caro* Ballerini, help has arrived.

Arguing for his alternative, Branca re-establishes his own authority, as well as that of his Italy, where he states there is less economic disadvantage than in the United States, and also more substantive equality between men and women, who after all must be recognized as different. Now Branca begins to discuss scholarly publications about women and gender studies, finding in them the same defects originally attributed to rash feminists, and arguing that scholarly and activist works will be far more valuable if they do not focus exclusively on women.

At this point, the semantic force of the photograph that accompanies the article, a detail from 'Il ballo della vita' ('The Dance of Life') by

Edward Munch, becomes clearer.[12] Standing at the left and right of this photograph, mere observers of the couples engaged in a dance, are two lone women. The woman on the left is dressed in white, like most of the other women in the picture; her arms are open in an inviting gesture at the level of her hips, and her expression is welcoming. The other woman is dressed in black, like the men in the picture; her hands are locked tight, again at hip-level, and her expression is grim. It seems that Vittore Branca and Luigi Ballerini (whose last name means 'dancers' in Italian) expect partners in the Dance of Life. Their invitation hasn't been accepted. The photograph is helping to rechannel anxieties, so that the fault lies not with men who fear being deprived of the companionship of women, but rather with the woman who risks gloomy isolation. Certainly no woman could dance alone.

In sum, Branca adopts two rhetorical strategies that, as we shall see, are associated with male voices in the *Decameron*. Like the Author of the *Decameron*, he creates, internal to his text, a female audience that he can control and with respect to whom he and his cohort are superior. Furthermore, Branca adopts strategies typical of the *Decameron*'s three male narrators. He tries to speak for women by claiming that they would be freed if they fulfilled their maternal impulses; as I show in chapter 3, 'Boccaccio's Sexed Thought,' the male narrators of the *Decameron* hasten to speak for women by suggesting that women will be freed if only they would give free reign to their sexual desires. The morality is different, but the rhetorical stance of the male speaker is essentially the same.

So if one hoped to displace such unconscious repetitions of unenlightened male rhetorical positions, what would one have to do? In this study, I maintain that we would have to recognize that the discourse about narration and reading in the *Decameron* is intimately bound to its production of a discourse about woman. In other words, we would have to recognize how central gender is to the construction of social reality in the *Decameron*. But most important, I would argue, we need to rethink our ideas about how meaning is created in the *Decameron*. We need to understand better the *Decameron*'s rhetoric – and to be quite clear, this is of prime importance whether or not readers are specifically interested in the *Decameron*'s rhetoric of gender and sexuality.

My book takes what has lain dormant in our readings of the *Decameron* – the polemicism of the narrators' voices – and reveals its vibrancy. One might say that although I recognize the importance of seeing how meaning in the *Decameron* emerges 'grammatically' (as Tzvetan Todorov and Cesare Segre, structuralist readers, would have it) and 'semantically' (as many more traditional readers would have it), I believe that many readers still have only a tenuous notion about how meaning in the *Decameron* emerges 'syntactically.' By combining a 'syntax of the *Decameron*' with semantic and grammatical analyses, I am claiming that we would come closer to a rhetorical reading of this work. Such a rhetorical reading is not limited to understanding what speakers choose to talk about (*inventio*), how they use to arrange their information and arguments (*dispositio*), what rhetorical and stylistic features they use in order to render their messages most effective (*elocutio*). Its principal and overarching task is another: to train our attention on how speech acts accomplish things, or, even more simply, to ask ourselves what these speech acts are doing, since in the case of literary narratives like the *Decameron*, they are clearly doing myriad things at once. Although readers have often slipped into thinking about the rhetorical strategies of the *Decameron* as if they were homologous with those of a single unifying Authorial voice, we can no longer afford to tolerate such imprecision. The *Decameron* frame narrators are not well-developed characters such as we might find in the later European novel, but they remain marked by individually distinctive rhetorical approaches. Even more important, we must recognize that it is over an extended arc of time that the frame narrators of the *Decameron* confront and work through the issues of concern to them. What can be accomplished rhetorically in the latter part of the *Decameron* is thus very much dependent on the groundwork that is laid early on – hence the extended attention that I devote to the first third of the work.

As I argued in 'The Untidy Business of Gender Studies: Or, Why It's Almost Useless to Ask if the *Decameron* Is Feminist,' far too many feminist readings of the *Decameron* have relied on an 'iconic' mode that will produce a 'misogyny quotient': How many empowered, outspoken, and desiring women on one hand, how many victims like Griselda on the other? In that essay, focusing on Day 8 of the *Decameron*, I proposed that a rhetorical analysis would offer us a more complex approach to an ever-shifting target. In the case of a feminist reading, such a rhetorical analysis would aim to identify how the discourse about woman is constructed via crucial (and often unforeseen) intersections of multiple narrative contributions. This, for example, is what I believe the stories of Day 8 of the *Decameron* do when as a group they exclude woman from being an active agent in economic, political, legal, and authorial economies of exchange.

Since writing that essay, I have thought a great deal more about what happens in more sophisticated analyses of Decameronian misogyny, such as those advanced by Millicent Marcus in her reading of the tale of the scholar and the widow (*Decameron* 8.7), widely perceived as the most misogynistic novella of the *Decameron*.[13] What Marcus shows is that, although a given utterance might seem 'misogynist' on the surface, said utterance could be interpreted as anti-misogynist if there is evidence that the author is encouraging the reader to take other extra-textual information into account in evaluating that utterance. To understand how a *Decameron* novella produces a discourse about woman, for example, we would have to identify how its utterances come to have meaning within codes that would have been recognizable in mid-fourteenth-century Italy. Marcus does this, revealing two readings at odds with each other: one based on mimetic principles (do as the story tells you the cruel male protagonist does), and one based on a more subtle semantic analysis that exposes the pathetic qualities of the cruel male protagonist. The choice between these two readings doesn't seem too difficult.

Yet it is crucial to recognize that a semantic study like Marcus's can be deployed – in ways that she could not have imagined and for which she cannot be held responsible – to unexpected political ends. It can seem especially compelling to two groups: to people who want desperately to believe Boccaccio wasn't misogynist (I myself don't care to answer this question, as it doesn't infringe on what I see as important about the *Decameron*), and to people who believe that contemporary critical methodologies have no place in the reading of medieval and early modern texts (I don't count myself among their number either). In feminist circles, moreover, a blanket denial of a novella's misogyny is almost certain to raise a few eyebrows. Misogyny isn't easily erased by the ironic reversal of the surface meaning of an utterance. So a key contribution like Marcus's may also have been utilized to less than productive purposes by readers who have continued to circle around the question of whether the *Decameron* is really misogynist or feminist. I therefore believe that feminist analyses of texts like the *Decameron* are going to come to a standstill unless we begin to *combine* semantic analyses (i.e., evaluations of an utterance in light of the codes that are crucial to giving it meaning) with syntactic ones (readings that judge the particular value and function that an utterance has within the temporal unfolding of the text).

As we shall see in the opening chapters, the *Decameron* 'frames' woman from the very beginning. At critical junctures, its narrators defame certain women and defend others, encouraging readers to take sides in the debate about woman.[14] But even more important, the *Decameron* delimits and shapes the questions the reader is permitted to ask about woman. Our task is to examine the very structure of the questions that the *Decameron* poses about reading and sexual difference. Only then will we be able to grasp the intellectual and political investments that contemporary readers have in trying to understand – or to ignore – these issues.

The *Decameron* offers us a glimpse into a fictional world where the views of male and female narrators are gendered. We see this in the exchange between Fiammetta and Dioneo, representative narrators of the *Decameron* and the focus of my discussion in chapter 2. I continue this exploration when I discuss the exchanges between male and female narrators in chapter 3. Given the title of that chapter, 'Boccaccio's Sexed Thought,' readers minimally familiar with Boccaccio are likely to think they can foresee where this is going. I don't mean to disappoint readers looking for something more risqué, but behind the select phrase 'sexed thought' there hovers not the promise of a seductive scene but rather the weight of a feminist exploration into 'il pensiero sessuato,' a phrase coined by Italian theorists of difference as they have called into question the masculine-neuter I.[15]

Contrary to what many readers think, the novellas about proactive women in the *Decameron* are offset by assurances from the female narrators that there are no transgressions. So we must ask, in these stories, Are women making any progress? As the *Decameron* progresses, what can we say about how women who attempt to take control are treated? I turn to this issue in chapters 4 through 6, using several examples: first, the case of stories told about transgressive women who cross-dress as men, then the cluster of stories on Day 6 that reflect on women's rhetorical power, then the issue of men, women, and figurative language in the *Decameron*. Although acknowledging that the stories use multiple strategies in order to both assert and temper the possibility of change (so that it is not always so clear whether a story functions in favour of the status quo or in resistance to it), I argue that ultimately the stories of the *Decameron* appear to close off the possibilities available to women. They appear to open up the possibility of the expression of female desire at the same time that they describe severe limits placed on the way in which women can speak out.

This leads me to my final chapter, 'Domestic Violence in the *Decameron*.' Here, I show that as the stories of the *Decameron* progress and women characters become increasingly empowered, the spectre of violence against them becomes more insistent. Readers have often had considerable difficulty in reading stories that showcase violence against women. Therefore, one of my objectives in this chapter, where I offer an extended commentary on Emilia's story of the Goose Bridge (*Decameron* 9.9), is to help readers understand better how misogynistic rhetoric works and how we, as readers, can best respond to it.

In my Conclusion, I step back in order to reflect briefly on the relative weight of these rhetorical analyses of the *Decameron*, the anxieties they may induce, the possible benefits they may bring, and the ways in which they might be used in order to open up new approaches to works as richly plurivocal and provocative as Boccaccio's *Decameron*.

chapter one

Woman as Witness

In his Introduction to Day 1 of the *Decameron*, the Author describes the outbreak of the Black Death in Florence in 1348: mysterious symptoms, the inevitability of death, the oppressive presence of the dead and the dying, the measures taken to avoid the plague, the abandoned city, the effects on morality. His is presumably an eyewitness account of a crucial and traumatic moment in Florentine history. In fact, however, this narrative is filtered through other literary and historical descriptions of plagues.[1] If we examine the principal subtext, Book 2, chapter 4 of the *History of the Langobards* (*Historia Langobardorum*) of Paul the Deacon (720–99?), we shall see that the Author of the *Decameron* is reworking his source material in ways that have crucial implications for the discourse about woman in this work.

Here, in translation, is what Paul the Deacon wrote about a plague in sixth-century Italy:

In the times of this man [Narses] a very great pestilence broke out, particularly in the province of Liguria. For suddenly there appeared certain marks among the dwellings, doors, utensils, and clothes, which, if any one wished to wash away, became more and more apparent. After the lapse of a year indeed there began to appear in the groins of men and in other rather delicate places, a swelling of the glands, after the manner of a nut or a date, presently followed by an unbearable fever, so that upon the third day the man died. But if any one should pass over the third day he had a hope of living. Everywhere there was grief and everywhere tears. For as common report had it that those who fled would avoid the plague, the dwellings were left deserted by their inhabitants, and the dogs only kept house. The flocks remained alone in the pastures with no shepherd at hand. You might see villas or fortified places lately filled with crowds of men, and on the next day, all had departed and everything was in utter silence. Children fled, leaving the corpses of their parents unburied: parents forgetful of their duty abandoned their children in raging fever. If by chance long-standing affection constrained any one to bury his near relative, he remained himself unburied, and while he was performing the funeral rites he perished; while he offered obsequies to the dead, his own corpse remained without obsequies. You might see the world brought back to its ancient silence: no voice in the field; no whistling of shepherds; no lying in wait of wild beasts among the cattle; no harm to domestic fowls. The crops, outliving the time of the harvest, awaited the reaper untouched; the vine-yard with its fallen leaves and its shining grapes remained undisturbed while winter came on; a trumpet as of warriors resounded through the hours of the night and day; something like the murmur of an army was heard by many: there were no footsteps of passers by, no murderer was seen, yet the corpses of the dead were more than the eyes could discern; pastoral places had been turned into a sepulchre for men, and human hab-itations had become places of refuge for wild beasts. And these evils hap-pened to the Romans only and within Italy alone, up to the boundaries of the nations of the Alamanni and the Bavarians. Meanwhile, the emperor Justinian departed from life and Justinian the younger undertook the rule of the state at Constantinople.[2]

The description of the plague in the *Decameron* concentrates on many of the same issues: the pronounced symptoms; the three-day limit on life; the flight from the habitations of men; the renunciation of basic familial duties; the attention to burial rites; the overwhelming number of the dead; the abandonment of dwellings to wild beasts. And yet in the *Decameron*'s reworking of this subtext, the Author is concerned with more than providing vivid descriptions of buboes and beasts.[3]

The dominant feeling of the Latin subtext is one of eerie barrenness and desolation. Even when the imagined sounds of trumpets and armed warriors creep in, the emphasis remains on the negation of sound and of any living presence, whether human or bestial. There are 'no foot-steps ... no murderer was seen.' Respected customs and boundaries have broken down. Intergenerational bonds lose their force, and the proper value given to countryside and city is no longer respected as pastoral places become sites of death and cities come to be inhabited by beasts. In the *Decameron*, there is desolation but there is also an overwhelming emphasis on excess and a breakdown of cognitive, emotional, moral, sexual boundaries: the bodies of the dead multiply, animals weighed down by a good day's meal take over, invading city and countryside, people are given to displays of moral and sexual excess.[4]

In focusing on moral matters, Paul the Deacon and the Author of the *Decameron* have different goals. The *History of the Langobards* recounts the breakdown of bonds between parent and child: children leave parents unburied, and even more unnaturally, parents abandon children to illness. The passage in the *Decameron* makes gender central to the issue of abandonment: 'l'un fratello l'altro abbandonava e il zio il nepote e la sorella il fratello e spesse volte la donna il suo marito; e, che maggior cosa è e quasi non credibile, li padri e le madri i figliuoli, quasi loro non fossero, di visitare e di servire schifavano' ('brother abandoned brother, uncle abandoned nephew, sister left brother, and very often wife abandoned husband, and – even worse, almost unbelievable – fathers and mothers neglected to tend and care for their children as if they were not their own' [1.Intro.27; trans., 9]). After two instances in which one (male) individual abandons another, the passage reaches a woeful crescendo, with women abandoning men, and men and women abandoning children. In lamenting the tragic state of events, the passage obliquely delineates the truly unspeakable: that sister might abandon sister and an aunt her niece (raising the issue of solidarity among women), and that a husband might very often abandon his wife and a grown child its mother (raising the possibility that women as well as men might justifiably see themselves as wronged by members of their families).[5] But the woman reader of this passage is not positioned as is the male reader. Denying her the possibility of positioning herself as 'victim,' the Author of the *Decameron* identifies her as the primary weak link in the marital bond.

From here the leap to the threat of women's sexuality is short.[6] The passage I have just been discussing does not allow for the possibility that a woman might be abandoned by her loved ones. The focus now settles on woman's lack of virtue:

E da questo essere abbandonati gl'infermi da' vicini, da' parenti e dagli amici e avere scarsità di serventi, discorse uno uso quasi davanti mai non udito: che niuna, quantunque leggiadra o bella o gentil donna fosse, infermando non curava d'avere a' suoi servigi uomo, qual che egli si fosse o giovane o altro, e a lui senza alcuna vergogna ogni parte del corpo aprire non altramenti che a una femina avrebbe fatto, solo che la necessità della sua infermità il richiedesse; il che in quelle che ne guerirono fu forse di minore onestà, nel tempo che succedette, cagione.   (1.Intro.29)

And since the sick were abandoned by their neighbors, their parents, and their friends and there was a scarcity of servants, a practice that was previously almost unheard of spread through the city: when a woman fell sick, no matter how attractive or beautiful or noble she might be, she did not mind having a manservant (whoever he might be, no matter how young or old he was), and she had no shame whatsoever in revealing any part of her body to him – the way she would have done to a woman – when necessity of her sickness required her to do so. This practice was, perhaps, in the days that followed the pestilence, the cause of looser morals in the women who survived the plague. (9)

As the Author reaffirms that men may not gaze upon women, he draws attention to the physical appearance and social status of both subjects, the woman being looked at, and the man who looks at her. The text encourages us, by means of subjunctives that follow the adverbs 'quantunque' and 'qual che,' to imagine just how charming and beautiful and noble the woman might be, and how young or old the man. There is no description of the woman's illness and bodily suffering. Her pain remains unspoken. To recognize it would be to grant her subjectivity, and that would be to acknowledge a transgression against *woman*, not a transgression against men's honour. So another account of shocking behaviour is substituted.

The look of the male servant is threatening because it transgresses the prescribed order of things, which is maintained by gender and class distinctions. As the Author goes on, we hear of other customs and practices that have gone by the wayside, mainly having to do with mourning and bearing witness to the dead. During the plague, the dying and the dead of the upper class have no one – no women, no friends, no clergy – to bear witness to their passing and hasty burial. As the Author of the *Decameron* goes on to note, the crisis was even greater for the lower (and possibly middle) classes, where decomposing bodies piled up in the streets, and biers became the final resting place of multiple corpses. The root of the problem, as the Author identifies it, is this: citizens – in particular women, and even more specifically women of the upper classes – have failed to meet the responsibilities of bearing witness to the dead.

The Author recounts numerous woes, shifting from one place to another (city to countryside, countryside to city), and ending finally in his pained cry about the places and the people that once were. In a final desperate attempt at relief from misery, the scene shifts to seven young women gathered in the church of Santa Maria Novella in Florence.

Veiling their true identities with the fictional names Pampinea, Filomena, Neifile, Lauretta, Emilia, Elissa, and Fiammetta, the Author then recounts how Pampinea pleads with her female companions to use 'natural reason' and leave the plague-stricken city for safer environs.

Like the Author earlier, Pampinea makes it woman's duty to bear witness, and she and her companions have continued to uphold this responsibility. They see the dead; they hear the friars chanting; they wear the garments of mourning. The rhetorical challenge will be how to relieve the women from this duty so that they may save themselves. Here she talks about how everywhere she and her companions see death and crime: dead bodies, exiles who flaunt the law, the scum of the city. No longer can woman bear witness. The dead are too many for her to bear witness at the private level. At the public level, the outlaws know that she is an ineffectual witness, since those who would enforce the laws are dead or dying. Furthermore, if the assumption is that the woman mourning the death of a loved one bears witness to the living members of her own community, here again the system has crumbled. Pampinea emphasizes that everywhere there is nothing but the dead and dying. Moving from scenes of death in church, and outside, to the private confines of her home, Pampinea describes her peak moment of horror thus:

E se alle nostre case torniamo, non so se a voi così come a me adiviene: io, di molta famiglia, niuna altra persona in quella se non la mia fante trovando, impaurisco e quasi tutti i capelli adosso mi sento arricciare, e parmi, dovunque io vado o dimoro per quella, l'ombre di coloro che sono trapassati vedere, e non con quegli visi che io soleva, ma con una vista orribile non so donde in loro nuovamente venuta spaventarmi.   (1.Intro.59)

And when we return home, I do not know if what happens to me also happens to you: coming from a numerous family, I now find no one at home but my maid, and I become so afraid that my hair stands on end, and wherever I go or sit in my house, I seem to see the shadows of those who have passed away, not with the faces that I remember, but with a horrible altered expression that has come to them from who knows where and which terrifies me.   (My translation)

Pampinea's crowning argument, reinforced by her claim that she does not know if her personal experience is shared by the other six women, is 'there is no one like me.' Hers is a plea that another person testify to her existence.

The Introduction reaffirms, both at the intradiegetic and diegetic levels, that it is woman's role to bear witness to the dead and their place in a social order that respects gender and class distinctions. This keeps women enclosed, be it within the home, the church, or the social order. Should she choose not to assume the role of witness to this social order, she must face the consequences. Who could bear witness to women? Not male servants (their look would be eroticized), not female servants (their look is not authorized). Since she may not write her own experience, woman must cede this responsibility of bearing witness to another – to the Author of the *Decameron*, for example, or, at the very least, to the trusted friend of the Author's, who offers the reliable report of what the women are doing in the church of Santa Maria Novella on a Tuesday morning. Now she will be 'written about.' And she will risk being the object of the unauthorized eroticized look. In effect, the choice for women is to testify to patriarchy or not to testify at all.

In making this claim, I am proposing a reading of the Introduction to Day I that is substantially different from the one offered by Aldo S. Bernardo in 'The Plague as Key to Meaning in Boccaccio's *Decameron*.'[7] Bernardo argues that the description of the plague is meant primarily as the background, 'an ironical and contrapuntal beat,' to the chaste and honourable behaviour of the ten Florentine narrators. In contrast, I would say that the description of the plague and its moral effects serves to identify conflicts in gender relations that will be 'worked through' – and not necessarily to woman's advantage – in the course of the *Decameron*.

This subtle manipulation of woman into the position of witness to the social order is difficult to perceive, because Pampinea is an 'authoritative' woman who speaks and invokes reason. She even does so in a church, the place where (according to Pauline dictates) women should not speak out. As she advocates for survival, Pampinea is also upsetting the conventional wisdom about women. Filomena, the first to see Pampinea's plan as controversial, argues that women, as defective beings, are incapable of carrying out Pampinea's plan successfully unless they have a male guide:

Ricordivi che noi siamo tutte femine, e non ce n'ha niuna sì fanciulla, che non possa bene conoscere come le femine sien ragionate insieme e senza la provedenza d'alcuno uomo si sappiano regolare. Noi siamo mobili, riottose, sospettose, pusillanime e paurose: per le quali cose io dubito forte, se noi alcuna altra guida non prendiamo che la nostra, che questa compagnia non

si dissolva troppo più tosto e con meno onor di noi che non ci bisognerebbe:
e per ciò è buono a provederci avanti che cominciamo.   (1.Intro.74–5)

Remember that we are all women, and any young girl can tell you that
women do not know how to reason in a group when they are without the
guidance of some man who knows how to control them. We are fickle,
quarrelsome, suspicious, timid, and fearful, because of which I suspect that
this company will soon break up without honor to any of us if we do not
take a guide other than ourselves. We would do well to resolve this matter
before we depart.   (15–16)

Elissa then seconds the necessity of having men as leaders; and going
beyond the folk wisdom of women as less able than men, she provides
biblical support for her assertion about men's superiority: 'Veramente
gli uomini sono delle femine capo e senza l'ordine loro rade volte riesce
alcuna nostra opera a laudevole fine: ma come possiam noi aver questi
uomini?' ('Men are truly the leaders [literally, the 'heads'] of women,
and without their guidance, our actions rarely end successfully. But how
are we to find these men?' [1.Intro.76; 16]). As is often pointed out,
Elissa is echoing Paul's First Letter to the Corinthians 11.3 ('But I would
have you know that the head of every man is Christ; and the head of the
woman is the man; and the head of Christ is God') as well as his Letter
to the Ephesians 5.23 ('the husband is the head of the wife, as Christ is
the head of the church').[8]

While Elissa proceeds to express her concern that not just any men
will do, three men appear in the church, as if magically or by *deus ex
machina*:

Mentre tralle donne erano così fatti ragionamenti, e ecco entrar nella
chiesa tre giovani, non per ciò tanto che meno di venticinque anni fosse
l'età di colui che più giovane era di loro. Ne' quali né perversità di tempo
né perdita d'amici o di parenti né paura di se medesimi avea potuto amor
non che spegnere ma raffreddare. De' quali l'uno era chiamato Panfilo e
Filostrato il secondo e l'ultimo Dioneo, assai piacevole e costumato ciascuno: e andavan cercando per loro somma consolazione, in tanta turbazione di cose, di vedere le lor donne, le quali per ventura tutte e tre
erano tralle predette sette, come che dell'altre alcune ne fossero congiunte
parenti d'alcuni di loro.   (1.Intro.78–9)

While there were these discussions among the ladies, oh look, three young men came into the church, none of whom was less than twenty-five years of age. In them, neither the perversity of the times nor the loss of friends or parents nor fear for their own lives had been able to cool, much less extinguish, the love they bore in their hearts. One of them was called Panfilo, another Filostrato, and the last Dioneo, each one very charming and well bred; and they were trying to find, for their greatest consolation in those turbulent times, whether they could see their ladies, all three of whom happened to be among the seven ladies previously mentioned, while the others were close relatives of one or the other of the three men.   (My translation)

How tangible is the promise of action and reasoned guidance from these men? This passage offers a complex answer.

On one hand, the women do appear passive, as if to suggest that they need masculine intervention. While the women try to decide how to act in response to the plague, their discussions simply 'happen,' as if to discount women's ability to think actively ('tralle donne erano così fatti ragionamenti'; 'there were these discussions among the women'). The men, however, already have transcended the stage where they are passive victims. With a love unperturbed by the terrible events of 1348, they are taking action: 'andavan cercando ... di veder le lor donne' ('they were trying to find ... whether they could see their ladies').

If this passage encourages us to see the men as more 'active' than the opposite sex, it also challenges the view of these men as more reasonable and more constant than the women. These men are interested primarily in the consolation that love and women can offer them. The interpolation of 'in tanta turbazione di cose' ('in those turbulent times') delays our recognition of this fact: 'andavan cercando per loro somma consolazione, in tanta turbazione di cose, di vedere le lor donne' ('they were trying to find, for their greatest consolation in those turbulent times, whether they could see their women').

Furthermore, the men's firmness of purpose – reinforced by an insistent, almost incantatory, alliteration on p – is certain to recall the Author's own declared resoluteness in love, which bore the same alliterative stamp. In the Preface to the *Decameron*, the Author had described his own resoluteness in love: 'il mio amore, oltre a ogn'altro fervente e il quale niuna forza di proponimento o di consiglio o di vergogna evidente, o pericolo che seguir ne potesse, aveva potuto né rompere né piegare' ('my love, more fervent than any other, which could not be broken or bent by any resolution, advice, public shame, or danger that might result from it' [Proemio, 5; 2]). And now, speaking about Panfilo,

Filostrato, and Dioneo, the Author says, 'né perversità di tempo né perdita d'amici o di parenti né paura di se medesimi avea potuto amor non
che spegnere ma raffreddare'). Furthermore, the alliteration of the
phrase used to introduce the young men ('e ecco entrar') recalls the
repeated appearances of the conjunction 'e' ('and') used to depict
the Author's affective reaction to the plague, which was described in the
Introduction with repeated paratactic constructions.[9] Now, if these
young men are in much the same situation as the Author, overwhelmed
by the devastation that love and death can bring, do they really have the
critical distance that would ensure successful judgment and action?

How then are power relations characterized when the women and
men interact? I would argue that in Boccaccio's writings, voyeurism is a
principal means of affirming power,[10] so we should hardly be surprised
to find that the scopic drive is of prime importance in this passage: 'Né
prima esse agli occhi corser di costoro, che costoro furono da esse
veduti' ('No sooner did the ladies spring to their eyes than they too
were seen by the ladies' [1.Intro. 80; my translation]). We are told, in
essence, that both groups see each other simultaneously. But is this gender parity? Again the passage provides a complex answer. The men are
'seen' by the women; the women 'spring' or 'rush' (*corser*) to the eyes of
the men. So the men are 'passive' objects of the look; the women are
'active' agents. On the other hand, the men remain constant, stable,
fixed; the women are represented as fluid and mobile.

This uncertainty about where power lies is reflected as well in the
numerical composition of the individual groups. One might think that
the sheer numbers emphasize women's dominance. But as Joy Hambuechen Potter has noted, 'The fact that there are *seven* women and
three men in itself symbolically asserts male, not female, superiority.
Seven is a well known and important number in the world: seven vices,
seven virtues, seven Liberal Arts etc. Three, however, is infinitely superior and more sacred, even in non-Christian numerological systems.'[11]

Pampinea, speaking to her companions, offers to include the men
in a way that seems to provide for balanced power relations: 'volentieri
e guida e servidor ne saranno, se di prendergli a questo oficio non
schiferemo' ('[they] would gladly be both our guides and servants if we
do not balk at accepting them for such service' [1.Intro.80; my transla-
tion]). This is a statement full of promise. Men will 'serve' in the leadership position that Filomena and Elissa had hoped for. They will be both
higher and lower than the women. What is the likelihood that men and
women could arrive at a common understanding of what it means to be

'both leader and servant'? Will the men live up to the women's implicit expectation (i.e., will they be reasonable, orderly, and amenable to doing the women's bidding)? Or is Pampinea in fact leading the women into an unwritten contract which, given anthropological and discursive realities of gender relations, will prove risky for the women?

Before the group is constituted, there is yet another twist. Neifile, of whom one of the men is enamoured, now articulates an objection to taking the men along. Although she acknowledges that the men are upstanding and honourable, and many good things can be said about them, she states:

> Ma, per ciò che assai manifesta cosa è loro essere d'alcune che qui ne sono innamorati, temo che infamia e riprensione, senza nostra colpa o di loro, non ce ne segua se gli meniamo.   (1.Intro.83)

> ... but it is quite obvious that some of them are in love with some of us who are here present, and I fear that if we take them with us, disgrace and disapproval will follow, through no fault of ours or of theirs.   (16)

Often read as 'merely' a demure woman's concern with her own chastity and honour (given that Neifile blushes deeply upon hearing Pampinea's proposal to accept the men's company), this objection is far more. Neifile is asserting that both sexes exist within social and discursive systems over which they do not have control.[12] It is she who calls our attention to the presence of the Other. Pampinea has proposed to leave the city, and has artfully countered various objections that might be moved. Filomena and Elissa have reintroduced objections; as they argue for taking men along, they reproduce discourses about the defects of woman and the virtues of man that would reinforce their arguments for male guidance. Neifile sees the other side of the picture, namely, how such a decision could, within the same social context, be deleterious. What Neifile knows – and her blush also tells us – is what Lacan also asserts: that the subject is lodged between *what she says* and *what is said.*

As the women decide what to do, and as Pampinea presents their proposal to the men, their utterances are marked simultaneously by silence. First, the women agree: 'non solamente *si tacquero* ma con consentimento concorde tutte dissero ...' ('not only did *they fall silent* but they all said with one mind ...' [1.Intro.86; my translation; emphasis mine]). Pampinea then approaches the men, and as if to point insistently to the peculiar combination of silence and speech, the Author writes: '*senza più parole* Pampinea. ... la lor disposizione fè manifesta' ('*Without further discussion*, Pampinea ... described their plan' [1.Intro.87; my translation; emphasis mine]). In both cases, what we see is not silence first and *then* speech, but silence and speech mapped over each other. The contradictory rules governing women's speech are being enacted. Silence is under erasure, for a silenced woman continues to speak. But her speech is under erasure, for even as she speaks, she can be considered to have said nothing.

As I have shown thus far, when the women are alone, their actions are judged against the social norms that regulate gender behaviour, their words (and their silences) continually displaced. The pattern continues when the women encounter the men. When the proposal to leave the city in the company of the men is greeted by the men, the men's reaction confirms how curious the proposal is: the men think that they are being ridiculed (*beffati* [1.Intro. 88]).[13] This, of course, should not surprise us, given that the proposal so obviously defies gender norms. What is remarkable is how gender norms are reinforced even when gender seems not to be at issue.

Consider, for example, the exchange between Pampinea and Dioneo as the group decides on its activities. Having heard the women's proposal to leave the city of Florence, the witty Dioneo threatens to leave the group unless certain conditions are met: having abandoned his troubled thoughts inside the city walls, he is here to amuse himself. Pampinea internalizes Dioneo's response 'as if' it were her own: 'non d'altra maniera che se similmente tutti i suoi avesse da sé cacciati' ('not otherwise than as if she similarly had driven all her troubled thoughts away' [1.Intro.94; my translation]).[14]

Who is the authoritative leader here? Pampinea is the first to exercise authority and to expand on women's ability to speak freely in a variety of ways. She is the one to establish the rotation of administrative and political responsibilities. She seems to tip the balance in favour of the women when she is made queen and orders 'everyone [lit. every man] to be silent' ('che *ogn'uom tacesse* [1.Intro.98; my translation]).[15] She proposes that the group tell stories for their pleasure and amusement, and she renders storytelling more than a frivolous activity for idle women when she chooses the term *ragionare* (to narrate, to argue, to discuss with a strong rational component) to describe what the group will do: 'voglio che libero sia a ciascuno di quella materia ragionare che più gli sarà a grado' ('I want each of you to be free to discuss any subject that most pleases you' [1.Intro.112; my translation]). But the fact remains that Dioneo has served as Pampinea's guide by shaping the possibilities for the group's future discussions.[16]

It is therefore misleading to assert the obvious, as does one reader, that '[t]he men play no part in planning the move to the countryside or in devising the machinery of the story-telling.'[17] The fact is that the men do not have to 'plan' and 'devise' in order to influence the discursive configurations. Their mere presence – even if 'marginal' – within a system that regulates gender behaviour will ensure that. The women may 'plan' and 'devise,' but the system will seek to designate them as supporting witnesses to the men. As we shall see, the same will be the case throughout the storytelling of the *Decameron*. In the following chapters, I propose that we track the gendered narrative perspectives of the *Decameron* to see how certain narrative perspectives – usually not those of the women – gain dominance.[18]

chapter two

Fiammetta v. Dioneo

If one had to select the two narrators of the *Decameron* who embody the different worlds that the *Decameron* explores, these would most certainly be Fiammetta and Dioneo. Noting that scholars have often identified Fiammetta and Dioneo as a couple, Janet Smarr writes, 'Whether or not these two are in love with each other, they represent two quite different attitudes which Boccaccio makes balance each other, just as he balances the structure of the book.'[1] As Smarr demonstrates, Fiammetta is pivotal to Boccaccio's vision of a humanity that is rationally governed and temperate. In order to highlight this function of hers, Boccaccio will structure a work so as to place into relief the relationship of Fiammetta and her male counterpart (Caleone in the *Filocolo*, Dioneo in the *Decameron*). In this symmetrical structuring, organized around a pattern of 9 + 1, Boccaccio offers two moments that reaffirm this superior order: the stories of marriage and love on Day 5 (when Fiammetta is queen and Dioneo sings) and the stories of magnanimous behaviour on Day 10 (when Dioneo tells the final tale of the *Decameron* and Fiammetta sings).[2] Seeing Fiammetta as the spokesperson for marriage and Dioneo as the representative for sexual pleasure, Smarr concludes that, '[i]n their combination, license and marriage or energy and order are bound together.'[3] Because of this, Smarr grants special consideration to Days 3 and 7, where the topics seem most congenial to the expressions of natural love and where Fiammetta and Dioneo sing together.

In the years since Smarr presented her analysis of Fiammetta and Dioneo, our views of marriage, order, and noble virtue in the *Decameron* have undergone something of a shift. In general, I believe we are less inclined to see in the *Decameron* any clear progress from a lower to a higher moral plane, or to emphasize its idealistic elements at the expense of all else. Thus, Robert Hollander and Courtney Cahill, reading Day 10 as an interrogation of the myth of order, cast a quizzical eye on scholars like Vittore Branca, Victoria Kirkham, Marga Cottino-Jones, and Teodolinda Barolini who see a triumphal focus on unequivocal virtue at the end of the *Decameron*.[4] Moreover, thanks to the heightened awareness provided by feminist responses to Boccaccio, we are likely to be troubled about the linking of violence – particularly violence against women – with stories about marriage and order in the *Decameron*.[5] In light of these increasingly complex readings of virtue, marriage, and order, readers might well feel less than fully comfortable with Smarr's relatively optimistic assessment of symmetrical balance in the *Decameron* or Fiammetta's place in guaranteeing that balanced order.

Still, Smarr offers a useful starting point for the argument of this chapter, namely, that Fiammetta and Dioneo are crucial to the development of a discourse about gender difference in the *Decameron*. Their discursive interactions bring to the fore all the important issues that Smarr identifies – principal among them whether we should view marriage as a positive social institution and whether we should allow that sexuality outside marriage is 'natural' – and with the added twist that we must not forget that the *Decameron* presents these views about sexuality as gendered.

In contrast to Smarr, who chooses ultimately to privilege the moments at the end of Day 3 and the end of Day 7 where Fiammetta and Dioneo sing together, I would like to focus for the duration of this chapter on a series of narrative moments in which the differences between Fiammetta and Dioneo become most evident. I shall begin by focusing on Dioneo and Fiammetta's first stories (*Decameron* 1.4 and 1.5). In polemical response to Dioneo's portrayal of the first woman character, Fiammetta introduces the terms of a debate about gender on Day 1 and she follows through with yet another counter-response on Day 2 when she uses her story of Andreuccio da Perugia (2.5) both to seal her criticism of Dioneo's views about gender and to broaden the scope of the gender debate. Dioneo's most poignant response to Fiammetta will appear only at the end of Day 8, but the narrative and discursive modes he adopts at this juncture have profound consequences for the storytelling on the last two days of the *Decameron*, when many of the gender issues are battled out with the greatest force.

As should be evident from this brief overview of this verbal sparring match, the discourse about gender in the *Decameron* emerges in a vein of dialectical and antagonistic exploration, as a series of statements and counter-statements about men and women, their attributes, characteristics, modes of interaction, and so forth. It is worth our while to consider these matters further because they have a definite bearing on what may be said not only about gender issues but also about the construction of meaning in the *Decameron*.

In his Preface to the *Decameron*, the Author addresses himself to an audience of lovesick women and promises them stories about 'piacevoli e aspri casi d'amore e altri fortunati avvenimenti' ('different cases of love, both bitter and sweet, as well as other exciting adventures' [Proemio 14; 3]). But the opening stories of the collection steer clear of matters of the heart. Ser Cepparello gives a false confession to a holy friar who takes it as evidence of his saintliness (1.1). Abraham the Jew interprets ecclesiastical corruption as the evidence that he should convert to Christianity (1.2). Then, with his parable about the three rings, Melchisedech disarms a hostile sultan (1.3). As a unit, these stories have shaped our reading of the *Decameron* as a metacritical reflection on the power of the word, the uses of narrative, and the pitfalls inherent in reading.[6]

Each of these stories, in its own modest way, supports the idea that narration and interpretation and the construction of social reality are the province of men – or at the very least, of individuals without gender. Simply by ignoring the female perspective that the Author's Preface led us to expect, these stories, along with the readings they have generated, displace woman just a wee bit more.

Still, at the centre of Day 1, behind the by now dominant concern about narration and reading, there emerges a strand of discourse about woman. Dioneo inaugurates the debate about sexual difference by telling the story of the monk and the abbot (1.4), the first novella of the *Decameron* to introduce a female character, and the first novella to speak of sex. In the story that follows, about the marchioness of Monferrato and her chicken banquet (1.5), Fiammetta will respond tit for tat, calling into question Dioneo's portrayal of woman and her sexuality.

Fiammetta is not only telling a story for the general edification and amusement of her companions; she is also directing it with implicit accusatory force at Dioneo. Using the terms of speech-act theory, we would say that her story is a perlocutionary as well as a locutionary act.[7] It does something (challenges Dioneo's views) at the same time that it states something (tells us about a woman's success). Fiammetta attempts to execute at the diegetic level what Melchisedech accomplishes at the metadiegetic level in *Decameron* 1.3. There, the sultan asks Melchisedech a question designed to undo him: which is the true faith, Jewish, Saracen, or Christian? Melchisedech immediately fathoms the trickiness of the question, tells the parable of the three rings, each one indistinguishable from the other, each one the sign of an authorized heir.[8] Likewise, when Dioneo tells of the monk and the abbot, his audience will have the opportunity to grasp the hidden force of the utterance and to offer one or more narratives in response.

Granted, Fiammetta may not be the first narrator of the *Decameron* to use storytelling as a polemical tool. On the basis of on Millicent Marcus's assessment of the novella of Melchisedech and the sultan (1.3), we should probably grant primacy to Filomena.[9] Declining to participate in the cosmic ambitions that Panfilo and Neifile had advanced in the first two stories of the *Decameron*, stories that showed readers of religious truths who were either deluded or willing to impose their interpretations on texts unlikely to support them, Filomena presents the ideal reader as a secular presence who is keenly aware of how meanings are generated.[10] Her story reminds us that social reality is constructed by means of agreements – however provisional, however constrained – about narratives that we produce.

For better or worse, however, Filomena's ideal author and reader happen to be men. So by the time Filomena finishes her story, the women readers of the Author's Preface look like a screen behind which the real male readers lie. Millicent Marcus describes those female readers of the Preface as a modest decoy for the ideal public that Boccaccio seeks to create through his narrations. In the tale of Melchisedech, we get our first glimpse of the powerful, learned, and well-disposed readers who constitute Boccaccio's ideal audience.[11]

In response to Dioneo, the narrator who introduces bawdiness and bodiliness into the ·*Decameron*, Fiammetta re-establishes difference as an important category in narration and reading. She reorganizes the reading relationship around the question of gender difference; she re-delivers the possibility of reading (and writing) as a woman.

Let us begin by considering the implications of Dioneo's first story. The plot, for those readers unfamiliar with it, is as follows: A young monk surreptitiously brings a young woman into his cell. He is seen by his abbot, who then plots to expose the monk's sin. The monk, aware that he has been observed, leaves his cell and supplies the abbot with the key to it. The abbot goes to the cell intending to ascertain the facts of the situation, but he too falls prey to sexual temptation. He takes his pleasure with the girl, placing her on top of him. Later, the abbot attempts to punish the monk for his sin, hoping thereby to be the only one to possess the girl. But when the monk obliquely rebukes his superior, the abbot realizes that it would be shameful to castigate the monk when he himself was guilty. The monk escapes punishment, and the girl is sent away from the monastery, only in all likelihood to be asked to return frequently.

Crucial to an understanding of this novella are its two sources, story 54 of the *Novellino*, 'Qui conta, come il piovano Porcellino fu accusato' ('How the country priest named Piglet was accused of wrongdoing') and the fabliau 'L'evesque qui beneï le con' ('The Bishop Who Blessed the Cunt'). Scant attention has been paid to them.[12] Uncomfortable with the salient sexual content of the fabliau, A.C. Lee, author of *The 'Decameron': Its Sources and Analogues*, seems only too relieved that Dioneo's novella does not require him to speak openly about a woman's sex.[13]

Yet it is not prudishness alone that has kept readers from thinking about this novella's sources and analogues. Even Guido Almansi, never one to shy away from licentious novellas, encourages us to turn away from the sources. He writes:

> The literary precedents which have been proposed for this story are of little help. There is, for example, the *fabliau, L'evêque qui bénit le con*, which is all in a farcical manner and concludes with a superbly blasphemous *grossiéreté* in the *benedictio vulvae* of the final episode. None the less, this *fabliau*, of little weight, is profanely and blandly unconcerned with the treatment of moral issues. Again, story LIV of the *Novellino* bears a certain relationship to the *fabliau* but it is extremely slight in construction and little can be made out of the analogue.[14]

For Almansi, both sources are 'of little help.' One is 'of little weight'; the other is 'extremely slight in construction' and 'little can be made' out of it. What is important to him is that the characters of the novella are elements in a functional scheme, rather than bearers of a well-delineated psychology. Pared down to their basic roles – the clever and lustful young monk, the young and beautiful girl whom he (and later the abbot) takes to bed, the hypocritical and self-deceived abbot – these 'narrative puppets' are manipulated according to artistic and combinatory possibilities. The goal, Almansi argues, is to render insight into the mechanisms of self-deception.[15]

I would agree with Almansi that *Decameron* 1.4 relies on characters that are rendered emblematic, and I would also agree that this novella, unlike its subtexts, pays more attention to the unfolding of the abbot's hypocrisy and self-deception. Nevertheless, I do not believe our questions should stop here.

Why, I would ask, among all the emblematic characters of *Decameron* 1.4, is it the figure of the young girl that is most significantly pared down? Why is it that she is reduced to her marked physical beauty and her unremarkable moral character?[16] Almansi would have it that '[s]he is a character possessing neither face nor personality; a passive victim of a 'texte en train de s'écrire' ('a text in the process of composing itself').[17] But before this girl is whittled down to nothing, let us take another look at the subtexts, where we shall see that such a reduction of the female character was hardly inevitable. In doing so, we shall see that the girl of *Decameron* 1.4 is not only a passive victim of a 'text in the process of composing itself' (as Almansi has argued), but a key element in what I would call a 'discourse in the process of articulating itself.'

In *Novellino* 54, the bishop, named Mangiadore (let us call him 'Hoggett') finds the country priest Porcellino (let us call him 'Piglet') guilty of having had affairs. Although we know nothing else about the bishop and the priest at this point, the names convey who the bigger pig is.[18] Porcellino's family finds a way to extricate him from this predicament. They hide him under the bishop's bed; so Porcellino is present when the bishop invites a woman – one whom he must pay, no less – to lie with him. Emerging at an opportune moment, Porcellino confronts the bishop, who is then properly shamed and lets him be, at least for a while.

In 'L'evesque qui beneï le con' ('The Bishop Who Blessed the Cunt'), the subordinate's resistance to the bishop is illustrated at much greater length.[19] When the bishop discovers that the priest has a woman to whom he is much attached, he responds by saddling the priest with penances designed to make the priest renounce his woman. First, the bishop maintains that the priest may not drink wine until he has stopped seeing the woman (24–33). The woman, Dame Auberee, tells her lover that if he cannot drink wine, he can chug it (40–57). Then the bishop tells the priest that he may not eat goose until he has stopped seeing the woman (58–63). The woman tells her lover that instead, he can eat gander, of which he has at least thirty (73–80). Finally, the bishop tells the priest that he may not sleep on a featherbed (84–5). The woman promises to make her lover a bed of cushions (94–101). After all threats fail, the fabliau turns toward exposing the bishop's hypocrisy. When the bishop comes to visit the village for a week, staying with a townswoman, the priest arranges to hide behind a curtain in her bedroom. From there, he observes how the woman refuses the bishop's advances until the bishop agrees to bless her cunt as if it were about to be ordained. The bishop offers his benediction, and as he pronounces the final words, 'Per omnia secula seculorum,' the priest responds 'Amen.' The bishop, first frightened, then amused, leaves the priest to drink wine as he wishes, eat goose and spicy chicks, and keep his woman, as long as the priest keeps out of his sight (218–25).

How is *Decameron* 1.4 different from its sources, and why have these differences been introduced?

Refashioning these two subtexts with a vengeance, Dioneo limits very significantly the roles given to the female characters, and he creates a male protagonist who, unlike his two priestly predecessors, is capable of carrying out every segment of his project independently. While it is true that Dioneo does not malign woman by representing the girl as avaricious (a commonplace in medieval misogynistic thinking that *Novellino* 54 invokes), he also does not represent her as having any substance. The nameless young girl of *Decameron* 1.4 pales in comparison to the shrewd Dame Auberee, whose masterful manipulation of linguistic differences enables her to evade a bishop's control. Throughout Dioneo's novella, the girl remains the object of male action, the instrument of male pleasure. Although presumably she speaks when she consents to accompany the monk back to his cell, her words are never reported in direct discourse; and once she is in the cell, she assumes a passive role, listening if all is going well, or crying if it isn't.

The main point, however, is not merely that the young girl is passive. Rather, it is that she, unlike the monk, is unaware that she is being looked at, and she does not have the option of placing herself in the position of 'he who looks.'

Dioneo's novella captures for us, in a nutshell, the problem of the look as explored by Sartre.[20] The abbot imprudently believes himself to be the sole bearer of the look. The monk, by contrast, knows that one can be both the bearer and the object of the look; he shows us how the look can overturn a hierarchy. But just as the novella illuminates the look, it leaves unexplored the problem of the way that the gaze so neatly elides woman.[21] In order to see this, we would have to go beyond considering who claims the position of subjective mastery (the abbot or the monk), in order to analyse the very terms on which this subjectivity is structured.

Who is the girl? For the monk, she is 'forse figliuol d'alcuno de lavora-tori della contrada' ('perhaps the daughter of one of the local workers' [1.4.5; 39]), while for the abbot, 'potrebbe essere tal femina o figliuola di tale uomo' ('she might very well be a respectable woman or the daughter of some person of importance' [1.4.14; 40]).[22] Agreed that she is beautiful, they can arrive at conflicting assessments of her social station because her subjectivity is irrelevant.

In one fleeting moment, we may harbour hopes that the girl's identity and station will be disclosed. The abbot enters the monk's cell with a plan to find out who the girl is: 's'avisò di voler prima veder chi fosse e poi prender partito' ('he decided first to see who the girl was and then make his decision' ([1.4.14; 40]). But all the abbot could 'see' when his eye fell upon her was a beautiful young girl. For him, she loses all subjec-tivity, becoming merely an object to be possessed ('guadagnata preda' or 'the spoils ... gained' [1.4.20; 41]).

In this novella where secrets are key to the development of the plot, only male secrets about sexual possession are granted any significance. The girl's mysterious identity comes to be irrelevant in the competition between males to assert superior knowledge and sexual rights. In exchange for its pleasurable exploration of difference (high/low, serious/comic, heavy/light, truthful/hypocritical), the novella asks the reader to accept a voyeuristic interest in secrets about sex (secrets that, even though they involve woman, are ultimately men's secrets) and to turn a blind eye to the secret of subjectivity (a secret that woman bears). The novella asks us to reaffirm men's control of secret space at the expense of woman.

It would be premature to call Dioneo's tale 'misogynist' on account of its representation of a passive woman. I believe it is dangerous to hang large theories about reading and sexual difference on such a small hook. Still, the novella raises red flags. To what degree do the narratives of the *Decameron*, in constructing the reader's pleasure, depend on the elision of woman's subjectivity? And when stories of the *Decameron* grant women subjectivity, will they construct it on a male model?

Meanwhile, for the next storyteller, Fiammetta, there is also a more immediate concern: Are women simply beautiful young playthings with no moral standards to speak of?[23] This is the question to which she responds when in *Decameron* 1.5, pointedly addressing herself to 'donne mie belle' ('lovely ladies' [1.5.4; 42]), she presents a woman of a differ-ent calibre.

Again, for those unfamiliar with Fiammetta's story, it is as follows: The king of France falls in love with a marchioness in a faraway land and arranges to visit her while her husband is away. The marchioness invites the king to dinner, and orders that chicken be served at every course. Confronted with this scene, the king inquires, with phrasing that allows him to broach the subject of sexuality and reproduction: 'Dama, nascono in questo paese solamente galline senza gallo alcuno?' ('Madam, are there only hens and no cocks born in this country?' [1.5.14; 44]). The marchioness replies, 'Monsignor no, ma le femine, quantunque in vestimenti e in onori alquanto dall'altre variino, tutte per ciò son fatte qui come altrove' ('No, my lord, but though women may differ in dress and rank, the women here are the same as they are elsewhere' [1.5.14; 44]). The king departs soon thereafter. Fiammetta concludes:

E senza più motteggiarla, temendo delle sue risposte, fuori d'ogni speranza desinò; e, finito il desinare, acciò che il presto partirsi ricoprisse la sua disonesta venuta, ringraziatala dell'onor ricevuto da lei, accomandandolo ella a Dio, a Genova se n'andò.   (1.5.17)

So he continued to dine with no hope of success and with no further attempts at jesting, for he feared her retorts; and immediately after dinner, in order to cover up a dishonest arrival with a hasty departure, he thanked her for the honor she had done him, she commended him to God, and he left for Genoa.   (44)[24]

The truncated rhythms that Fiammetta uses in this concluding sentence of the novella are the parting touch for a woman trying to clip a man's wings: 'fuori d'ogni speranza *desinò* ... *a Genova se n'andò*' ('So without teasing her further, fearing her retorts and discouraged, *his dinner he ate* ... and *for Genoa he left*' [1.5.17; my translation; emphasis mine]). Can Fiammetta rid herself of Dioneo as perfunctorily as the beautiful and worthy marchioness has rid herself of the king of France? She can try, braving the challenge by offering an alternative account of women's virtues.

The vast majority of the women of the *Decameron* are physically beautiful, of course. But according to whom? And what does their beauty entail? As I shall argue in the next chapter, 'Boccaccio's Sexed Thought,' were we to examine the novellas told on Day 2 of the *Decameron*, when more women populate the stories, we would see that the three male narrators of the *Decameron* highlight women's carnality, which they link directly to women's sexual availability. We would also see that the seven women narrators do not concentrate on women's beauty in the same way. Even when they mention corporeal beauty, they remain focused on women's character and intellect. And in none of their stories on the Second Day do women consent to sexual relations not subsequently legitimated by marriage.

Now I find it curious that whenever Fiammetta says that the marchioness is 'most beautiful,' she takes care to specify that the source of this information is a man. In the context of a discussion of the marquis of Monferrato, 'fu per un cavalier detto che ... quanto tra' cavalieri era d'ogni virtù il marchese famoso, tanto la donna tra tutte l'altre donne del mondo era bellissima e valorosa' ('one knight remarked that there existed under all the stars in the world no couple equal to the Marquis and his lady; for inasmuch as he was renowned among knights for every virtue, his lady was likewise considered most beautiful and worthy among all the women of the world' [1.5.6; 43]). Upon being received by the marchioness, the king judges her to be 'bellissima e valorosa e costumata' ('beautiful, virtuous, and courtly' [1.5.11; 43]), even more so than the report had claimed. And the third time her beauty is mentioned, it is in the context of the king's observation of her at dinner: 'con diletto talvolta la marchesana bellissima riguardando, sommo piacere avea' ('from time to time he would gaze at the beautiful Marchioness with delight' [1.5.13; 44]).

Whereas the men of the novella are primarily interested in reporting on and evaluating and deriving pleasure from the marchioness's beauty, the single other female observer and narrator – Fiammetta herself – never remarks on it. When she refers to the woman as anything other than 'la gentil donna' or 'la donna' or 'la marchesana', she comments on her moral and intellectual qualities alone. The marchioness is, according to Fiammetta, 'savia e avveduta' ('prudent and wise' [1.5.9; 43]) and 'valorosa' ('worthy' [1.5.10; 43]). The king seeks bodily pleasures rather than virtue; otherwise, why is it that when he receives a report about the virtue of the marquis of Monferrato, equal to the beauty of the marchioness, he chooses to seek her out? Moreover, the marchioness is a woman of insight. She can judge evidence and see into the king's heart, even before she meets him. She knows full well that it is her reputation for beauty that draws him: 'né la 'ngannò in questo l'aviso, cioè che la fama della sua bellezza il vi traesse' ('nor was she deceived when she concluded that he was drawn there by the renown of her beauty' [1.5.9; 43]). With respect to her perspicacity, she is the equal of the wise Melchisedech, who had grasped straightaway the insidiousness of the sultan's question to him (1.3.9).

Also important to Fiammetta's defence of woman is her assertion of the marchioness's rhetorical skill. For the very first time in the *Decameron*, a woman uses her signifying abilities to achieve what she desires. (And note well: what she desires is freedom from unwanted sexual attention.)

This is indisputably a pro-woman story, is it not? Before we rush to respond in the affirmative, we should weigh the matter more carefully.

As will have been clear to the reader from my own presentation of Fiammetta's discursive strategies, Fiammetta devotes considerable narrative energy to undoing the notion that beauty signals sexual availability. In comparison, the exploration of woman, language, and subjectivity gets short shrift. What this means is that, at least at first glance, Fiammetta's narrative tends to encourage us to focus on the Imaginary (the realm of ego-identifications) rather than on the Symbolic (the realm of language and subjectivity). This may not be the most effective response to Dioneo's novella, especially since, as I argued above, his novella is also organized so as to make us focus on the Imaginary rather than the Symbolic.

Furthermore, in fashioning the marchioness's retort, Fiammetta adopts strategies whose overall effectiveness is debatable. Yes, the king of France did get the point when the marchioness used her chicken dinner to express her opinions about sexual difference. But because this is the very first instance where figurative language is used to describe sexual difference, and because figurative language (especially about sex) will be crucial territory in the struggle for control of meaning and mastery, this novella will also derive its meaning in retrospect, as its encoding of women's and men's uses of language will be reaffirmed by some, contested by others. The marchioness, who prevails with her immediate visitor, loses ground when her retort is seen in the context of the *Decameron*'s discourse about men, women, and figurative language.

Why might the marchioness's strategy fall short of the mark? First, as with any utterance, there is a potential for failure (which, depending on the context of the utterance might be called a 'misfire' or 'abuse' or 'infelicity').[25] With Shoshana Felman, I would hasten to add that this is not 'because *something is missing*, but because *something else is done*, or because something else is said.'[26] The marchioness organizes her chicken dinner, and produces a message about women and difference (women are fundamentally the same even when you dress them up differently). But she also sends an inadvertent message as she maps figurative language about women onto alimentary and bestiary semantic fields. What are the consequences of the metaphorical equations 'woman = comestible' and 'woman = animal'? Both of these metaphors, which linger on in later figural renderings of woman in the *Decameron*, deny subjectivity to woman. Again, these metaphors are not decidedly preferable to Dioneo's mapping of an enclosed space (a cell to be opened with a key) as feminized and sexualized.[27]

Second, although Fiammetta grants woman the right to speak, her story maps out sexual difference along the axis of silence versus speech. When the marchioness plans the chicken banquet as a framing event, a good portion of her contribution is non-verbal. It is a man who introduces the language of hens and cocks in order to speak figuratively about sexual difference. (Never mind at this point that silence is as much a speech act as a verbal utterance. The narrators of the *Decameron* will not explore this possibility until Day 3, and when they do, it will be a male narrator, Filostrato, who shows how a man's silence can function as a speech act [3.1].) This opposition between female silence and male speech continues even when the marchioness utters her witty remark. The marchioness declines to use her chickens to talk about sex, even though the king of France has broached the subject of chicken sexuality and reproduction. She turns the king's statement around, preferring to comment instead on the differences instituted by dress and status. In doing this, she limits the range of the king's metaphor; now there is no point in his talking about sex anymore, much less trying to do it. But she also, at least provisionally, situates the female speaker as someone who may not use figurative language to talk about sex. This is not entirely unproblematic, because as we shall see later in the *Decameron*, such figurative language tends to remain the prerogative of male speakers (3.1, 3.10, 4.Introduction, 5.4, 7.2, 10.10, Author's Conclusion), the female speaker ventriloquized by a man (2.7), and of the déclassé female speaker (2.10, 6.Introduction, 8.2).

The rhetorical problem of *Decameron* 1.5 has now taken shape. Fiammetta resists Dioneo's representation of woman, but with discursive strategies whose achievements are disputable, dubious. By this I do not mean that we should forthwith dismiss her rhetorical achievement. Rather, we must allow for it to be debated. Her response to Dioneo can be registered, and its value determined more precisely, only as other voices join in. The fate of her discursive strategies is now at least partly in the hands of others.

Upon hearing Fiammetta's tale, the women of the group praise the action of the marchioness (1.6.2). Nevertheless, Fiammetta's critique of gender relations recedes as the next three narrators turn their attention elsewhere. In 1.6, Emilia tells how a worthy man confounds the evil hypocrisy of the religious with a witty response. In the seventh and eighth tales of Day 1, told by Filostrato and Lauretta, men use witty remarks to confound hypocrisy and avarice, and to reinforce virtue in a religious and political context. By this time we may wonder whether Fiammetta's questions have been forgotten or displaced. Although Elissa returns cautiously to the subject of gender relations in *Decameron* 1.9, her very brief story about the woman of Gascony and the king of Cyprus has never been read with an eye to its participation in a discourse about gender, justice, and political authority; moreover, because it is the shortest tale of the collection, it is certain to be insufficient to the enormity of the project of rethinking gender and power and institutions. In the final story of Day 1, wherein Mastro Alberto puts Madonna Malgherida in her place after she unwisely mocks him for having fallen in love with her (1.10), Pampinea returns to the issue of gender relations that Fiammetta had addressed, this time to co-opt the syntactic structure of Fiammetta's novella (wherein a character of one sex uses a witty remark as a form of personal defence against a character of the opposite sex).[28] In so doing, Pampinea relays a message about women diametrically opposed to Fiammetta's: she calls into question women's verbal abilities and reinforces male authority.

That Boccaccio should show us the risks and vulnerabilities of entering the interpretive fray is part of the brilliance of his *Decameron*. Here is Judith Butler writing in 1997 about 'the equivocity of the utterance': 'If utterances bear equivocal meanings, then their power is, in principle, less unilateral and sure than it appears. Indeed, the equivocity of the utterance means that it might not always mean in the same way, that its meaning might be turned or derailed in some significant way.'[29] This sounds remarkably similar to what the *Decameron* is proposing in the mid-1300s, does it not?

Again, here is Butler writing about the consequences of linguistic vulnerability:

For if one always risks meaning something other than what one thinks one utters, then one is, as it were, vulnerable in a specifically linguistic sense to a social life of language that exceeds the purview of the subject who speaks. This risk and vulnerability are proper to democratic process in the sense that one cannot know in advance the meaning that the other will assign to one's utterance, what conflict of interpretation may well arise, and how best to adjudicate that difference. The effort to come to terms is not one that can be resolved in anticipation but only through a concrete struggle of translation, one whose success has no guarantees.[30]

Again, I would have us note that these conclusions are the same ones we are forced to embrace in our reading of the *Decameron*, most especially in our reading of the polemical exchanges among its narrators. The meaning assigned to any particular narrative contribution will depend on the place that readers and respondents will assign to it in their continuing dialogue.

The risk of linguistic vulnerability, the challenge to use narratives to fashion human identity and social reality – these are constants of our current thinking about the performative nature of language, as they were for Boccaccio when he wrote the *Decameron* in the mid-1300s. But what specific conclusions are we to draw about misogynistic and pro-woman discourses in a work such as the *Decameron*? At the very least, what can we conclude about Fiammetta's intervention?

On Day 1, Fiammetta looks to be the lone voice of resistance to a discourse dominated by male concerns and biases. Obviously, there are many narrative exchanges to come; the case of Fiammetta v. Dioneo cannot be decided definitively at this early point in the *Decameron*, in part because we do not yet know if Fiammetta has more to say in response to Dioneo, in part because we do not yet know whether Dioneo will respond, and how. But this much we can say: Differing with Dioneo, Fiammetta makes visible the tensions around gender ideologies and politics. She moves toward naming the problem. Because her response is directed at Dioneo, the only other narrator to address the issue of sexuality, she encourages us to establish a specific subject who might be accountable for a specific act.

This impulse to assign accountability for misogynistic discourse is not uncommon. As with all speech that is hateful, what does this desire for accountability mean, and where does it lead us in our thinking about political responses? Here, we should pose the question that Judith Butler so aptly formulates regarding the performative force of utterance: 'If the injury can be traced to a specifiable act, it qualifies as an object of prosecution: it can be brought to court and held accountable.'[31] Again, with Butler, we ought to ask, 'Do we accept the notion that injurious speech is attributable to a singular subject and act?'[32]

Yet to what extent is Dioneo responsible for the potentially anti-woman discourse that he speaks (or, more aptly, that speaks through him)? Who could serve as prosecutor of such an offence? Fiammetta may position herself in an adversarial role with respect to Dioneo. He may be summoned. But what if he chooses, like some other narrators, not to respond? After all, misogynistic discourse, as R. Howard Bloch has argued, consistently deflects responsibility: 'it is a citational mode whose rhetorical thrust displaces its own source away from anything that might be construed as personal or confessional. No one admits to anti-feminism. No one says, "I am a misogynist."'[33]

Finally, who would be the judge that could review the case, resolve it, or dismiss it? Later, when Fiammetta takes her place as queen on Day 5 of the *Decameron*, she will sit 'pro tribunali' (5.Intr.5; 314), in the place of honour, like a judge before his tribunal. Who or what might she judge, and how would she deliver her opinion?

The case of 'Fiammetta v. Dioneo' must be consigned to the reader, who shall be called upon to take the difficulties in the presentation of evidence and the delivery of an opinion into account. Of course, as a gendered being, the reader must also acknowledge his or her own implication in the case. The reader is not safely confined to the judge's bench. In this case, as in others in these fictional worlds, the reader may also be prosecutor, supporting witness, defendant, plaintiff, or some perplexing combination thereof. What the reader can discover, as a result, is not the absolute truth about the case, not whether Fiammetta is right and Dioneo wrong, not whether the *Decameron* is misogynist or feminist, but rather some dimly illuminated truth about the process of reading and weighing evidence that will tell us as much or more about a particular reader in a particular social and historical setting as it will tell us about a particular textual conflict. And if we are fortunate, in this investigation that will have to take us far beyond where we currently are in our thinking about the *Decameron*'s gender ideologies, these judicious readers will be able to disclose to us the process by which a text such as the *Decameron*, although it is obstructionist in its attempt to deflect certain questions about woman and gender, also grants us insight into the rhetorical construction of a social reality that is configured differently for men and women.

Let us turn now to Fiammetta's story about Andreuccio da Perugia on Day 2 of the *Decameron*. My initial claim is simple enough: that Andreuccio da Perugia, the naive and bumbling protagonist of one of the best-known novellas of the *Decameron*, could be identified as a casualty of fourteenth-century sex wars. I shall argue my point by examining the relation between this novella and some key stories that precede it, both in the *Decameron* and in the French fabliau tradition. I would not have us be content to stop here, however, and that is why I shall also argue that Fiammetta's novella of Andreuccio da Perugia, while it encourages the reader to delight momentarily in her superiority to Andreuccio, also, by means of its nuanced conclusion, calls into question too-hasty proclamations of victory.

Let us begin by thinking about how stories about women get generated in the early portion of the *Decameron*. On Day 1, women appear when they become the objects of male sexual attention. A young monk notices a young girl in the fields and took her to his cell (1.4). Word of a marchioness's beauty brings the king of France to her land (1.5). A woman of Gascony is raped and then seeks justice (1.9). And master Alberto falls in love with Madonna Malgherida when he sees her at a feast (1.10). In a cluster of stories at the beginning of the Second Day (*Decameron* 2.2, 2.3, and 2.4), something quite startling happens: women see men.

For what purpose? These sightings by women are not simply a reversal of the mechanism we saw on the First Day. On Day 2, a woman's look does not initiate the major storyline. Rather, her look allows for resolution of a plot line that has heretofore involved only men. In *Decameron* 2.2, told by Filostrato, Rinaldo d'Asti falls victim to highway robbers; but he can be saved because a widow sees him, and offers him shelter and sexual pleasure. *Decameron* 2.3, told by Pampinea, focuses at great length on the political and financial hardships of a Florentine banking family in England and, in particular, on the hardships of a certain Alessandro; he manages to avoid financial ruin because he merits the attention of an abbot who proves to be the daughter of the king of England and a marriage prospect. Then, in *Decameron* 2.4, Lauretta tells of a merchant, Landolfo Rufolo, who accumulates wealth in a piratry scheme, but very nearly loses his life in a shipwreck on the high seas; a lowly washerwoman saves him from a watery death. As a unit, these stories reaffirm that, with the help of a woman who comes to his aid at an unexpected moment (and who may even make sexual advances toward him), a male protagonist can overcome the adversities of Fortune. Even more, these stories offer reassurance that when women become bearers of the look rather than its objects, they will exercise the look only to accommodate and encourage male desire.

Once again, as on Day 1, Fiammetta challenges this view. Her novella of Andreuccio da Perugia (*Decameron* 2.5) is a pivotal contribution to the storytelling of Day 2.[34] Fiordaliso, the Sicilian prostitute, merely *looks* like Good Fortune to the naive and bumbling Andreuccio, whose perpetual misreading of signs drives the novella ahead. Moreover, Fiammetta takes advantage of a second chance to counter Dioneo's story about the monk and the abbot (*Decameron* 1.4). As I argued in my discussion of *Decameron* 1.4 and 1.5, Dioneo rewrites his sources, in particular the French fabliau 'L'evesque qui beneï le con' ('The Bishop Who Blessed the Cunt'), in order to render the female character far less substantial or clever than the men; with her novella about a virtuous marchioness, Fiammetta tries to cast woman in a more positive light. Now, on Day 2 of the *Decameron*, Fiammetta will continue this nascent battle between the sexes. This time, she will respond tit for tat: she too will revise a French fabliau, and this time the revisions will be to the detriment of the male character.[35]

Fiammetta's source is 'Boivin de Provins,' a fabliau that pits against each other two tricksters: Boivin, a pleasure-seeking wastrel ('mout bon lechierres' [v. 1]), and the prostitute Mabile. Boivin decides to go to the fair at Provins, not to participate in merchant activity, but to be the subject of narrative activity: 'Porpenssa soi que a Prouvins / A la foire voudra aler, / Et si fera de lûi parler!' ('He decided he would go / To the fair at Provins / And there he would make a name for himself' [lit. 'he would make himself the subject of talk' [vv. 2–4]). So he disguises himself ably as a peasant, in clothes that the narrator of the fabliau believes to be of one piece. (This 'seamlessness' of his garments, apparently a gratuitous detail, will turn out to be significant later, when we see Boivin in action.) Having acquired a large purse and put into it twelve deniers, Boivin heads straight to the street where prostitutes live:

> Et vint en la rue aus putains,
> Tout droit devant l'ostel Mabile,
> Qui plus savoit barat et guile
> Que fame nule qui i fust.
> Iluec s'assist desus un fust
> Qui estoit delez sa meson;
> Delez lui mist son aguillon,
> Un poi torna son dos vers l'uis.

(20–6)

And he came to the street of whores
Right in front of the house that belonged to Mabel,
Who knew more about trickery and guile
Than any woman who ever was.
There he sat down on a log
Which lay in front of her house.
He laid his stick beside him
And turned his back a little toward the door.

The opening scene very ably describes the competing sexual powers of Boivin and Mabile in terms of physical objects: he has his staff and purse (*aguillon* and *borse grant*), she her house and the log next to it on which he sits (*meson* and *fust*). Boivin's phallic power, represented mainly by his staff, has been amply displayed as Boivin arrives 'tout droit' ('directly,' but also 'straight' and 'upright') in front of Mabile's house. He chooses to place a check on that phallic power. He puts his staff down in order to sit on the log by Mabile's house, and he makes himself more vulnerable by turning his back a little.

Boivin now recounts out loud the 'truth' of his financial dealings, partly to suggest his gullibility, partly to testify to his recently acquired wealth. Upon hearing this, two pimps summon Mabile. Continuing his monologue, Boivin laments the absence of a niece named, coincidentally enough, Mabile: 'S'or eüsse ma douce niece, / Qui fu fille de ma suer Tiece, / Dame fust or de mon avoir / ... "Ahi! douce niece Mabile ... !"' (If I had my dear niece now, / Who's the daughter of my sister, Tess, / She would now be the mistress of all my money / ... "O dear! Sweet niece, my Mabel ... !"' [105–7, 112–13]). This quickly leads to a reunion of niece Mabile and her 'uncle.' She asks him his name, and he says,

> – 'Je ai non Fouchier de la Brouce.
> Mes vous samblez ma niece douce
> Plus que nule fame qui fust!'
> Cele se pasme sor le fust.
>
> (127–30)

> 'My name is Fouchier de la Brouce;
> But you look like my dear niece
> More than any woman who ever was.'
> She fainted upon the log.

Boivin, who identifies himself as 'Fouchier de la Brouce' (126), has exposed his nature. As Howard Bloch notes, this name 'suggests his fictitious status, his status as fiction, betraying as it does the character of the swindler (compare with "fauchier"), of the fornicator (compare with "foutier"), and of the trickster (compare with "fou-chier")' (98). Mabile fails to catch these allusions and thus does not foresee her future subduction by Boivin. She foreshadows her vanquishment by falling into a fainting spasm on the log. The equivocal rhyme on *fust* (meaning both *was* and *log*), which had also been used when Boivin first appeared on Mabile's doorstep (24–5), reappears as the power dynamics between them are shifting (129–30).[36]

Promising him the hospitality of Saint Julian, the pimps invite Boivin into Mabile's house. Boivin has every reason to expect to be well treated, since, as Arturo Graf noted, the offer of the hospitality of Saint Julian involved not only good lodging, but also pleasurable companionship. Mabile entertains him with a grand meal, then offers him a young girl, Isane, whom she claims is a virgin. Throughout this display of cordiality, the battle for power continues. Mabile uses winks and gestures (which she naively believes Boivin does not see) to affirm her superiority over her guest; in particular, she gestures to Isane that the girl should cut the man's purse. Meanwhile, Boivin keeps up his verbal trickery with laments of his dead family members. He is clearly ahead in this struggle, since his rhetorical deception (like the vestments he wears) is made up out of whole cloth.[37]

Now, as Boivin and Isane are left alone, the claim of sexual superiority will be decided. Boivin, in a gesture of self-castration that will give him the edge, cuts the strings to his purse. Then he demonstrates that his phallic power is nonetheless intact:

> Puis si commence a arecier,
> et cele la borse a cerchier.
> Que qu'ele cerche, et cil l'estraint,
> De la pointe du vit la point.
> El con li met jusqu'a la coille,
> Dont li bat le cul, et rooille
> Tant, ce m'est vis, qu'il ot foutu.

(275–81)

> Then he began to get hard,
> And she, to search for the purse.

> While she was searching and he was embracing her,
> With the point of his penis he pricked her.
> He put it into her cunt all the way up to his balls,
> With which he beat her ass and banged
> So much that, in my opinion, he screwed her.

After pulling up his britches, Boivin 'sees' that his purse has been cut, and cries to his 'niece' that the young woman is responsible. Mabile opens the door, and threatens to beat him with a stick; he leaves. Mabile, certain that the purse is soon to be hers, demands it of Isane, who of course does not have it. So Mabile beats the girl and tears her clothes. Such is the fate of those who tell the truth; integrity of body and apparel is the privilege of those who, like Boivin, deal in unassailable falsehoods. Finally, as other people approach, the scene turns into a general brawl: Boivin's pretense of violence toward himself has been unleashed as uncontrollable violence among his opponents, who are less able to control the distinctions between truth and deceit.

The end of the fabliau coincides with the end of the story as Boivin tells it:

> Boivin s'en vint droit au provost,
> se li a conté mot a mot
> de chief en chief la verité.
> E li provos l'a escouté,
> qui molt ama la lecherie.
> Sovent li fist conter sa vie
> a ses parens, a ses amis,
> qui molt s'en sont joué et ris.
> Boivin remest trois jors entiers,
> Se le dona de ses deniers
> Li provos dis sous a Boivins,
> Qui cest fablel fist a Provins.

(369–80)

> Boivin went straight to the magistrate
> And told him the truth, word
> For word from beginning to end
> And the magistrate, who greatly loved
> A bawdy story, listened to him.
> He kept making him tell the whole experience

To his relatives and to his friends,
Who enjoyed it very much and laughed about it.
Boivin stayed there three whole days;
And the magistrate gave ten sous
Of his own money to Boivin,
Who made this fabliau in Provins.

The listener is encouraged to take pleasure in Boivin's superior deceptiveness and sexual power. Do we actually know what the 'truth, word / For word from beginning to end' is? Could Boivin be making up a story out of whole cloth again, just as when he told Mabile the 'truth' about his finances and family? Who knows? We needn't care, because in hearing Boivin recount his adventure, we get pleasure from his fictions without having to pay inordinately.[38]

Fiammetta mutates the crafty and clever Boivin de Provins into the laughably naive Andreuccio da Perugia. Convinced that his ostentatious display of money is proof that he is a serious horse trader, Andreuccio is easily taken advantage of by someone who sees this display as proof of his gullibility. He is all too willing to assume that an invitation to an unknown woman's house is proof of his magnetism; it never occurs to him that she might be interested in something else in his pocket. He imprudently chooses to remain silent about his departure for a district of Naples inauspiciously called 'Malpertugio' ('Evil Hole'), and when he arrives there, he has no inkling that these are not the environs of the well-to-do.

The question of the reader's pleasure is more complicated than we might expect, however. It is true that the reader is encouraged to take pleasure first in the superior deceptiveness of Fiordaliso, the Sicilian prostitute who, with a good deal of planning and a little luck, tricks the gullible Andreuccio out of his five hundred florins. Fiordaliso, the first *female* voyeur of the *Decameron*, sees without being seen.[39] And the reader can identify with her, for like all readers, she finds out information without (presumably) having to reveal any. But when Fiordaliso disappears from the narrative, the reader is left with Andreuccio. Now what, if not to participate in Andreuccio's education as a critical reader? Andreuccio falls once (into the latrine, after he fails to judge the signs that would tip him off about Fiordaliso), and yet again (as he is left in a well by the grave-robbers), and even yet again (when he is abandoned in the tomb of the archbishop of Naples, after he chooses to remain with the grave-robbers). Finally, one would think, he will learn to be more prudent. As he hides the archbishop's ring from the grave-robbers and as he tricks another grave-robber into thinking he is one of the living dead, Andreuccio discovers what Boivin and Fiordaliso have known all along: that things are not always what they seem.

At the end of the story, Andreuccio is in possession of a ring worth more than five hundred florins; he has recovered his losses. Some readers maintain that Andreuccio has learned his lesson, that he has become, in the words of Giovanni Getto, 'un abilissimo interprete e maestro,' 'a most proficient interpreter and master.'[40] But it is not clear that Andreuccio is much less naive at the end than he was in the beginning.

To read this novella as if it were about the successful education of a critical reader requires that we ignore what happens after this momentary resolution. Andreuccio wanders aimlessly through the streets of Naples, just as he had done earlier, after he had fallen into the latrine outside his 'sister's' house. It is almost dawn, and therefore nearing the time when it will be light enough to begin to see, but he is wearing the archbishop's ring – surely a large one – on his finger nonetheless. How different is this from when he had displayed his money for all to see when he arrived in Naples? As it happens, Andreuccio then comes upon the inn where he had been staying. He tells the innkeeper the whole story – just as he had earlier, when he had foolishly told his woes to the grave-robbers, who then proceeded to take advantage of a poor unsuspecting sop. It is only because the innkeeper is not inclined to take advantage of his guest that Andreuccio escapes the cycle of victimization. Andreuccio comes to a happy end, but it isn't by his own doing that he makes it out of Naples alive. Given how little he seems to have learned, one has to wonder whether Andreuccio will manage to keep his ring when he returns to Perugia.[41]

The novella of Andreuccio da Perugia demonstrates masterfully not how a protagonist can triumph over misfortune, but rather how complicated it is to calculate losses and gains. Anyone familiar with balance sheets and financial statements is certain to know that the mere presence of assets is not a reliable indicator of financial strength, nor is debt a crippling factor. Gains and losses that appear on paper are not always such; they may be passive, not realized. So it is too in a world in which one attempts to calculate degrees of mastery and submission, triumph and failure, liberation and oppression. Whereas previous stories on Day 2 show an astute protagonist threatened by misfortune but then restored to his initial state (Martellino in 2.1 and Rinaldo d'Asti in 2.2), or show how he can be elevated to a new status that permits him to withdraw from the risky world of mercantile exchange (Alessandro in 2.3 and Landolfo Rufolo in 2.4), Fiammetta's story about Andreuccio da Perugia, which stages two different stories of gain, is dedicated to showing how we might fool ourselves into thinking of our protagonist as a winner. To do this, Fiammetta forges a delicate balance in the power relations between the crafty Sicilian prostitute and Andreuccio. Fiordaliso tells the superior story about herself and leaves with a handsome sum. The foolish Andreuccio, who is also most willing to tell of himself, regains his wealth. No wonder then that a reader as insightful as Millicent Marcus vacillates between Andreuccio and the Sicilian prostitute when she tries to name the active hero of this novella, the person who authors his (or her) destiny.[42]

Fiammetta also resists the drift of the early novellas on Day 2, where good things happen when people speak in orderly fashion.[43] Martellino owes his life to an orderly narration; his friends Marchese and Stecchi tell their innkeeper of Martellino's plight ('come il fatto era gli raccontarono' [2.1.30]), and subsequently the innkeeper has them tell a certain Sandro Agolanti ('ogni cosa per ordine dettagli' [2.1.30]), who arranges for Martellino's release. When Rinaldo d'Asti finds himself at the woman's castle after he has been robbed, Rinaldo tells her all in orderly fashion ('per ordine ogni cosa narrò' [2.2.32]), and in response she treats him extraordinarily well. In *Decameron* 2.3, the daughter of the king of England manages, by means of an eloquent speech to the pope, to attain her desires. In Fiammetta's story, orderly narration is effective – but not quite in the way we might have imagined. Fiammetta reminds us, first of all, that orderly narration is not a reliable indication of truth, virtue, or success. Andreuccio, hearing the young Sicilian woman's orderly narration ('questa favola così ordinatamente, così compostamente detta da costei' [2.5.25]), makes the mistake of thinking that her story is true because it is well told. She is successful; but he pays the consequences. Fiammetta also reminds us that orderly narration does not ensure triumph over adversity. Andreuccio offers the grave-robbers a systematic account of what he had found after he got out of the well where they had abandoned him ('ordinatamente disse come era avvenuto e quello che trovato aveva fuori del pozzo' [2.5.50]). The grave-robbers still remain intent on taking advantage of Andreuccio, lovely narration or not.

Fiammetta will also take her distance from other narrators' ideas about critical reading. Filostrato and Pampinea have broached some epistemological and practical questions about reading, such as: What sort of knowledge can we derive from the reading of signs, and how reliable is it? Soon thereafter, they abandon these questions about intellectual knowledge, preferring to turn instead to descriptions of pleasurable sexual encounters. In *Decameron* 2.2, told by Filostrato, Rinaldo d'Asti carefully considers the speech and comportment of his travelling companions and, since signs are not always what one takes them to be, he gets robbed by the very men he thought he could trust. Filostrato continues not by exploring interpretive matters in greater detail, but by granting Rinaldo d'Asti comfort and pleasure in the arms of a widow. Likewise, in *Decameron* 2.3, the matter of critical reading arises briefly as the abbot carefully considers his travelling companion Alessandro, weighing his speech and behaviour, and determining him to be worthy of love (2.3.20–2); Alessandro remains completely unaware of the necessity of critical reading, and has to wait for the abbot/princess to enlighten him. What could have turned into a sustained exploration of critical reading is put aside in favour of a description of the sexual encounter between the abbot/princess and Alessandro.

Contesting this nascent trend, Fiammetta frustrates those who are looking for a story about sex rather than reading. Once Andreuccio discovers (*ahimé!*) that the beautiful woman who has invited him into her abode is his sister, Fiammetta is in a position to force us to reflect long and hard on the education of a critical reader. She is the first narrator of the *Decameron* to do so. When to speak, when to remain silent, when to be honest, when to be deceptive? The answers to these questions can materialize only in a practice that is constantly sensitive to difference, to small but significant shifts in meaning and in context.

Moreover, Fiammetta renders it difficult for the narrators of the *Decameron* to think about women as merely supporting the fortunes of men who move in the world of trade and finance. As a result, women and their fortunes become a more stable focus of the narration. As I argue in the next chapter, the narrators, in the wake of Fiammetta's story, have a more complicated framework for thinking about men, women, and fortune, and they begin to explore how gender structures the experience of loss and misfortune. Overwhelmingly, the stories of Madama Beritola (*Decameron* 2.6), Alatiel (2.7), Madonna Zinevra (2.9), and the wife of Ricciardo Chinzica (2.10) ask how *women* respond to the blows of fortune, in a way that Pampinea's story of a princess/abbot and Fiammetta's story of a Sicilian prostitute could not yet do. Women characters are no longer figured simply as helpers in a plot line dedicated to males and their concerns. Male characters are no longer indisputably winners. Narrative and social roles, having been expanded, will become a subject for ongoing investigation and debate.[44]

So if we step back for a moment, we see that the strategy of Fiammetta's novella about Andreuccio da Perugia is two-pronged. The story is a second barb thrust at Dioneo and the male ego, another vindication of woman's intellect and her resistance to male desire. Here its message about the sexual difference seems cut-and-dried. But in its foregrounding of questions of critical reading, the novella refuses such unequivocal answers.

As we recognize this complicated narrative strategy, we can explain better why it is that many readers might prefer to read Fiammetta's novella as the story of an uncomplicated and straightforward triumph, rather than a story about the problematic murkiness of reading and narration.[45] In the latter part of Day 2, the narrators of the *Decameron* conveniently illustrate this for us. Even as they imagine a world made more complex by gender and sexual difference, they try to re-establish, with broad strokes, the order and stability that seemed to reign before Fiammetta introduced troublesome differences. They downplay the point about critical reading that Fiammetta had made. Critical reading seems not relevant to the resolution of their protagonists' dilemmas. This is not to say that the reader of the *Decameron* is freed from the responsibility of judging and weighing evidence, but rather that the novellas offer listeners and readers no model for what a critical reading might look like. This is especially striking in novellas like *Decameron* 2.8 and 2.9, stories about a man falsely accused of rape and a woman falsely accused of infidelity, precisely because one feels that a critical reading of the evidence might have saved the protagonists from misfortune.

And *pace* Fiammetta, the narrators of the second half of Day 2 reaffirm the value of orderly narration. Madama Beritola is saved by a story told by a nursemaid who, called forth by Currado, 'ordinatamente ogni cosa gli disse e le cagioni gli mostrò per che quella maniera che fatto aveva tenuta avesse' ('told him everything in detail, explaining, as well, her motives for behaving as she had' [2.6.73; 107]). In *Decameron* 2.7, Antigono helps Alatiel construct a story that will save her honour ('ordinatamente ciò che da far fosse le dimostrò,' 'he explained in detail what she had to do' [2.7.102; 123]), and she recounts this story fully when she is before the king and queen ('secondo l'ammaestramento datole da Antigono rispose e contò tutto' [2.7.104]). Finally, Sicurano, having organized and requested a meeting ('questo ordinato avea e domandato' [2.9.63]) begins to tell her story of betrayal and loss to the sultan in generic terms, then substantiates it by exposing her breasts and revealing herself as the protagonist of that story.

With the exception of Fiammetta, the narrators of Day 2 bypass questions of critical reading, and reject the idea that orderly narration could ever be detrimental to the protagonists of their novellas. What does this mean? It means that just as readers get introduced to a more intricate social reality – one that takes account of gender and sexual difference, one that acknowledges the contrary uses to which language can be put – they may not have the tools they need to comprehend adequately the workings of this system. That, in a nutshell, was Andreuccio's dilemma, when he moved from the limited social world of Perugia to the city of Naples. One could say that Fiammetta has presented her companions with a richer view of rhetoric and social reality; but she can not oblige them to assume this view. Indeed, it seems that they do not mind visiting a place where more complex readings are required, but ultimately they prefer to return home to well-worn standards.

Dioneo does not respond immediately to Fiammetta, either after her story on Day 2 or after her stories from Day 3 through Day 5. On Day 2, he makes it clear he has some other fish to fry, as he announces in the final story of the day that he will rethink his narrative options and offer a response to Filomena's story about Zinevra and Bernabò. On Day 3, with a story about the jealous Catella who tries to trick her husband into making love to her and in fact is tricked into an encounter with her lover Ricciardo, Fiammetta explores the difficulties that women find themselves in as a result of discursive systems that ensure male dominance. Then (as I have shown elsewhere), Dioneo uses his story of Alibech and Rustico in order to reflect on the relation between words and deeds, and, more precisely, on the discontinuity between them.[46] In *Decameron* 4.1, Fiammetta reveals the price that a woman pays when she exceeds the bounds placed on her by a male-authored system (one that, in this case, is doomed to tragic ends). On that same day, Dioneo, introducing one of the first active female servant characters of the *Decameron*, shows how crafty women willing to use their bodies and their speech can manipulate male authorities to their own (comic) ends (4.10). On Day 5, when she is queen, Fiammetta overturns Filostrato's trajectory toward tragedy by offering the group the possibility of a happy ending; in her own story about Federigo degli Alberighi (5.9), she deftly manoeuvres her audience into approving Monna Giovanna's choice of this flawed comic hero as a husband.[47] In an abrupt turnabout, Dioneo offers a pivotal novella about the wife of Pietro di Vincio-lo (5.10) in which he calls into question the primacy of heterosexual love at the same time that he validates the carnal desires of married women. On Day 6, Fiammetta calls attention to the value given to male (as opposed to female) ugliness when she tells a story about how the repulsiveness of the Baronci family is testimony to their nobility (6.6). Dioneo, going against the propensity for the witty remark rendered succinctly, dominates the day with a long story about Brother Cipolla (6.10) in which he also manages to introduce the first really ugly woman of the *Decameron*, the kitchen-maid Nuta, whom he portrays as comparable in ugliness to the Baronci. By Day 7, when Fiammetta tells, for the first time, a story that resolutely applauds a woman's adultery on account of the extreme jealousy of her husband (7.5), Dioneo explicitly directs his attention toward another of the female narrators, Elissa, whose contribution he recognizes and amplifies when he tells of a Sienese man named Tingoccio who discovers after his death that sexuality is not sinful in precisely the way he had feared (7.10). On Day 8, Fiammetta also focuses on the contribution of another narrator, trying as she does in *Decameron* 8.8 to displace some of the misogynistic force of Pampinea's novella about the scholar and the widow (8.7) by offering a more 'comic' form of vengeance. At this point, Dioneo chooses to return to the plot situation that Fiammetta had raised on Day 2 with Andreuccio da Perugia: a northern Italian merchant tricked by a Sicilian woman craftier than he. As we shall see, Dioneo's retelling of this story will prove seminal for storytelling in the final days of the *Decameron*.

In the Author's rubric, the gist of Dioneo's story on Day 8 is communicated thus: 'Una ciciliana maestrevolmente toglie a un mercatante ciò che in Palermo ha portato; il quale, sembiante faccendo d'esservi tornato con molta più mercatantia che prima, da lei accattati denari, le lascia acqua e capecchio' ('A Sicilian woman masterfully relieves a merchant of all the goods he has brought to Palermo; pretending to have returned to Palermo with even more goods than he had the first time, he borrows money from her and leaves her with nothing but water and hemp' [8.10.1; 544]).

As Dioneo rethinks what happens to a Sicilian woman who tries to trick a merchant, there is something of the element of surprise on his side. After all, sixty-four stories separate Andreuccio from his counterpart Salabaetto, and one Sicilian prostitute from another. Madam Fiordaliso had escaped with Andreuccio's five hundred florins and there is no reason to think that she – or a proxy for her – would be summoned to justice. Now Dioneo, speaking on behalf of Florentine men, and offering his story as the final touch to a series of reflections about giving people their due, makes certain that his protagonist, a Florentine merchant, will triumph. Salabaetto profits economically as well as intellectually from his initial experience of having been duped; the deceptive Sicilian woman is made to pay.[48]

Dioneo marshals a host of details from Fiammetta's story of Andreuccio da Perugia (2.5).[49] As we read, we suspect time after time that Salabaetto may suffer the same fate as Andreuccio. Alerted already at the introduction of the character of the Sicilian woman (*ciciliana*), who appears only in *Decameron* 2.5 and 8.10, the reader is sensitized to the parallels between the two tales. Iancofiore, like Fiordaliso, commands the voyeuristic gaze – that is, she observes without being observed – and she controls how messages are transmitted to their intended publics. Both Salabaetto and Andreuccio, meanwhile, go to their trysts with these women without notifying anyone; their naivety – and in particular their inability to interpret signs – is placed in relief.[50]

Most suggestive for the reader are the objects and activities that play a central role in both tales: the ring, the dinner, the perfumes, a silver belt with a purse, and of fundamental importance, of course, the 'cinquecento fiorin d'oro,' the five hundred gold florins. Those five hundred gold florins are a clear indication of potential danger, at least for the audience. Trained in critical thinking in the course of the tale of Andreuccio da Perugia, the reader feels a sense of impending doom as Dioneo tells how Salabaetto has 'pannilani ... che potevano valere un cinquecento fiorin d'oro' ('a quantity of woolen cloth ... that was valued at five hundred gold florins' [8.10.9; 545]), and again when Dioneo notes that Salabaetto, in response to Madonna Iancofiore's request for a thousand gold florins, replies, 'Madonna, io non vi potrei servire di mille ma di *cinquecento fiorin d'oro* sì bene' ('Madonna, I could not give you a thousand gold florins, but I can certainly spare *five hundred*' [8.10.31; 549; emphasis mine]).

All these similarities notwithstanding, Salabaetto is not quite as naive as Andreuccio. He has a friend, the treasurer named Canigiano, who, commenting on Salabaetto's story of having been deceived, notes its triple series of mistakes and laments them ('Male ... male ... male,' 'Very bad ... very bad ... very bad'). He offers a remedy: 'The fact is, we have to find something else' (literally, '*to see* something else' [*vuolsi vedere altro*, 8.10.43]). He sees what Salabaetto must do to avoid being a victim like Andreuccio: 'sì come *avveduto* uomo, *prestamente* ebbe pensato quello che era da fare e a Salabaetto il disse' (*'clever* man as he was, he *quickly* saw what had to be done, and he explained it to Salabaetto' [8.10.43; 550]). In doing so, he is discerning and quick of mind, as Madonna Fiordaliso had been when she moved quickly (*prestamente*) to put her hands on Andreuccio's money and equally quickly (*prestamente*) to close the house up behind him [see 2.5.40; 91]). Salabaetto is adroit like the Andreuccio who took sound advice and departed Naples immediately (*prestamente*) for Perugia (2.5.85; 97), not gullible as Andreuccio had been when earlier he assumed that Madam Fiordaliso was in love with him and declared himself available (*'prestamente* rispose che era apparec-chiato,' 'he *immediately* replied that he was ready' [2.5.11; 87; emphasis mine]).

Salabaetto astutely internalizes Iancofiore's tactics and uses them against her. Like Andreuccio, who is 'tricky' ('malizios[o]') in the moment that he acquires the ring worth five hundred florins (2.5.78; 96), Salabaetto is 'shrewd' ('malizioso') when he arranges to meet with Iancofiore a second time (8.10.46; 551). He encourages Iancofiore to plead with him at length ('poi che una buona pezza s'ebbe fatto pre-gare,' 'after he allowed her to beg him for quite some time' [8.10.57; my translation]), a tactic that Iancofiore had used before introducing her request for a thousand gold florins ('Poi che la donna s'ebbe assai fatta pregare,' 'After allowing him to beg her for quite some time' [8.10.30; 548]). Although Iancofiore attempts to take the upper hand with a speech rivalling Fiordaliso's in *Decameron* 2.5, her efforts here and later are in vain. The deception that Fiordaliso perpetrated in the tale of Andreuccio is destined to be avenged. Throughout the tale of Salabaetto and Iancofiore, the reader is drawn into trying to protect the male pro-tagonist from becoming like Andreuccio, and therefore into accepting the punishment of Iancofiore, who loses a tidy sum (1000 florins of her own in addition to the 500 florins she had wrongfully acquired from Sa-labaetto), though in recompense she becomes, by default, the owner of barrels of sea water and bales of hemp worth approximately 200 florins.

Dioneo's story stands as the crowning achievement of a day dedicated to showing how the forces of economic exchange and accountability (*ragione*) work to exclude women. In a world ruled by *ragione* – under-stood principally as accountability in financial transactions, but also as the informing principle of evaluative and jurisprudential activities – women remain as the medium of exchange and they are barred from controlling that exchange. *Ragione* remains within a masculine domain, thus conferring ultimate control upon men.

Moreover, the two stories of Day 8 that focus on revenge against women – Pampinea's story of the scholar and the widow (8.7), and Dioneo's story of Salabaetto and Iancofiore (8.10) – permit us to see how misogyny is fuelled by letters, given that they link male reasoning and accounting to 'scholarly' and legal documentation.

The scholar of *Decameron* 8.7 affirms the power of his pen: 'E dove tutti mancati mi fossero, non mi fuggiva la penna, con la quale tante e sì fatte cose di te scritte avrei e in sì fatta maniera, che, avendole tu risapute, ché l'avresti, avresti il dì mille volte disiderato di mai non esser nata. Le forze della penna son troppo maggiori che color non estimano che quelle con conoscimento provate non hanno' ('And even if all my plans had failed me, my pen would not have done so, and with it I would have written so many things about you and in such a fashion that when you came to learn about them, which you would have, you would have wished a thousand times a day that you had never been born. The powers of the pen are far mightier than those people suppose who have not known them through experience' [8.7.99; 517–18]). In keeping with this, the suffering widow becomes like writing material: 'parve nel muoversi che tutta la cotta pelle le s'aprisse e ischiantasse, come veggiamo avvenire d'una carta di pecora abrusciata se altri la tira,' 'when she moved, it seemed as if all of her cooked skin was cracking and splitting, like a piece of scorched parchment being pulled apart' (8.7.114; 520).

The importance of maintaining control over writing is reaffirmed again by Dioneo in *Decameron* 8.10. There, in his opening comments to the story, Dioneo tells of the customs-house account books that serve as sources of important information both about the goods and about the merchants who own them (8.10.4–8). The information in these accounting statements, which are open to the public, can be used by women like Iancofiore who wish to deceive foreign merchants like Salabaetto. Salabaetto realizes only after he has been tricked that he has no recourse because he has no witnesses and no documentation in writing (8.10.40). However, following the advice of his treasurer friend, Salabaetto, having had 'everything registered under his own name' ('fatto ogni cosa scrivere a sua ragione' [8.10.44; 550]), puts his new goods into the warehouse. Iancofiore continues to pay attention to writing as before; she stipulates that all transactions with Salabaetto, the customs officers, and the usurer be recorded. But her plan backfires. It is Salabaetto who makes certain that he retains the 'key' (8.10.62), symbol of the instrument of access to the entire system.

Here men control the instruments of exchange and reproduction;

women are divested of the power to control writing, as well as of the power to see and denounce deception. Such moments underline the ways in which mercantile, legal, and scholarly writing could contribute to women's loss of status in the late Middle Ages.

I noted earlier that Dioneo's narrative technique in *Decameron* 8.10 has a profound impact on the subsequent storytelling. Beginning in Day 9, in which Emilia permits the group to tell stories without having to labour under a specific topic, the storytellers now, as never before in the *Decameron*, dedicate their energies to revisiting earlier moments, often in order to rewrite them. They recharge specific phrases with new meaning and reshape narrative situations to their own liking. Thus, in *Decameron* 9.1, a story about Madonna Francesca and her two unwanted lovers, Filomena responds to Emilia's story of Madonna Piccarda and the Rector of Fiesole (8.4), making a woman's triumph from the degradation of other women. *Decameron* 9.2 revisits Dioneo's story of the monk and the abbot (1.4), and in doing so, reveals some salient differences between secret sexual relations in male and female religious communities. Filostrato and Fiammetta return to the Calandrino cycle, this time to place Calandrino in a feminized role, first by making him pregnant (9.3) and then by permitting Tessa to take her vengeance on him (9.5). Both Neifile and Lauretta choose to revisit the subject of the homosocial relationship between two men (see 9.4 and 9.8), already inventively explored by Filostrato in *Decameron* 4.9; but the two women narrators on Day 9 deftly eliminate women from the equation, refashioning their stories in exclusively male comic-realist environments. Panfilo offers another sexual comedy, modelled on a French fabliau (9.6); his contribution takes up some strands that Pampinea had already addressed early in Day 3, when she had described the secret encounter between a stable-hand and a queen. As if in response, Pampinea will take up a more tragic moment from Panfilo's tale on Day 4 (Gerbino's dream) and rework it into a terrifying lesson for women who fail to heed their husbands (9.7, about the wife of Talano d'Imole).

True, a certain amount of 'rewriting' had already taken place in the *Decameron*. But nowhere is it as evident as in Day 9, when it appears linked to Dioneo's efforts, and therefore the result of something we could call the 'Dioneo effect.' Because Dioneo tracks the story of Andreuccio da Perugia so closely in *Decameron* 8.10, he spawns a way of thinking about the narrators' *very own stories* as material to be recreated, permitting some narrators to redirect them onto potentially anti-woman terrain (as Dioneo does Fiammetta's story), and empowering other narrators to reorient, with pro-woman twists, stories that have been less than complimentary to women. As a result, Dioneo assumes a function in the *Decameron* that looks quite like the functions that the Author himself is privileged to hold.

As we read through the polemical exchanges offered by the narrators of the *Decameron*, we inevitably find ourselves asking, 'So, in the end, do men or women come out on top?' For example: Should we delight in Dioneo's reaffirmation of carnal sensuality and will to power? Or, along with Fiammetta, should we draw a line against Dioneo's less than gracious representation of women? Should we support Fiammetta (who tells how a crafty woman triumphs over her male victim and brings him to greater cautiousness) or Dioneo (who retells her tale as a triumph of male mercantile reasoning over female deception)? Even if the *Decameron* does much to aid and abet the reader wishing to take sides in these sex wars, our attention would be better trained on more fruitful questions: Should we embrace Fiammetta's rhetoric or Dioneo's? Which rhetoric does the *Decameron* encourage us to accept?

Putting my analysis of a particular exchange between Fiammetta and Dioneo into the larger context of their interaction in the *Decameron*, I would offer the following observations.

When it comes to the subject of gender and sexual relations, Dioneo's views get reinforced because he gets the first and the last word. When he introduces the first woman character of the *Decameron* and the first representation of heterosexuality, he initiates the debate on gender even if he does not take account of gendered views. That puts Fiammetta into a position where whatever she says is belated, already a reaction to something else, already secondary and 'dependent.' But then Dioneo is also permitted to have the final word. In his verbal sparring match with Fiammetta, he is the one who sums up the positions most forcefully with his story of Salabaetto and Iancofiore (8.10), which is permitted to stand as the lapidary response to Fiammetta's story of Andreuccio da Perugia (2.5). Given that, early in the *Decameron*, he offers always to be able to tell the final story of each day, he is privileged to tell the final story of the entire collection. His account of the patient Griselda has often been interpreted as the *Decameron*'s vision of ideal womanhood, indeed, as its vision of an ideal humanity. Fiammetta's song at the conclusion of Day 10 could be read as a commentary on and a response to Dioneo's final novella. Yet even here, Fiammetta's contribution appears secondary. Few readers have paid as much attention to the songs and the frame narrative as they have to the novellas themselves. Dioneo secures the final word as he invites Fiammetta to reveal the autobiographical content behind her song.

This leads me to my next point: Fiammetta's stories only infrequently prove as vital or consequential as Dioneo's. Consider the story of the marchioness of Monferrato and the chicken banquet, which Fiammetta tells in response to Dioneo's story of the monk and the abbot. How many people would remember and repeat this 'witty remark'? Many contemporary readers (my students principal among them) find this story a bit peculiar. (And theirs may be a generous response, at least in comparison to the reaction of readers who think the story is lame.) Fiammetta's story of Andreuccio da Perugia is one of the very best in the *Decameron* – but how many people would recognize Fiammetta's subtle rewriting of a French fabliau in response to Dioneo's rewriting of a French fabliau? Fiammetta tells a variety of entertaining but less than fully memorable comic stories that involve the responses of jealous mates or family members: the story of Catella and Ricciardo (3.6), the story of the woman who tricks her impossibly jealous husband (7.5), the story of Spinelloccio and Zeppa engaged in mutual adultery (8.8), and, to some extent, the story of Calandrino in love with another woman (9.5). Each of these stories (like the story of Andreuccio da Perugia on Day 2) is an attempt to displace ways of thinking that dominate in previous stories of each of these days. To be frank, Fiammetta's stories of human relationships have not been highly memorable among the *Decameron*'s readership; their exploration of character and motivation is not as subtle as can be found in other stories of the *Decameron* (and even some other stories by Fiammetta). Her contribution is different. She frequently speaks at a pivotal juncture, reflecting on material that has appeared previously, rethinking it in subtle and sophisticated ways, sending the stories in new and interesting directions, complicating what has gone before. Still, precisely because she occupies this intermediary position, she never gets the upper hand.

Dioneo is allowed a coherent ideological position, as he is ever in favour of carnality, sexuality, and freedom from authorities and institutional restraints. Because his ideological position is relatively transparent, he is perhaps the single narrator who has earned essays and volumes of criticism dedicated to him alone. Fiammetta is given a complex and potentially contradictory position.[51] Resistance to Fiammetta is likely to be greater not because of the content of her message but because it is simply more difficult to unravel. One could say that it is precisely the complexity of Fiammetta's rhetorical stance that makes the *Decameron* the compelling and engaging work of literature that it is.

If one accepts Janet Smarr's view of Fiammetta and Dioneo (to which I referred in my opening remarks to this chapter), one might well assume that Fiammetta's is the rhetoric in support of social order and marriage while Dioneo's is the rhetoric of sexual liberty. I hope that, in the wake of what I have written here, the reader will acknowledge that the situation is quite a bit more complicated. Smarr describes what may well be the ideological underpinnings for Fiammetta and Dioneo. To describe their rhetorics, however, is a different matter.

Even Wayne Booth, writing about the *Decameron* in *The Rhetoric of Fiction*, falls prey to this confusion of ideology and rhetoric. Writing in the early 1960s, long before most of the contemporary critical studies on the *Decameron*, he too focuses on 'the lovely lady' Fiammetta and 'the lusty young courtier' Dioneo, obliquely typing them as representative poles of the *Decameron* whose rhetorics can profitably be compared. Dedicating his remarks chiefly to several stories by Fiammetta (Monna Giovanna and Federigo degli Alberighi in *Decameron* 5.9, and the woman who tricks her jealous husband in 7.5), Booth is concerned to show that the stories of the *Decameron* are not governed by a single moral code. Fiammetta's moral code is clearly not that of Dioneo's, but even more unsettling to Booth, it seems, is the fact that Fiammetta does not appear to have an absolute moral code at all. In his discussion of *Decameron* 5.9, Booth claims to be exploring Fiammetta's rhetorical techniques in arguing for a beautiful and virtuous woman's acceptance of the flawed comic hero who has long loved her, on one hand, and, on the other, for the punishment meted out to an excessively jealous husband. Yet Booth's assessment of Fiammetta's rhetoric is hampered by his desire to see all rhetoric attuned to a coherent ideology. Since Fiammetta, like all the female narrators of the Decameron, proves an advocate both of fidelity and infidelity, of chastity and fulfilment of desire, what Booth finds is that he, like Erich Auerbach before him, can find no basic moral attitude and no consistent approach to reality in the tales of the *Decameron*. The complexity of voices and moral views is too great. In contrast, one could question the moral choices of a narrator like Dioneo, consistently an advocate of carnal love, but at least one knows where he stands on the issue of carnal sensuality.

Both Auerbach and Booth invite the *Decameron* to provide a single coherent moral message, and then they are inevitably disappointed when the work fails to live up to the terms they themselves have set.

Auerbach in particular seems distressed that, in the *Decameron*, all is not subjugated to a higher tragic vision as it is in Dante. Booth is more open to the possibility of a tolerant and comic vision of the world, but even he concludes that '[t]hese extremes by no means exhaust the variety of norms that we are led to accept by the shifting rhetoric as we move through the *Decameron*. The standards of judgment change so radically, in fact, that it is difficult to discern any figure in Boccaccio's carpet.'[52] Nevertheless, there is a figure in Boccaccio's carpet, and it becomes visible to us when we acknowledge the kinds of differences that in the *Decameron* are born of gender and remain part and parcel with gender. When readers like Auerbach and Booth perceive a lack of moral coherence in the *Decameron*, I believe that what they are really responding to are the apparently contradictory moral positions that female narrators of the *Decameron* assume. Thus, in the following chapter, I invite readers to reflect on the way that gender is far more controversial in the *Decameron*'s views of sexuality and moral choice than has previously been thought.

chapter three

Boccaccio's Sexed Thought

Opinion from diverse quarters has it that a lot of sex is happening in the *Decameron*. First-year students reading the *Decameron* at Cornell University marvel at how quickly the characters fall in love (usually upon seeing an incredibly beautiful or handsome person for the very first time, and sometimes without seeing them at all); they are even more puzzled at how quickly those characters fall into bed. Thomas Bergin notes that the ten storytellers 'are much interested in sex,' and he calculates that 'of the one hundred tales told 67 percent present situations where a sexual relationship (one cannot always call it love) is central to the action.'[1] Aldo Scaglione has asserted that the *Decameron* represents a 'total surrender to the erotic instinct.'[2] Indeed, sex is so dominant a theme in the stories that many readers wonder how the narrators can talk so much about sex without engaging in it.[3]

Readers who reaffirm the dominance of eros in the *Decameron* like to point out that both women and men experience the same carnal longings. They typically cite the following stories: Alatiel (*Decameron* 2.7); Bartolomea of Pisa (2.10); Masetto da Lamporecchio and his nuns (3.1); Alibech and Rustico (3.10); the Author's novella in his Introduction to Day 4 (i.e., the so-called *novelletta delle papere*); Ghismunda and Tancredi (4.1); the novella of the nightingale (5.4); Madonna Filippa (6.7); and the cluster of stories in Day 7, all of which testify to women's uncurbed sexuality and deceptiveness. In most of these stories, women actively seek sexual satisfaction; in several notable cases, they seek to justify their choices before others.

Some readers of the *Decameron* go even farther, attributing to *women* the main impulse toward a positive and active sexuality. The actress Franca Rame is representative. In the last portion or 'Sixth Day' of

Dario Fo's *Manuale minimo dell'autore* (*Tricks of the Trade*), Rame points to the *Decameron* as an example of powerful storytelling by women who understand the subversive force of the obscene:

> In Boccaccio sono le donne che tengono il gioco del *Decameron* ... (Fiorina è la signora delle favole): sono loro che prendono più spesso dei maschi la parola per il racconto ciclico delle novelle. E quasi sempre le storie raccontate da quelle ragazze sono più spassose e provocatorie, specie sul piano dell'erotismo, di quelle degli uomini.
>
> Ma Boccaccio non se l'è mica inventato di sana pianta il rito della 'conta', cioè delle veglie durante le quali ci si raccontavano favole struggenti e fabulazzi osceni. Presso i contadini, fino a cinquant'anni fa, è sempre esistita la tradizione che vedeva le donne più prestigiose, la sera, nelle stalle, raccontare favole e moralità, e, appena i bambini s'erano addormentati, storie oscene. L'osceno è sempre stato, non smetterò mai di ribadirlo, l'arma più efficace per abbattere il ricatto che il potere ha piazzato nel cranio della gente, inculcandole il senso di colpa, la vergogna e l'angoscia del peccato. Che grande trovata quella di farci nascere già colpevoli, con una colpa (quella originaria) da scontare o lavare! Machiavelli consigliava al Principe: 'Date a un popolo la convinzione d'essere colpevole, non importa di che, e vi sarà più facile governarlo.'
>
> Distruggere, col far ridere, questa angoscia è sempre stato l'impegno principale dei comici, specialmente di sesso femminile.

In Boccaccio, it is the women who are in charge of the situation in the *Decameron*, and it is they who speak more than the men in the cyclical recitation of the stories. Generally, the women's stories are more erotically entertaining and spicy than those of their male counterparts.

Boccaccio was not the inventor of the custom of storytelling. Until about fifty years ago, among peasant peoples it was common for the higher-ranking women to gather others together in the stables, and recount fables and moral tales until the children went to bed and then to get down to more obscene stories. The obscene has always been, as I will never tire of repeating, the most effective of all weapons in the struggle to free people from the disease with which Power infected people when it planted in their minds a sense of guilt or shame, and an anxiety over sinfulness. What a splendid device that was to have us all born guilty, with a sense of sin (original) to be cleansed or of a penalty to pay. Machiavelli advised the Prince: 'Give the people a sense of guilt, it doesn't matter of what, and it will be much easier to govern them.'

To destroy this anxiety through laughter has always been the principal
task of comic writers and performers, especially the women among them.[4]

Still, the supporters of eros have disregarded some crucial details.
First: Very many of the erotic stories in the *Decameron* are told by the
three male narrators, Filostrato, Panfilo, and Dioneo. (I am hard
pressed to find evidence to support Franca Rame's claim that '[g]ener-
ally, the women's stories are more erotically entertaining and spicy than
those of their male counterparts'; but then, in the passage I have
quoted, she also misrepresents Machiavelli.) Second: Two of the male
narrators in the *Decameron* impose constraints on the narration that
might produce some of the same effects as a 'willing' surrender to eros.
When Filostrato is crowned king of Day 4, he requires that the group tell
of unhappy love (which elicits, obviously, a certain number of stories
that show the effects of the surrender to passion); and on Day 7, Dioneo
obligates his companions to tell stories about duplicitous wives.

There are finer distinctions to be drawn, and I set out here to demonstrate how the *Decameron* draws them along gender lines. Men and
women, the *Decameron* tells us, have different experiences of the social
reality they inhabit. As we shall see when we compare the stories of male
and female narrators, the *Decameron* describes a world where the two
sexes hold divergent views of sexuality, moral choice, language, and
truth.

Day 2 of the *Decameron* is very largely a man's world. Men and their concerns dominate, especially in the first half of the day. One might have
foreseen this implicit bias, given the way that Filomena, the reigning
queen, had formulated the topic: 'chi, da diverse cose *infestato*, sia oltre
alla sua speranza *riuscito* a lieto fine' ('men, who having suffered a variety of misfortunes, achieve a happiness beyond their dreams' [I.Conclu-
sion.11; translation mine; emphasis mine]).[5]

The bias toward men and their fortunes remains constant even when
the stories include female protagonists. After all, if 'Fortune is a woman,'
as Machiavelli asserted, the struggle against Fortune is a struggle to be a
true man. By no means is this goal easily achieved. As Millicent Marcus
has noted in her discussion of Day 2 of the *Decameron*: 'The image of man
which emerges from fortune's tale is an inert one, in contrast to the
robust, assertive hero who prevails in the bulk of the stories.'[6] If
Decameron 2 is the site of a lack, what it lacks, this statement charges, is
true masculinity. It offers not real men, but an image of man; not an

active presence, but an inert one; a story told by Fortune, rather than one told by the characters themselves. Other of the *Decameron*'s protagonists are now marked as heroes, bearing the emblems of agency (they 'assert' and 'prevail') and substance (they are 'robust,' and can be found in the 'bulk' of the stories). They adhere to the ideals of clever industriousness and wit, and ability to mould one's environment, that some readers have proclaimed the hallmark of the *Decameron*.[7]

We might well summarize the goals of the storytelling on Day 2 as follows: to be active rather than passive; to speak (and to speak well) rather than 'be spoken'; to control the look rather than to be its object; to control the forces of exchange rather than to be traded or exchanged. These are all modes that have been gendered as masculine in our culture, so it follows logically that, in reading Day 2, readers tends to favour characters who fit the mould of the manly (if not actually male) hero.

What does it mean then for women to struggle with misfortune and adversity? We can answer this question only if we recognize that loss means something fundamentally different for the men and women of *Decameron* 2. Buffeted by fortune's blows, men usually lose their material goods: their money, their clothes, their horses.[8] If the things they lose cannot be fully restored to them when they return to their original state, they receive new clothes and better possessions. Women, whose battle with Fortune emerges in the latter part of Day 2, lose not only their material goods (on which the narrators tend not to focus anyway), but also their husbands and children. Women lose their connectedness.[9]

This is not to say that men do not experience loss, even loss of self. Martellino, Landolfo Rufolo, and Andreuccio da Perugia are good examples to the contrary, for they all have close brushes with death. However, in no case is a male victim of Fortune dehumanized and reified in the way female victims are. In *Decameron* 2.6, Madama Beritola becomes animal-like, as indicated by her new name, Cavriuola ('Madam Doe'). Reduced to eating herbaceous vegetation, Madam Doe evokes traditional representations of the madman.[10] Alatiel of *Decameron* 2.7 becomes an object, a 'beautiful thing,' to be exchanged among men.[11] Both Beritola and Alatiel lose, at least temporarily, the ability to speak and to narrate coherently; they are cast out of the social communities that recognize them as fully human participants. By contrast, none of the male victims of fortune is excluded from social and linguistic communities in this way, even when they venture abroad. Since social affiliations and language are key to overcoming misfortune on Day 2, it is no wonder that women might have more difficulty countering misfortune and that in several stories (*Decameron* 2.3 and 2.9), they must dress as men in order to succeed.

In its representation of women and their misfortunes, the *Decameron* reflects the social reality of its times; therefore, it portrays women and men responding to adversity in different ways. Yet there is more. As early as Day 2, the stories reveal a marked gender divide among the narrators.

In the stories they tell about women, the three male narrators speak largely with one voice. Sexuality is a source of comfort, and the female characters exist, it seems, for the express purpose of satisfying male protagonists and their own carnal needs. Filostrato tells of Rinaldo d'Asti who, robbed of all his possessions, is invited into a widow's house for what will prove a mutually satisfying sexual encounter. Panfilo tells how Alatiel loses her virginity and then loses man after man; continued sexual contact is sufficient to make her forget her woes. In Dioneo's story, Bartolomea discovers that the pirate who has kidnapped her is better able to fulfil her sexually than was her husband, and she happily remains with him. Only one of the male narrators, Filostrato, has a woman initiate sex, but all of them emphasize that sex is of prime importance to women. Dioneo even goes so far as to allege that women can, at least metaphorically, enter the world of male deeds when they participate in the 'work' of sex.[12]

Consistent with their emphasis on female sexuality, the male narrators render physical beauty of cardinal importance. Filostrato offers his widow as 'del corpo bellissima quanto alcuna altra' ('as physically beautiful as any other woman' [2.2.19; my translation]). From Panfilo, Alatiel receives comparable praise as 'la più bella femina che si vedesse in que' tempi nel mondo' ('the most beautiful woman ever seen in the world in those times' [2.7.9; 110]). And Dioneo, with characteristic irony, describes Bartolomea as 'una delle più belle e più vaghe giovani di Pisa, come che poche ve n'abbiano che lucertole verminare non paiano' ('one of the most beautiful and charming young girls of Pisa [a city in which, by the way, most of the women look like gecko lizards]' [2.10.6; 153]).

As these beautiful women are having sex, none of them, curiously enough, ever gets pregnant. This is most remarkable in the case of Alatiel, who had 'lain with eight men perhaps ten thousand times' (126). Could it be that female fertility would prove deleterious to male sexual fantasies about women? The male narrators circumvent this possibility entirely on Day 2, offering instead some other implicit downsides. These beautiful and lust-driven women are fickle, quick to change lovers at a moment's notice. As the widow of *Decameron* 2.2 awaits a visit from her lover, a marquis, her mind is 'filled with the thought' of him (72), but when he fails to appear, she accepts Rinaldo d'Asti as a gift of Fortune. Alatiel passes from lover to lover, shedding a few tears at the demise of each one, but easily consoled with sex. Bartolomea announces forthrightly that she is much happier with the pirate who keeps her satisfied sexually.

In addition to being fickle, women are – according to the male narrators – secretive and deceitful. As the widow gives Rinaldo clothes and money and shows him the way out, she entreats him to secrecy ('che questo tenesse celato' [2.1.40]). Alatiel protects her reputation, with the help of one of her father's advisers, by offering a fictive account of her stay in a religious community, where the nuns served 'san Cresci in Valcava, a cui le femine di quel paese voglion molto bene' ('St. Peter-the-Big-in-the-Valley, for whom the women of the country had great affection' [2.7.109; 125]). When Bartolomea's husband comes to retrieve her from the pirate, she claims at first never to have seen him before. She agrees to speak with him, but finally threatens further distortions of the truth, as she concludes: 'e per ciò, come più tosto potete, v'andate con Dio, se non che io griderò che voi mi vogliate sforzare' ('so, with God's blessing, be off with you as quickly as you can or I shall scream and say that you are trying to rape me' [2.10.41; 158]). Taken as a unit, these three stories reaffirm in variegated ways that there is indeed a truth, and women are responsible for concealing it from men and from society at large.

What of the portrayal of women in the stories told by female narrators? Here they emerge in a different light. Whereas all the male narrators underscore the physical beauty and sexual availability of women, none of the female narrators do – not even Fiammetta, in whose story the Sicilian prostitute Fiordaliso figures prominently. (Fiordaliso may be a prostitute, but she deftly extricates herself from a sexual encounter with the all-too-willing Andreuccio by telling him that she is his sister.) The female narrators are more likely to focus on a composite picture of a woman's mental, moral, and physical qualities. In exploring human sexuality, they place the prime focus on the desire for long-term intimate relationships. The princess of England in *Decameron* 2.3 will not continue the sexual encounter she has initiated until she has assurances that Alessandro will marry her. Likewise, Giannetta, the daughter of the count of Antwerp in *Decameron* 2.8, repeatedly refuses to consider a lover unless his intentions are honourable. In *Decameron* 2.6, two young lovers,

Giannetto and Spina, engage in illicit premarital sexual relations; but as soon as Spina's father raises the possibility of marriage (now that he has discovered that Giannetto is actually a nobleman reduced to a servile state), Giannetto most willingly agrees, as his love for Spina has been constant.

Like the men, the female narrators see women as the repository of secret information. There is, however, a crucial difference. Instances of female deceit are offset by accounts of truthful and honourable women. This is most evident in *Decameron* 2.8. Elissa begins by telling how a spurned woman falsely accused the count of Antwerp of sexual assault. But she portrays all the other women of the story as upstanding; moreover, the original accusatrix repents on her death bed and reveals her previous duplicity.

Indeed, according to the female narrators, women speak the truth openly should they be fortunate enough to find someone to listen to them. Women explain why they have been deceptive – why they have been forced to assume other identities, and why, in some cases, they have constrained others to do so as well. These disclosures of the truth bring plots to resolution. In *Decameron* 2.6, a nurse claims Madama Beritola's children as her own and renames one of them in order to save them from harm at the hands of political enemies; eventually, when the political situation returns to normal, she reveals who they are and why she behaved as she did. The two women who cross-dress as men (the princess of England in 2.3 and Madonna Zinevra in 2.9) reveal their true identities when they can appeal to the authority of men other than their controlling fathers and husbands. Madonna Zinevra's case is particularly striking, since she has had to resort to deception in order to survive and eventually to expose the man who has defamed her. By no stretch of the imagination can her deception compare to the guile of the man who had made a false accusation or to the brutality of the husband who had ordered her killed when he believed she was not faithful to him.

In *Decameron* 2.6, 2.8, and 2.9, the female narrators acknowledge that children are born of sexual relations. They grant children a space in which to exist. In their stories, women bear children, nurse them, live and sleep in close proximity to them, show tremendous concern for them. As least one female narrator, Elissa, imagines that a man could be as committed to this ethic of care (see her Gualtieri in 2.8). Furthermore, both Emilia and Elissa imagine how the life of children in future generations might proceed, and they affirm the crucial role that children can play in the return of the parent to his or her original state (2.6 and 2.8).

At this early point in the *Decameron*, the evidence suggests that the female narrators conceive of human experience in terms noticeably different from those embraced by the men. They distance themselves from the men's view of women as highly sexualized beings; instead, they portray women's sexuality as directed toward the creation and maintenance of long-term relationships. They seem aware, as the men do not, of the connection between sexuality and reproduction. And in response to the men's implicit assertion that women are secretive and deceptive, the female narrators acknowledge that women are not always truthful; but they investigate women's legitimate reasons for deception, and they show women who are motivated eventually to reveal their secrets.

If we accept that human experience – particularly in the realm of sexuality – is articulated very differently by the *Decameron*'s male and female narrators, we will no longer be able to argue that the *Decameron* celebrates a 'total surrender to the erotic instinct.'[13] No longer will we be able to read the stories of Masetto serving his willing nuns (3.1), Alibech and Rustico 'putting the devil into hell' (3.10), or Madonna Filippa flaunting her goods publicly (6.7) without some awareness of the tremendous investment that the male narrators of the *Decameron* have in asserting women's carnality.

Certainly, someone is likely to say, even if this gender divide appears on Day 2, there is no guarantee that it applies to the remainder of the *Decameron*. After all, on Day 2 the narrators are still struggling to define who they are and what they believe. They have shown how humans respond to adversity, but they will have many more opportunities to describe the possibilities of human wit, creativity, and intelligence. Furthermore, they have not yet experienced the events that will shape their storytelling in key ways. They have not yet made the move to a lovely garden at the beginning of Day 3, or to the Valley of the Ladies at the end of Day 6; both locations will prove influential in the group's considerations of sexuality. They have not yet dealt with the noisy interruption of their servants, which will take place at the beginning of Day 6; that will be the occasion on which issues of everyday reality (and especially gender and class) will be brought to the forefront. Finally, they have not yet told stories under the leadership of any of the men, which means they have not yet dealt with topics that they would have rather avoided (such as 'unhappy love' on Day 4, or 'tricky wives' on Day 7).

Many more stories remain to be told about sex, and one might imagine that later in the *Decameron* – perhaps on the days that focus more explicitly on sexuality, such as Day 3 and Day 7 – we would see the female narrators coming to an agreement of sorts with the three men. In order to test this hypothesis, I propose that we now turn to a closer examination of these later moments, which might seem to contradict the evidence I have presented so far.

With the exception of the story told by Neifile, who is the reigning queen, all the stories on Day 3 focus on illicit sexual relationships.[14] Throughout, it appears that women as well as men welcome the pleasures of sex, regardless of moral or ethical considerations. Reinforcing this idea, several of the female narrators explicitly conclude their tales of illicit love with statements of their own hopes for sexual fulfilment (3.3, 3.6, 3.7). Would this not suggest that the female narrators have conceded their point and that they are now fundamentally in agreement with the three men?

I would grant that on Day 3 the female narrators do not hold to the ideals of female honour they sought to depict on Day 2. Nevertheless, I would urge us, once again, to look more closely at the representation of sexuality. It remains gendered.

In the stories told by men, the women remain ever willing to engage in sex without delay. In Filostrato's tale of Masetto da Lamporecchio (3.1), the nuns initiate a sexual encounter with him, after having summarily considered – and dismissed – their vows of chastity and the possibility that they might become pregnant. In Panfilo's story about Friar Puccio, a monk named Dom Felice expresses his desires for Friar Puccio's wife and straightaway finds that she is 'disposta a dover dare all'opera compimento' ('well disposed toward bringing his work to fruition' [3.4.11; 185]). Dioneo describes Alibech as an exceedingly willing young girl (though granted, she is too innocent to know what she is doing).

Because women are so willing to engage in carnal activity, the obstacles that appear in the men's stories are best described as 'external' or 'logistical.' How to get into a convent, not how to seduce the nuns. How to find a secluded place away from a husband, not how to convince the wife. How to most smoothly get a naive young girl to submit to sex. The objects of male desire present difficulties only because, as Filostrato and Dioneo show, it requires considerable effort to satisfy women whose carnal desire has been awakened. Masetto's nuns prove so sexually demanding that Masetto is forced to seek an alternate solution; Alibech's sexual desire, once aroused, is insatiable.

At least one male narrator, Filostrato, does concede that sex is linked to reproduction. Masetto, who generates a brood of little monks ('monachin' [3.1.42]), manages the situation in a way most advantageous to himself, as he remains a rich patriarch without having to shoulder a father's burdens ('vecchio, padre e ricco, senza aver fatica di nutricare i figliuoli o spesa di quegli' [3.1.43]). These children remain 'trophy offspring,' testimony to Masetto's virility.

Again, the female narrators offer a different picture of human sexuality. Neifile tells of a woman who uses the pretext of an illicit relationship in order to reconcile herself with her estranged husband (3.9). Pampinea and Fiammetta tell of women who have illicit sexual encounters, but, in both cases, the women believe they are with their husbands (3.2 and 3.6).[15]

When the female narrators tell of transgressive sexual activity that is actively chosen, they elaborate on the preparatory mechanisms, rendering the actual sexual encounter of lesser interest. In her story of a stable-hand who surreptitiously enters the bed of Queen Teodolinda, Pampinea illustrates at length the ways in which the stable-hand seeks to please the queen. Filomena, who tells about a woman who successfully tricks a friar in order to be with her lover, seems to take much more pleasure in relating how the ignorant friar was tricked than in describing the encounter between the woman and her lover; indeed, when the woman and her lover meet, they engage in devastating jokes at the expense of 'Brother Ignoramus.'

In the women's stories, the main obstacles are posed by the objects of desire themselves – unless they are entirely unaware of what is happening, like the queen of *Decameron* 3.2, who is literally in the dark. The man loved by the lady in *Decameron* 3.3 'was not aware of all this [i.e., her love for him], and paid no attention to her' ('di ciò non accorgendosi, niente ne curava' [3.3.7; 177]). About Zima, in 3.5, we discover that 'for some time now, he had been in love with, and courted unsuccessfully, Messer Francesco's wife' ('avea lungo tempo amata e vagheggiata infelicemente la donna di messer Francesco' [3.5.5; 190]). Catella is more interested in her husband than in Ricciardo Minutolo (3.6). Madonna Ermellina decides she will no longer be the mistress of Tedaldo degli Elisei (3.7). In 3.8, Ferondo's wife does not immediately comply with the abbot who loves her passionately.

When women do participate in illicit relationships, the female narrators tell of how they must be convinced that they are doing the right thing. Francesco Vergellesi's wife is resistant, until she sees Zima's persistence (3.5). Ferondo's wife seems quite bewildered by the abbot's advances toward her in 3.8; she becomes more receptive to him when he gives her gifts, and she does not concede herself to him until after her husband has 'died' and gone to Purgatory. (It appears that she actually believes that her husband has departed for the other world.) Madonna Ermellina resists the attention of Tedaldo degli Elisei, the man who declares his love for her. It is only after a lengthy story of misrecognitions, mistaken identities, fortunate rescue attempts, and Tedaldo's reappearance as if from the dead that Ermellina embraces Tedaldo (and then, only after her husband encourages her to do so in public).

The evidence that I have presented here leads me to view Day 3 as the site of male and female perspectives at odds. At first glance, my argument would seem to have much in common with David Wallace's, for he too maintains that the unity of Day 3 is illusory. Noting that the storytelling of Day 3 is situated in a lovely garden, he writes that

> for the medieval Christian, such a place was also a reminder of loss: since the Fall brought us east of Eden, men and women have never recaptured the idyllic harmony of their former innocent state. All ten tales in the third day are dedicated to the difficult dynamics of masculine-feminine relations.[16]

But having made this point, Wallace does not move to explore perspectives gendered as male and female. Instead, he turns his attention to the unifying threads:

> All ten [stories] feature attempts (nine successful) at illicit, deceptive or coercive love. Some of these stories, especially the first and last (Masetto among the nuns; Alibech among the hermits) have been found immoral: but every *novella* raises difficult questions about sexual relations and the mores devised to govern them.[17]

Wallace locates many themes of Day 3 in the final story of Day 2, about Bartolomea and her impotent husband (2.10), which he reads as an exposure of medieval misogyny. (In order to do this, of course, Wallace has to gloss over the ways in which Dioneo's story is not necessarily pro-woman.) In Wallace's view, *Decameron* 2.10 can be likened to multiple moments on Day 3: 'Anti-feminist commonplaces are to be found throughout the third day, but so too is a recognition that they are devised to save and protect men from moments of truth and inadequacy in their encounters with women.'[18] This paves the way for Wallace's reading of *Decameron* 3.1 (Filostrato's story about Masetto) and 3.10 (Dioneo's story about Alibech and Rustico) as critiques of masculine fantasy, not as assertions of it. What Wallace says about Masetto, he could well say about Filostrato and Dioneo too: '[T]he male voice speaks, then, only to disclose that masculine sexuality cannot sustain the pretensions of masculine fantasy.'[19]

Although Wallace's intentions seem worthy, there is something very curious about the way he chooses to unmask misogyny. His reading of Day 3 proves masculinist at heart; it reveals how our own implicit biases can interact with the gender biases already present in the text.

Wallace showcases *Decameron* 3.1 and 3.10, which he describes as 'brilliant responses to the topic proposed for the third day';[20] he reminds us that these two stories are told by men, Filostrato and Dioneo; and he describes these two male narrators as aware of the polemical force of their narratives. These two stories earn lengthy commentary.

Wallace then proceeds to explore two other novellas, *Decameron* 3.6 and 3.7. These stories are told by two women, Fiammetta and Emilia, but Wallace does not point this out. He does not describe these novellas as brilliant, nor does he assert that the female narrators are aware of what they are doing. Rather, Wallace seems drawn to these stories because of the stratagems employed by their *male* protagonists: Ricciardo Minutolo uses Dantean tactics to trick a married woman into a sexual encounter with him; Tedaldo employs a 'similarly complex pattern of deception,' in which he devises an elaborate public ceremony to mask his plan to regain the favour of a married woman who has abandoned him.[21]

What is happening here? One might think that the comparison is between apples and oranges: stories told by men versus stories told by women. In fact, we are being asked to compare good apples and bad apples: stories in which men discover their proper place versus stories in which men refuse to be bound by limits. There is nothing inherently wrong with such a comparison. But strangely enough, the good apples emerge from the stories told by Filostrato and Dioneo. For Wallace, these are 'Edenic narratives' where the protagonists discover their postlapsarian limits in the realms of sex and language. In the stories of the female narrators, there emerges a darker, less appealing vision, as men manoeuvre social and political situations to their advantage.

Implicit in Wallace's reading is the charge that Fiammetta and Emilia are not sufficiently critical of misogyny because they present a darker vision of humanity and because they do not show men whose desires have been curbed. I would counter that for narrators like Fiammetta

and Emilia, Edenic fantasies could never have been part of the landscape to begin with; these narrators are far too mindful of the restrictions under which women operate in civic communities like Naples and
Florence. Indeed, what does it mean to say that men like Masetto da
Lamporecchio and Rustico discover the limits of male fantasy, if these
discoveries never extend beyond the isolated communities in which
Masetto and Rustico live? What does it mean to say that the limits of
male fantasy have been exposed, if civic communities and institutions
remain fundamentally supportive of male desire?

I would agree with Wallace that there are moments when the
Decameron can offer a critique of masculinist values. I would even agree
that the argument can be made that male narrators of the *Decameron*
(like Filostrato and Dioneo on Day 3) participate to some extent in this
critique. Still, we ought to consider why it is that readers of *Decameron* 3
find the stories by the male narrators more compelling and memorable
than the stories by the female narrators.[22] We should also turn a more
discerning eye on the critiques of male fantasy. What do we gain if we
give more weight to critiques of male fantasy that emerge in stories (told
by men) that reaffirm women's overriding and singular carnality? Why
are we less attuned to the stories (told by women) that show women
caught in conflicting emotions about their sexuality and the social institutions that regulate it?

For my next arguments on gendered views in the *Decameron*, I turn to
Day 7, when Dioneo has the group tell stories 'delle beffe le quali o per
amore o per salvamento di loro le donne hanno già fatte a' lor mariti,
senza essersene essi o avveduti o no' ('about the tricks which, either out
of love or for their own self-preservation, wives have played on their
husbands, whether these tricks were discovered or not' [6.Concl.6; 410–
11]). Readers of Day 7 have seen its message about woman to be
extraordinarily consistent: women exercise control; they demonstrate
superior ability.[23] They have sought mainly to describe *how* women
achieve this control. According to Giovanni Getto, the women of Day 7
reaffirm their powers through manipulation of signs; in several notable
cases (7.4, 7.8, 7.9), they even succeed in substituting illusion for reality.[24] Barbara Zandrino sees the women's trickery as the result of their
superior intelligence (or men's inferior intelligence, as the case may
be).[25] David Wallace explores how the women control domestic space.[26]

Decameron 7 shows what all women can accomplish – or does it? Seeing these women in control of language, space, and their own wits,

twentieth-century readers might wish to cast their lots with them. Can we be so absolutely certain that the narrators of the *Decameron* would do the same? I think not.

How can we have forgotten that some of the women object to Dioneo's topic as ill suited to them? True, the women drop their objections after Dioneo counters with a long and multi-pronged defence. However, as we know from Day 4, when Filostrato managed to persuade his reluctant companions to accept his proposed topic (tragic love), there can be continued resistance even as the narrators seem to play along. Pampinea's tale about Frate Alberto (4.2) fulfils the letter of Filostrato's mandate but contradicts its spirit. So isn't it also possible that, on Day 7, the narrators might resist Dioneo even as they comply?

Obviously, I would not even pose the question but for the fact that I do not judge the narrators to be clearly aligned with the characters they portray in their stories. Throughout Day 7, the narrators rely heavily on comic and parodic sources, mainly from the French *fabliaux*. This in itself should make us wary of taking the narrators' judgments at face value. As Day 7 opens, we see characters whose class status would automatically distance them from the aristocratic narrators.[27] Emilia presents Tessa, who is married to Gianni Lotteringhi, a wool weaver (7.1); Filostrato tells of Peronella, a weaver married to a bricklayer (7.2); in 7.4, Lauretta chooses to tell a story about 'una semplicetta donna,' 'a simple woman' (7.4.4; 431). Furthermore, by their settings, the opening four novellas emphasize the ideological divide between the noble Florentine narrators and their characters. The first novella of Day 7 is set in one of the poorer quarters of Florence; the several novellas that follow are set in locations marked as significantly 'other' in character: Naples (7.2), Siena (7.3), Arezzo (7.4). This tactic seems unusual, given that the primarily Florentine settings on Day 6 had served to reinforce the narrators' understanding of themselves as a community.

As is her wont, Fiammetta, who tells a central story on Day 7, paves the way for a new development. She proposes an analogy between all women and the lower classes:

Esse stanno tutta la settimana rinchiuse e attendono alle bisogne familiari e domestiche, disiderando, come ciascun fa, d'aver poi il dì delle feste alcuna consolazione, alcuna quiete, e di potere alcun diporto pigliare, sì come prendono i lavoratori de' campi, gli artefici delle città e i reggitori delle corti, come fé Idio che il dì settimo da tutte le sue fatiche si riposò, e come vogliono le leggi sante e le civili, le quali, allo onor di Dio e al ben comune di ciascun riguardando, hanno i dì delle fatiche distinti da quegli del riposo.   (7.5.4)

Like everyone else, after being closed inside the house all week, attending to the needs of the family and the household, these young girls wish to enjoy the peace and quiet of a holiday and to enjoy themselves, as do the laborers in the fields, the artisans in the cities, and the magistrates in the courts, and just as God Himself did when He rested from all His labors on the seventh day, and as it is prescribed in both canon and civil law, which, in consideration of the reverence due to Him and for the common welfare of everyone, has distinguished days of labor from those of rest.   (435)

No longer is it so clear that the poor and the labourers are different from women. By suggesting that all women are like the labouring classes and reminding us that even superior authorities like magistrates and divinities can be seen as labourers, Fiammetta manages to shift the focus more firmly toward the merchant class and the nobility. Pampinea introduces a knight and his wife (7.6), Filomena tells a story of a son of a nobleman reduced to being a merchant on account of poverty (7.7), and Neifile tells the story of a merchant who marries into an aristocratic family that presents itself as none too noble and courteous (7.8). But even after Fiammetta makes the bold move of equating women with the lower classes, there will continue to be ways for the narrators to distance themselves from the characters of Day 7. The stories of the latter half of this day still tend to take place in other cities (Rimini, Paris, Bologna, Argo). Even more important, the degree of interpersonal violence is suddenly raised. In *Decameron* 7.7, Egano, pretending to be an adulterous woman, gets beaten and verbally abused. In 7.8, a maidservant, substituted for an adulterous woman, gets beaten and has her hair cut off. In 7.9, a married woman proves herself to her lover by killing her husband's best sparrow hawk, yanking out a lock of his beard, and extracting one of his best teeth. I would submit that these particular instances of violence are, for the *Decameron*'s Florentine narrators, marked as unacceptable for members of the nobility.

Finally, there remain differences in the way that male and female narrators portray the sexual act. The women narrators of the *Decameron* focus more on women's desire to save themselves (presumably from potentially threatening husbands) than on women's desire to achieve sexual satisfaction with their lovers. Indeed, there are only two occasions on Day 7 when accounts of sex turn especially graphic, and both are provided courtesy of men. Filostrato shows Peronella's lover having sex with her while her husband scrapes the inside of a barrel into which she leans (7.2). Panfilo offers the most unreserved expression of sexual desire in *Decameron* 7.9, when he tells how Lidia and Pirro engage in sexual intercourse in broad daylight, before the eyes of Lidia's astonished husband. Both Filostrato and Panfilo portray sexual activity as happening in the presence of husbands, in defiance of them. Their tales, placed in the second and ninth positions, have the effect of framing the day, almost in the way that Filostrato and Dioneo did on Day 3, with their tales of Masetto and Alibech. Nevertheless, theirs is one point of view, not wholly endorsed by the female narrators.

Even the Author's rubrics respect the difference between the men's and the women's views. Only in the rubrics for the men's stories does the Author represent women as agents. For Filostrato's story, the Author writes, 'Peronella mette un suo amante in un doglio tornando il marito a casa' ('Peronella hides her lover inside a barrel when he discovers that her husband is coming home' [7.2.1; 421]). And for Panfilo's story, he offers, 'Lidia moglie di Nicostrato ama Pirro' ('Lidia, the wife of Nicostrato, is in love with Pirro' [7.9.1; 458]). In a striking reversal, the Author's rubrics for the women's stories – at least in six of the seven cases – focus clearly on the agency of male protagonists, not on their wives.[28] The rubric for Pampinea's story is only superficially an exception, for here the Author names Isabella as the grammatical subject, but renders her the object of male agency by adopting the passive voice: 'Madonna Isabella, con Leonetto standosi amata, da un messer Lambertuccio è visitata e torna il marito di lei' ('While she is with Leonetto, Madonna Isabella, who is loved by a certain Messer Lambertuccio, is visited by him just as her husband is about to return home' [7.6.1; 442]). The Author's rubrics underscore the gender divide that is already present in the men's and women's stories about sex.

Let us consider then how the *Decameron* orchestrates the alternative views presented by the female narrators. As the *Decameron* begins, the most pressing issue is a rhetorical one: how one might use language well in order to improve the condition of individuals and communities. During Day 1 and the first half of Day 2, concerns specific to women as a group remain overshadowed by matters perceived to be more 'universal': the disintegration of individual virtue, social life, and political institutions. The importance of gender to this rhetorical project becomes clear early in the *Decameron*, but it emerges almost as a secondary thought, largely in the wake of several key contributions from Fiammetta (1.5 and 2.5).

The women's point of view emerges with greatest force in the latter part of Day 2. Following Day 2 of the *Decameron*, the possibility of a critical response is increasingly limited. Day 3 does much to guarantee that women and men will work within a system whose terms remain defined by men;[29] it also discourages any radical rethinking of terms. Days 4 and 5 focus predominantly on sexual love (whether by design, in Days 4, 5, and 7, or by fortuitous event, in Day 3). In this forum, perhaps as a consequence of the topic, ever less space is provided for the female narrators to communicate their differences. As we look to Day 6, where readers have found proclamations of the liberating possibilities available to women who express their sexual desires, we find that these stories underscore the limits placed on woman's speech and her critical faculties.[30] Most disturbingly perhaps, as the *Decameron* proceeds to its denouement and increasing numbers of women seek to speak out or otherwise control their own circumstances, the spectre of violence against women becomes more insistent.[31]

My main purpose so far has been to demonstrate that we can no longer read the *Decameron* as if gender were largely irrelevant to the construction of meaning. As Carol Gilligan might assert, the *Decameron* represents men and women speaking 'in different voices.'[32]

I refer to Carol Gilligan, author of *In a Different Voice*, because she has reaffirmed the gender differences that theorists of moral development seemed wont to ignore. Citing the authoritative words of Virginia Woolf, Gilligan argued, 'It is obvious that the values of women differ very often from the values which have been made by the other sex ... it is the masculine values that prevail.'[33] On the basis of a very small number of interviews conducted in pilot studies, Gilligan asserted that women are inclined toward an ethics of care and attachment, while men are inclined toward an ethics of justice. As she reflected on the stories women told, she heard affirmations of connectedness and relationship; she noted that men, by contrast, offer stories of achieved separation to counter dangerous moments of affiliation. Because Gilligan also undertook to reveal the limitations of Lawrence Kohlberg's theories and evaluations of moral development, her claims have been fiercely debated, and most especially by Kohlberg and his supporters.[34] But even these oppositional voices have found themselves compelled to acknowledge the basic validity of Gilligan's thesis: that we err if we believe that a masculine view is the universal view, and that we must therefore account for women's experience and vision of the relation between the self and others.[35]

This is an important point from which readers of the *Decameron* could learn, since up until now there has been no acknowledgment that male and female narrators in the *Decameron* express fundamentally different views. Moreover, many readers of the *Decameron* remain unaware that they have tended to align themselves with perspectives that the *Decameron* marks as masculine. This said, I would advance two weighty caveats.

First and foremost, learning from Gilligan does not mean applying her theory wholesale to narratives about moral choice in the fourteenth century. It is not a cultural given that women always, and of necessity, conceive of their moral and experiential worlds in terms of care; nor are all men in every time and every place caught up only by the concerns of justice. Moreover, it is highly unlikely that these concepts, as we might understand them in the twentieth century, could transfer easily into fourteenth-century Italian terms. Mindful of these cultural and histori-cal differences, I have refrained from offering Gilligan's categories of (masculinized) justice and (feminized) care as useful tools for analysis of gender difference in the *Decameron*. In my discussion of *Decameron* 2, for example, the categories of 'justice and care' would apply only to a limited degree, to the extent that the women narrators do emphasize care. Gilligan's finding that women tended to seek 'connectedness' while men sought 'separateness' would also be only partially applicable to an analysis of *Decameron* 2. Whereas connectedness is of vital impor-tance to women characters in the *Decameron*, the categories of disjunc-tion and separateness do not apply to the male characters – and this is clearly the effect of different social and historical circumstances.

Second, and no less important: The *Decameron* offers us a *fictional rep-resentation* of gendered voices. It is not a given that fourteenth-century Italian men and women would have constructed their moral and experi-ential universes exactly as the *Decameron* suggests they would. Imagine extrapolating about contemporary moral values from the viewpoints expressed by a mixed group of ten college undergraduates and gradu-ate students. Obviously some of their views would ring true for us on a larger scale; but in other cases, we would see their views as representa-tive not of society at large but of their own socio-cultural backgrounds and of their individual experiences. Likewise with the views of the ten narrators in the *Decameron*. (Would it be possible to compare the views expressed in the *Decameron* to the views of real-life men and women? Perhaps, but this approach is significantly hampered on account of the dearth of fourteenth-century Italian women who recorded their experiences in writing.)

Once we acknowledge that the *Decameron* certainly does not reflect our moral and experiential reality and that it will reflect the moral and experiential reality of the Middle Ages and Renaissance only in part, what can we say about it? If it is not true and constant to its own time, what is the point of pausing over the scenarios that it places before us?

To this I would answer: What is of prime importance is the fact that the *Decameron* makes us aware that moral and experiential universes are constructed around categories like gender (and class, civic and national identity, religious identity, and so forth). The *Decameron* depicts how social and discursive power is divided between the sexes. The fictional storytellers of the *Decameron* are marked by their gender and by their express views on sexuality and sexual difference. Over this tension, other splits emerge: among the male narrators, whose views slowly begin to differentiate, and among the female narrators, who have always, since the beginning of their association, shown us that there is not full agreement among them.

Do the *Decameron*'s representations of gender difference and human sexuality provide new insights or are they ultimately in the service of traditional forms of gender domination? Here things get nebulous. The cloud cover grows yet thicker when we take account of the fact that Boccaccio, through his Author and his ten narrators, provides women with the opportunity to speak their desire – but the voice of female desire appears to emerge more clearly when female desire is consistent with male desire.

Nevertheless, our responsibilities remain clear. Hearing the polyphony of this great work of European literature, we need to recognize that the *Decameron* is not only the affirmation of universal human truths that transcend individual and social differences, but also an exploration of how stories are generated by difference itself. In many cases, we will find familiar accounts of gender that we have inherited and which we have been encouraged to embrace. But other viable (though perhaps less familiar) accounts also emerge, and then we must ask why some accounts have seemed more compelling to us. In recognizing that we have choices as readers – and that a work like the *Decameron* even offers us some of these alternatives – we will go a long way toward recognizing that even stories that have been used in the service of gender domination need not continue to be employed in this fashion.

chapter four

To Transvest Not to Transgress

Boccaccio's transgressive women have found a special place in the hearts of readers, some of whom are so delighted at the prospect that women are taking any action at all that they cannot pause to ask whether there is justification for the women's choices. How far did the author of the *Decameron* intend to go when (in the guise of his ten narrators, of course) he chose to portray 'deviant women,' women who depart from traditional codes for femininity and who may even assume roles traditionally reserved for men? Probably not as far as many readers think. I have already argued (in the previous chapter), and I shall continue to argue, that if we examine how the women narrators represent deviant female behaviour, we find that the deviations are counterbalanced by reassurances that women are not really overstepping their bounds.

At this juncture, I would like to focus on two stories where women don male garb: *Decameron* 2.3 and 2.9, stories told by Pampinea and Filomena, outspoken women who serve as the queens of Days 1 and 2 respectively. In *Decameron* 2.3, an impoverished Florentine loan shark named Alessandro happens to meet up with an abbot who turns out to be an English princess rebelling against the will of her father. She declares her love to Alessandro and then eloquently defends her cause before the pope, who agrees to marry the couple. In *Decameron* 2.9, Bernabò bets on the chastity of his wife Zinevra, loses the bet when he is tricked by Ambrogiuolo, and orders Zinevra killed. After convincing her assassin not to kill her, Madonna Zinevra disguises herself as a man and flees Genoa, eventually putting her talents to good use in the service of the sultan. Later, when she happens to encounter the man who falsely accused her, she arranges to expose him and to defend her deceived husband. She prevails: her accuser is punished; she and her husband return home.

Pampinea and Filomena are mobilizing and reshaping a variety of textual sources, from the legend of the cross-dressed Saint Eugenia to the stories of the 'wager cycle.'[1] On the surface, it appears that these two narrators wish to reaffirm the proactive woman who transgresses gender roles.[2] But as Pampinea and Filomena tell of the infractions of gender roles, they reaffirm the necessity of those roles and they reaffirm virtues – among them loyalty, chastity, and deference to men – that traditional gender roles help to foster. The princess and Madonna Zinevra must break the rules of the system in order to abide by it.

These stories strike me as worthy of in-depth commentary on two counts. First of all, consistent with what I have been arguing so far, when female narrators provide examples of women who successfully bend gender roles, they also reassert the limits beyond which women ought not proceed. I am intrigued by the rhetorical strategies that the female narrators adopt in order to render deviant female behaviour acceptable to us, and so I shall comment on this aspect of these stories at some length. But there is another aspect of these stories that is even more intriguing to me, and that is the way in which both narrators use scenes of revelation and divestment in order to accentuate points of epistemological and hermeneutic resistance. For if we would like to think we have really gotten to the bottom of the matter when the female protagonists return to being women, such moments of textual density encourage us to reconsider.

I am particularly interested in *Decameron* 2.3 because, as a narrative, it is 'deviant.' It has not emerged as one of the more inspiring tales of the *Decameron*; it does not conform to most readers' ideas of what a good novella should be like. It is not difficult to understand why. The novella offers an equivocal message about Fortune, which is presumed to be the implicit topic of the Second Day; it avoids in-depth psychological probings; and when we compare the novella's principal male character, Alessandro, to some of the other successful protagonists of Day 2, it is evident that he cannot compete in cleverness or in dramatic experience.[3] Where is the compelling interpretive framework that would allow us to make sense of this story?

I would submit that the novella can not be understood within the interpretive frameworks that have thus far been applied to it. In searching for evidence of a unified message in a unified artistic effort, the reader is almost certain to be disappointed by the novella's deviance.

The novella has a divided message and its artistic efforts are therefore equally divided. To think otherwise is to remain unmindful both of Pampinea's purpose in telling the story and of the Author's purpose in including it in the *Decameron* as he does.

Pampinea's story is a response to the story that precedes hers, Filostrato's novella of Rinaldo d'Asti. Claiming he would address 'sacred things' ('cose catoliche' [2.2.3]), Filostrato had proceeded to tell of a man who had benefited from the intervention of the heavens. Rinaldo d'Asti is robbed of all his possessions and abandoned, but he manages – thanks to Saint Julian – to find comfortable lodging with a charming widow for a single night. Then he is restored to his previous condition. In responding to this story, Pampinea has her work cut out for her. How will she counter Filostrato's narrative about female carnality and consensual illicit sex? How will she present the viewpoint of an aristocratic woman like herself, without alienating the pro-male contingent of her audience?

Pampinea sets out to appeal to a dual audience – those who want to hear about the world of male-dominated finance and politics and those who want to hear a story of romance between star-crossed lovers. But she makes sure that the appeal to the male sector of her audience dominates. She begins with an all-male setting, focusing on men who might be part of the Lamberti or Agolante family businesses both in Florence and in England. (Why equivocate about Alessandro's family affiliation? To create a greater possibility that the Florentine listener will identify with the male protagonists.) These prodigal men and their fortunes are the cardinal hinge of the story, allowing the introduction of their nephew, Alessandro, who is responsible for the English portion of the family business. Alessandro appears to be the only decent fellow in the lot, but even he cannot manage when warfare breaks out in England, creating an impossible financial situation. After a long wait for a peace that now seems impossible, Alessandro decides to leave England. As he is returning to Italy, he meets up with the abbot who will turn out to be a woman – and a princess no less – who wishes to marry him. The princess's offer of marriage will prove beneficial not only for Alessandro, but also for his entire family.

Because Pampinea begins and ends by focusing on men, and because she delays introducing her female character until her story of male financial and political woes is well advanced, she can level several implicit criticisms against men and male views. Her abbot/princess is a better critical reader than Rinaldo D'Asti – or, at the very least, luckier.

She eyes her travelling companion and sizes him up correctly. More important, however, the abbot/princess has standards of sexual behaviour that are stricter than those of the widow in *Decameron* 2.2. Although the abbot/princess, like the widow of *Decameron* 2.2, initiates the sexual encounter, she stops Alessandro as he moves to kiss her. She is not interested in a one-night stand:

> Avanti che tu più mi t'avicini, attendi quello che io ti voglio dire. Come tu puoi conoscere, io son femina e non uomo; e pulcella partitami da casa mia, al Papa n'andava che mi maritasse: o tua ventura o mia sciagura che sia, come l'altro dì ti vidi, sì di te m'accese Amore, che donna non fu mai che tanto amasse uomo. E per questo io ho diliberato di volere te avanti che alcuno altro per marito: dove tu me per moglie non vogli tantosto di qui ti diparti e nel tuo luogo ritorna.   (2.2.33)

> Before you come any closer, listen to what I have to tell you. As you can see for yourself, I am a woman and not a man; I left my home a virgin, and I was going to the Pope to be married, and through your good fortune or my own misfortune, whatever the case may be, I fell so much in love with you when I saw you the other day that no woman ever burned with more love for another man. For this reason I have decided to take you as my husband over all other men; so if you do not wish to take me as your wife, leave here immediately and return to where you were.   (78)

Obviously, Pampinea is shoring up the virtue and chastity of her female protagonist, in order to portray her as superior to Filostrato's widow. But what about the possibility that the princess might be seen as excessively forward in her interactions with Alessandro? Pampinea offers reassurances about the princess's look and her speech.

Pampinea never requires the reader to acknowledge that a *woman* is the bearer of the look. The abbot/princess does not really even look at Alessandro at first; rather 'gli venne nel cammino presso di sé veduto Alessandro' ('as they were on the road, it happened that the sight of Alessandro presented itself alongside him' [2.3.20; my translation]). Throughout this passage in which Alessandro is described in detail, we repeatedly hear that these are the *abbot's* musings. The reader who might be worried about women looking upon men is reassured. This is a role reserved for men.

Pampinea faces a greater challenge when she has the abbot/princess speak on her own behalf. As is clear throughout Day 2, a woman who speaks to further her own personal interests must exercise care. If she takes advantage of men, like the Sicilian prostitute in the novella of Andreuccio da Perugia, the man must be a figure from whom the audience can distance itself.[4] If a woman might even remotely call male authority into question, it is wise not to use direct discourse in order to report her speech. In the novella of Madama Beritola, Currado's wife, by dint of persuasive arguments, leads him to change his mind about murdering his daughter and her lover (2.6.39–40; 102); the nursemaid who had fabricated new identities for Madama Beritola's sons (2.6.27–31; 101) later reveals in detail what she did and why (2.6.73–4; 106–7). None of these narratives are reported directly in the text. Only in the stories by Pampinea and Filomena do honourable women speak in direct discourse at any length, and when they do, they are exceedingly careful not to offend their male interlocutors.

It is worth our while to examine closely the speech that the abbot/princess delivers before the pope in *Decameron* 2.3:

'Santo Padre, sì come voi meglio che alcuno altro dovete sapere, ciascun che bene e onestamente vuol vivere dee, in quanto può, fuggire ogni cagione la quale a altramenti fare il potesse conducere; il che acciò che io, che onestamente viver disidero, potessi compiutamente fare, nell'abito nel qual mi vedete fuggita segretamente con grandissima parte de' tesori del re d'Inghilterra mio padre (il quale al re di Scozia vecchissimo signore, essendo io giovane come voi mi vedete, mi voleva per moglie dare), per qui venire, acciò che la vostra Santità mi maritasse, mi misi in via. Né mi fece tanto la vecchiezza del re di Scozia fuggire, quanto la paura di non fare per la fragilità della mia giovanezza, se a lui maritata fossi, cosa che fosse contra le divine leggi e contra l'onore del real sangue del padre mio. E così disposta venendo, Idio, il quale solo ottimamente conosce ciò che fa mestiere a ciascuno, credo per la sua misericordia colui che a Lui piacea che mio marito fosse mi pose avanti agli occhi e quel fu questo giovane' e mostrò Allessandro 'il qual voi qui appresso di me vedete, li cui costumi e il cui valore son degni di qualunque gran donna, quantunque forse la nobiltà del suo sangue non sia così chiara come è la reale. Lui ho adunque preso e lui voglio, né mai alcuno altro n'avrò, che che se ne debba parere al padre mio o a altrui; per che la principal cagione per la quale mi mossi è tolta via, ma piacquemi di fornire il mio cammino sì per visitare li santi luoghi e reverendi, de' quali questa città è piena, e la vostra Santità, e sì acciò che per voi il contratto matrimonio tra Alessandro e me solamente nella presenza di Dio io facessi aperto nella vostra e per conseguente degli altri uomini. Per che umilmente

vi priego che quello che a Dio e a me è piaciuto sia a grado a voi, e la vostra
benedizion ne doniate, acciò che con quella, sì come con più certezza del
piacere di Colui del quale voi sete vicario, noi possiamo insieme all'onore di
Dio e del vostro vivere e ultimamente morire.' (2.3.37–41)

'Holy Father, as you know better than all others, anyone who wishes to live
a good and honest life must avoid, insofar as he is able, everything which
might lead him to do the opposite; to this end, I myself, being a person
who wishes to lead a totally honest life, set out dressed in the clothes you
see on me now to seek the blessing of your holiness for my marriage, but I
have fled in secret, taking with me a large part of the treasures belonging
to my father, the King of England, who planned to have me marry the King
of Scotland, who is an extremely old man, whereas I as you can see, am so
young. What caused me to flee was not so much the old age of the King of
Scotland but rather the fear that if I were married to him, because of the
fragility of my youth, I might commit some act contrary to divine law and
against the honor of the royal blood of my father. In this frame of mind I
was on my way here when God, Who alone knows what is best for all of us,
moved, as I believe, by His compassions, set before my eyes the man whom
He chose to be my husband, and that person is the very man,' she said as
she pointed to Alessandro, 'whom you see standing by my side, whose manners and valor are worthy of any great lady, even if his blood is perhaps not
as obviously noble as that of a person of royal birth. Therefore, I have taken
him and it is he I desire, nor will I ever accept any other man no matter
what my father or others might think; thus the main reason for my journey
has been removed, but I should like to make my journey complete by visiting the holy and sacred sites of which this city abounds and by meeting
your holiness so that through you, the marriage contract made between
Alessandro and me, in the presence of God alone, may be made public in
your presence and in the presence of all men. I humbly beseech you, then,
that what was found pleasing to God and to myself may also find favor with
you and that you give us your blessing, so that with more certainty of pleasing Him whose vicar you are on earth, we may, to the glory of God and
yourself, live together until death do us part.' (79)

This speech is a tour de force. Throughout her presentation, the
abbot/princess addresses the pope deferentially. The pope is the spiritual leader of all Christendom; he above all knows the good toward
which all honest men strive. She has always sought his authoritative
blessing for her marriage, even before God presented Alessandro to her.

God has solved her dilemma, but her situation would not be complete without visiting the sacred sites of Rome and obtaining the pope's blessing. Having gained his goodwill through the repeated use of *captatio benevolentiae*, the princess refutes any negative representation of herself. She is not a rebellious daughter who has refused the husband that her father, the king, has chosen for her; not a thief who has pilfered the royal treasure; not a runaway dressed as a man; not an upstart who has decided to marry a commoner. Rather, she portrays herself as respectful of spiritual precepts, a virtuous young woman, intent only on saving her soul, and ever amenable to God's will.

The princess does not deny the accusations that could be made against her. On the contrary: she admits them all. Yet she consistently deflects attention away from the most egregious aspects of her behaviour. She does not want to marry an extremely old man, not because he is old, but because she fears for her virtue. She is dressed in the vestments of a male abbot, but she refers to these merely as 'the clothes you see on me.' Alessandro is of the mercantile/business class, but she refers to him as a person 'whose blood is perhaps not as obviously noble as that of a person of royal birth.' When she announces her intention to take Alessandro as her husband, she admits she will not change her mind, but she does not go so far as to tell the pope she would defy his authority. Rather, she states that she will not 'accept any other man no matter what my father *or others* might think' (emphasis mine).

Furthermore, the abbot/princess never casts men in a bad light. She does not openly criticize her father's decision, nor does she focus on the physical limitations of the king of Scotland. Her strategy is to identify superior male authorities, and use them to her advantage. Of course, it cannot hurt to ask the pope to rule against the king of England, since thirteenth- and fourteenth-century popes had a keen interest in asserting their own superiority. Nor can it hurt to invoke the wishes of God himself. To say otherwise would be to contradict the very principles on which papal authority is based. The princess reaffirms that men run the show – she just has to figure out how to play them off against each other.

In keeping with the desire to shore up male privilege, Pampinea asserts that it is men – not women – who benefit from a strong proactive character like the princess of England. Even when the princess describes to Alessandro how she fell in love with him, she emphasizes his fortune, her loss: 'o tua ventura o mia sciagura che sia, come l'altro dì ti vidi, sì di te m'accese Amore, che donna non fu mai che tanto

amasse uomo' ('whether it be on account of your good fortune or my
own misfortune, the other day when I saw you, Love made me burn for
you so much that no woman ever loved a man as much' [2.3.33; my
translation]). The princess asks the pope for his blessing so that she and
Alessandro can 'insieme *all'onore di Dio e del vostro* vivere e ultimamente
morire' ('*to the glory of God and yourself,* live together until death do us
part' [2.3.41; 79]). After the wedding, Alessandro's entire family in Florence is redeemed from debt and Alessandro is appointed Duke of
Cornwall, a position that – as Pampinea and her companions were sure
to know – had been created by royal charter in 1337, and has since been
reserved for the heir apparent to the English throne.[5]

Possibly because the princess of England is the most rebellious female
figure of Day 2, Pampinea must work harder to persuade her audience
to accept the princess's transgressive behaviour. She does so by evoking
an even more 'monstrous' threat – homosexuality – so as to establish a
distance from that spectre.

Alessandro, having no place to sleep, finally retires to the abbot's
room at the suggestion of the innkeeper. The abbot is awake, thinking
of his desires, and resolving in favour of acting upon them. Having
decided to have Alessandro at all costs, the abbot tells Alessandro to
come lie down next to him, which Alessandro agrees to do (though
after a long protestation that Pampinea renders very briefly [2.3.29]).
The scene creates a sense of wonderment in the reader, who may well
not remember the rubric, where the abbot is in fact revealed to be a
woman. Is it possible that Pampinea is about to introduce a scene of
homosexual love? The reader's own bewilderment is then reproduced
by Alessandro himself as the abbot begins to touch him: 'Alessandro si
maravigliò forte e dubitò non forse l'abate, da disonesto amore preso,
si movesse a così fattamente toccarlo' ('Alessandro, who was amazed at
this, feared that the abbot had been seized by some unnatural passion
or else he would not have grabbed him in this manner' [2.3.30; 78]).
The abbot, or rather the daughter of the king of England, reveals the
presence of her femaleness (her breasts), not the absence of her maleness
(a missing penis): 'prestamente di dosso una camiscia, ch'avea, caccia-
tasi, presa la mano d'Alessandro, e quella sopra il petto si pose dicendo:
"Alessandro, caccia via il tuo sciocco pensiero, e, cercando qui, conosci
quello che io nascondo"' ('then, quickly opening his own shirt, he took
Alessandro's hand and placed it upon his breast, saying: "Alessandro,
get rid of that foolish idea; put your hand here and find out what I am
hiding"' [2.3.31; 78]). For a reader who might fear – as Alessandro

seems to – that something untoward is about to take place, the discovery that the abbot is a woman is tremendously reassuring.

Nonetheless, aspects of Pampinea's story are less than reassuring. Compare the princess's revelation of her sex to that of Eugenia, the cross-dressed saint on whom the princess is modelled. In the legend of Saint Eugenia, there is a single public revelation scene: Eugenia, who has taken on the persona of Brother Eugene at least in part to avoid an arranged marriage, reveals her sex after she is falsely accused of sexual assault; she does so by opening her robe to the waist. In *Decameron* 2.3, there is a *double* moment of revelation. First the abbot reveals to Alessandro, in the privacy of their shared room, that he is a she; the revelation of the woman's breast is key proof. Then the abbot, whom Alessandro now knows to be a woman, goes before the pope and reveals not only her sex but also her parentage and status. In this public forum, no physical exposure seems to be necessary, or at least Pampinea does not comment on it. Monica Donaggio judges the princess's revelation of her sex to be less compelling than Madonna Zinevra's in *Decameron* 2.9, simply because Madonna Zinevra manages to keep her secret longer and because the public revelation of her sex seems more dramatic. But I think Donaggio has missed the point. The double revelation of the princess's sex in *Decameron* 2.3 has the effect of reminding us – as surely Alessandro must have felt when he got more details the second revelation around – that we may not have gotten to the bottom of things. Truths that have been revealed are merely partial; the process of revealing truth is ongoing. We can never rest easy, thinking that there is a telos, that we have reached a point where we can judge matters to be settled.

And there is at least one more nagging question. Presumably, the princess was travelling as an abbot who, not yet being of age, needed the pope's special dispensation to assume his duties. In separate moments, the princess tells both Alessandro and the pope that the purpose of her trip to Rome was to have the pope marry her ('al Papa n'andava che mi maritasse' [2.3.33], 'per qui venire, acciò che la vostra Santità mi maritasse' [2.3.37]). But she also tells the pope that she fled England because she did not wish to marry the man her father had chosen for her. If she was going to Rome to be married, who, precisely, did she have in mind to marry before she met Alessandro on the road? Or to pose the question on philological grounds: What, precisely, does the phrase 'che [il Papa] mi maritasse' tell us about the princess's intentions and motivations?

A review of the English translations shows us just how stubbornly opaque this phrase is. Does the princess mean that she intended that the pope 'might marry [her] off,' as Guido Waldman would have it?[6] Waldman's reading allows us to think of an innocent princess rebelling against her father only to submit to the pope's higher authority. This reading might be supported by the passages in which Pampinea comments on how the sight of Alessandro engenders strange new feelings in the abbot ('nuove cose' [2.3.24] and 'nuovi disii' [2.3.28]). The suggestion is that the princess really might have been expecting to receive a husband only upon her arrival in Rome and she might have been truly surprised by the appearance of a man for whom she feels an unusual desire. But Waldman's reading is not the only possible one. Does the princess mean to say, as Mark Musa and Peter Bondanella maintain, that she wants the pope to grant his holy blessing to her marriage? This might leave open the possibility that the princess may even have planned all along to choose her own marriage partner. In keeping with such anticipatory design, perhaps, is the alacrity with which she produces a marriage ring. No sooner does Alessandro agree to be her husband than she efficiently seals his expression of consent, apparently without even getting out of bed: 'Essa allora levatasi a sedere in su il letto, davanti a una tavoletta dove Nostro Signore era effigiato postogli in mano uno anello, gli si fece sposare' ('She then sat up in bed and, in front of a small picture of Our Lord, she placed a ring in his hand and had him marry her' [2.3.35; my translation]).[7] Since clandestine marriages were illegal but not invalid, this exchange between the princess and Alessandro is proof that they are married even before they arrive in Rome, where Alessandro, upon hearing the princess's speech to the pope, marvels that his *wife* is the daughter of the king of England ('udendo *la moglie* esser figliuola del re d'Inghilterra' [2.3.42; emphasis mine]).

The conflict between these two readings, offering a princess potentially innocent and potentially Machiavellian, is such that G.H. McWilliam intervenes to clarify. In doing so, he alters the sense of the text. In his translation, the princess declares, 'I myself, being one who desires to live a thoroughly honest life, have come all this way in the clothes you see me wearing, ostensibly to seek Your Holiness's blessing for my marriage. But in reality, I have fled, taking with me a considerable part of the treasures belonging to my father, the King of England.'[8] In the original Italian, there is no clear distinction between an 'ostensible' and an 'actual' motivation (although it is true that the force of the subjunctive 'mi maritasse' might be marshalled in favour of an ostensible motivation). McWilliam resorts to a suspect reordering of the syntax of the princess's admissions, and the vital phrase on which his reading depends ('But in reality ...') has no foundation in the Italian text.

So to sum up regarding *Decameron* 2.3: Pampinea tells us that we needn't worry about women's deviance, for women who dress up as men will not undo the social order. But Pampinea offers less reassurance about hermeneutic matters, for what she tells us, in essence, is that there is no way to get to the naked truth. That, I think, is even more daring than the appearance of a character that does not conform to accepted social roles.

Let us turn now to *Decameron* 2.9, told by the queen of Day Two, Filomena, who claims that her story will prove the truth of the proverb 'The deceiver is at the mercy of the deceived.' The story begins in Paris, with Italian merchants talking about the wives they have left at home. They are certain that their wives are cheating on them – for they know how women are and how they themselves are. Only one man, Bernabò from Genoa, begs to differ, offering a lengthy praise of his wife Zinevra. He is dismissed by Ambrogiuolo of Piacenza, who continues to maintain women's inferiority. In the back and forth that follows, which is going nowhere, Bernabò, certain that Ambrogiuolo will not be able to seduce his wife, sets a wager on his wife's chastity. The terms of the bet are worked out and Ambrogiuolo sets off for Genoa. There he manages to introduce himself into Zinevra's house in a chest from which, at night, he emerges. He gets a good look at the room, takes some of her possessions (a belt and a purse), and examines her body as she sleeps. After two days, he is carried out in the chest. Returning to Paris, he produces his 'proof' (the description of the room, the objects, and a description of a mole under Zinevra's breast). Bernabò, crushed by the news, pays up and then arranges for his disloyal wife to be killed by a servant. But threatened with death in a craggy wilderness outside Genoa, Zinevra pleads for her life, offers her clothes to the servant (so he can use them as proof that he has killed her), and flees Italy disguised as a man, Sicurano da Finale. Because she is so accomplished, she eventually ends up as one of the most trusted employees of the sultan. This puts her in a position where one day, at a merchant fair in Acre, she happens to recognize her own belt and purse in the possession of an Italian merchant named Ambrogiuolo. Asked about them, Ambrogiuolo claims that he seduced a certain Madonna Zinevra to get them, and that subsequently her husband had her killed. By now the pieces are coming into place. Sicurano da Finale orchestrates an audience at which he manages to have Ambrogiuolo and Bernabò tell their stories in the presence of the sultan, then Sicurano asks the sultan for permission to produce the lady. To the astonishment of all, Sicurano reveals himself to be Zinevra. The story ends happily as the sultan forgives Bernabò (upon Zinevra's request), redresses Zinevra as a woman, and punishes Ambrogiuolo severely (he is smeared with honey and left to be eaten by insects). Bernabò and Zinevra then return to Genoa, where they live happily ever after.

Filomena, like Pampinea, has a variety of strategies for diffusing deviance and reassuring us about gender roles. She highlights the world of men and their concerns by introducing them first and dedicating plenty of narrative energy to their affairs. She portrays Zinevra as intelligent, talented, and masterfully persuasive, with the proviso that Zinevra remain properly virtuous, deferential, and loyal to her spouse despite his very notable failings (among which, his having arranged her murder). Using the example of a woman from the northern Italian merchant class, Zinevra reaffirms that northern Italian women would probably never really overstep gender boundaries but for the fact that their very survival might depend upon it.

Filomena maintains a sense of seamlessness throughout. The novella is composed of different dramatic scenes, but to most readers the pieces appear to fit into a coherent whole. This is indispensable to the overall rhetorical strategy of the novella. Although there are multiple characters, the triangle of Bernabò, Zinevra, and Ambrogiuolo emerges as very well defined, thanks to their distinctive discursive styles. Crucial is the figure of Zinevra, established as the reader's primary focal point when she is described, in captivating detail, in a long passage of indirect discourse that reveals Bernabò's views about her. Indeed, if the reader negotiates without too much difficulty the transitions from Paris to Genoa, from Genoa to the craggy wilderness, from the craggy wilderness to the sultan's lands, and from the sultan's lands back to Genoa, it is because each of these transitions is firmly anchored in Zinevra. She is the organizing principle of the narrative. Through her, we can explore the question posed at the beginning of the novella: Is Bernabò's praise of her grounded in reality or not? The novella seeks to show us that it is. Other perspectives (be they Ambrogiuolo's, the sultan's, or Filomena's) are marshalled to show that Zinevra is as beautiful, accomplished, chaste, and loyal as her husband had claimed she was. So we derive a dual pleasure from this novella: we get to experience the changes, including a gender, language, and culture change, and ultimately we get to revel in the fact that in the end everything comes back securely to itself (or at least so it would seem).

The primary attempt to reassure is grounded in the claim that Filomena makes for her own novella, that is, that it proves the validity of the proverb 'lo 'ngannatore rimane al piè dello 'ngannato' ('the deceiver is at the mercy of the one he deceives' [2.9.3; 140]). Filomena's 'proof' lies in the coherence of the character she portrays. Because she is able to show that Bernabò's praise of Zinevra is trustworthy, because she is able to show not only to her reader but also within the world of the novella that Ambrogiuolo is deceptive, she can claim victory for truth. Still, the reader who pauses over this proverb will certainly find herself puzzled, since the story refuses to snap tidily into the ethical pronouncement that it is supposed to sustain. Hypothesis and evidence are discontinuous, and glaringly so.

It is problematic to assert that this novella proves how 'the deceiver is at the mercy of the one he deceives,' because multiple characters deceive and are deceived. Ambrogiuolo deceives Bernabò, but then the novella is driven ahead by several more deceptions: the servant, inspired by Zinevra, deceives Bernabò about the fate of his wife; Zinevra deceives the sultan and others into thinking she is male; Zinevra deceives Ambrogiuolo into thinking that she has no ulterior motive as she confers favours upon him. As the novella progresses, each of Zinevra's deceptions is peeled away to reveal the true deceiver. It becomes clear that Zinevra is not interested in furthering the fortunes of Ambrogiuolo, it becomes clear that she is not dead, and it becomes clear that she is not male. At the end, we are left with a speechless Ambrogiuolo at the feet of Zinevra, a deceiver brought down by the deceived.

How did it happen that Zinevra would prove to be most the most powerfully persuasive character? The key lies in her understanding of the relation between experience and narration, matter and language, body and clothes. She knows what Bernabò does not know (that language and clothes shape our reality) and what Ambrogiuolo does not know well enough (that bodies still matter).

The pivotal moment lies in the rhetorical strategy that saves Zinevra's life. Here is what she says to the servant assigned to kill her:

Ahi! mercé per Dio! non volere divenire micidiale di chi mai non t'offese, per servire altrui. Idio, che tutto conosce, sa che io non feci mai cosa per la quale io dal mio marito debbia così fatto merito ricevere. Ma lasciamo ora star questo; tu puoi, quando tu vogli, a un'ora piacere a Dio e al tuo signore

e a me in questa maniera: che tu prenda questi miei panni e donimi solamente il tuo farsetto e un cappuccio, e con essi torni al mio e tuo signore e
dichi che tu m'abbi uccisa; e io ti giuro, per quella salute la quale tu donata
m'avrai, che io mi dileguerò e andronne in parte che mai né a lui né a te né
in queste contrade di me perverrà alcuna novella.   (2.9.39–40)

Ah! Have mercy, for God's sake! Don't let yourself become the murderer of
someone who has never offended you just to serve another. God, Who
knows all, knows that I have never done anything for which my husband
should so reward me. But never mind that at the moment; now, if you are
willing to do so, you can please God, as well as your master and me, all at
the same time, in this way: take these clothes of mine and leave me only
your doublet and a cloak, return to your lord and mine with these clothes
and tell him you have killed me; I swear to you, by the life you have given
me, that I shall disappear and go somewhere where neither he nor you nor
anyone in these parts will ever again hear news of me.   (147)

Zinevra's solution depends on two crucial moments in which clothes
stand in for bodies: (1) the servant producing Zinevra's own clothes as
'proof' that she is a dead body, left as food for the wolves; and (2)
Zinevra donning the servant's male attire as 'proof' that she is no longer
Zinevra but a man. The former mimes the rhetorical strategy by which
Ambrogiuolo tricks Bernabò.[9] Bernabò is an unlettered speaker for
whom bodies, language, and clothes can sometimes function as equivalents, even though bodies are privileged entities. Bodies secure his metaphysical world, as we see when he bets his own head against his wife's
chastity. For Bernabò, who rightly recognizes that in certain sorts of dis-
putes, language can furnish no absolute proof, his own body serves as
the bottom-line guarantee of the inviolability of Zinevra's body. Having
decided that further words are pointless, Bernabò declares:

Il quistionar con parole potrebbe distendersi troppo: tu diresti e io direi, e
alla fine, niente monterebbe. Ma poi che tu di', che tutte sono così
pieghevoli e che 'l tuo ingegno è cotanto, acciò che io ti faccia certo della
onestà della mia donna, io son disposto che mi sia tagliata la testa se tu mai
a cosa che ti piaccia in cotale atto la puoi conducere; e se tu non puoi, io
non voglio che tu perda altro che mille fiorin d'oro.   (2.9.21)

This arguing with words could go on forever: you would speak and I would
reply and at the end it wouldn't make a bit of difference. But since you

declare that all women are so pliable and that your own wit is so great, in order to convince you of my wife's honesty, I am prepared to have my head chopped off if you can ever convince her to commit such a pleasurable act with you; and if you fail, I do not ask you to lose more than a thousand gold florins. (143–4)

Ambrogiuolo's deception of Bernabò depends then on several successful substitutions. First, he convinces Bernabò to substitute five hundred gold florins instead of his body (the fruits of his livelihood instead of his life). Later, Ambrogiuolo produces both clothing (Zinevra's belt and purse) and narrative descriptions (of Zinevra's room and her body) as evidence that he has possessed her. What Bernabò is unable to see, however, is that clothing and narrative descriptions, although they may construct bodies, are not proof of them. Just as he is deceived into believing that Zinevra has betrayed him, he can be fooled into thinking that she is dead because the servant produces her clothing as evidence.

Still, Zinevra retains the upper hand. Even though her experience has been misrepresented by men producing narratives about her and using her clothing to shore up these narratives, the Zinevra who presents herself as Sicurano da Finale remains an individual, sexed female, who has experiential knowledge of the truth. She knows that Zinevra is alive; she knows that she is female despite her male appearance; she knows that Ambrogiuolo has not possessed her. But how does one communicate one's experiential knowledge of the truth? This was, in fact, Bernabò's problem. His view of female sexuality was different from that of his fellow merchants in Paris because of his *particular* experience of having a wife of Zinevra's calibre. Nevertheless, his knowledge of his own truth – a truth grounded in his own experience – was dismissed by his fellow merchants as impossible. His experience of the truth was not recognized as a shared truth; therefore, from the point of view of fellow merchants such as Ambrogiuolo, it could not exist.

How can we convince others of experiential truth in the absence of normative paradigms that would already render such truths absolute? I believe this is what Filomena is getting at when she introduces her novella with the following statement:

Suolsi tra' volgari spesse volte dire un cotal proverbio: che lo 'ngannatore rimane a piè dello 'ngannato; il quale non pare che per alcuna ragione si possa mostrare essere vero, se per gli accidenti che avvengono non si mostrasse. (2.9.3)

There is a proverb often heard among the common people: that the deceiver is at the mercy of the one he deceives. This proverb would not seem possible to prove if it were not for the actual cases we have to demonstrate it. (141)

The truth of this statement, says Filomena, may seem evident only because of things that are 'accidental' in the Aristotelian philosophical sense: not constant, but unpredictable, exceptional, different. How is it that the truth can be confirmed even by individual cases? This is the problem that the story has to confront. It does this by working through the issue of gender and sexual difference; it does this by asking, 'What is a woman?'

This issue comes to a head when Sicurano da Finale (that is, Zinevra in disguise) receives permission from the sultan to bring forth Zinevra. Weeping, Sicurano da Finale throws himself at the feet of the sultan. We are told then that 'quasi a un'ora la maschil voce e il più non volere maschio parere si partì' (2.9.67). Here the Italian text proves resistant. How should we interpret and translate this phrase, in particular, the concluding portion of it ('il più non volere maschio parere si partì')?

For Franca Brambilla Ageno, the phrase as it stands makes no sense. Noting that Boccaccio is a most distracted author who frequently makes errors, she argues that Boccaccio, thinking that Zinevra *no longer* wished to be male ('*non* voleva *più* maschio parere' [my emphasis]), must have inserted that 'no longer' ('più non') into the sentence he was writing, but without the awareness that he was saying exactly the opposite of what he really wanted to say. In other words, according to Brambilla Ageno, Boccaccio wrote that Sicurano relinquished 'the desire no longer to appear male' but really he wanted to write that Sicurano 'no longer desired to appear male.'[10]

Vittore Branca also acknowledges the difficulty of the passage. In a footnote to *Decameron* 2.9.67 in the Mondadori edition, he writes: 'Ma la frase, così come è attestata dall'autografo e dalle più autorevoli testimonianze manoscritte, rimane oscura, perché sembra che quel "non" sia di troppo, o almeno pleonastico, come del resto avviene correntemente nel *D*. (cfr. la novella III 7, 5)' ('But the phrase, which appears in the autograph manuscript and in the most authoritative manuscripts, remains unclear, because it seems this "non" is unnecessary, or at least pleonastic, as does happen not infrequently in the *Decameron* [cf. *Decameron* 3.7.5]').[11] Since Branca allows that the 'non' might be pleonastic (i.e., that it has no force as a negative), the English translation

supported by his reading remains essentially the same as in the case of
Franca Brambilla Ageno: 'he relinquished the desire to appear male.'

Whatever way we look at this passage, it is evident that the matter is
complicated, hard to read and to register. Along with Vittore Branca
and Franca Brambilla Ageno, we might see this passage as affirming that
when Zinevra wishes to be a man she does so successfully and when she
wishes to return to being a woman, she merely lets the masculine guise
fall away. Nevertheless, I am not so sure that this is the only interpretation of a cross-dressed woman's desire. It seems to me quite possible that
a woman's assumption of masculinity could be linked to a desire *not* to
come into view as male. This would require that, aware of the slippage
between a body sexed female and a gender identity that is male, we
allow for the possibility that a subject whose body is sexed female could
experience an assumed male identity as a form of alienation, as an
imposed monstrosity.[12]

I am hesitant to say what sort of desire emerges when the sultan
grants that Zinevra may come forth because I do not believe we can
offer a uniform response to the question of what a subject performing a
gender identity *really* desires. In this regard, Vittore Branca's reference
to another case of pleonastic *non* (this time in *Decameron* 3.7) is instruc-
tive. The example, which appears in Emilia's tale about Tedaldo degli
Elisei and Madonna Ermellina, reads thus: 'qual che la cagion fosse, la
donna avendo di sé a Tedaldo compiaciuto un tempo, del tutto si tolse
dal volergli più compiacere, né a non volere non solamente alcuna sua
ambasciata ascoltare ma veder in alcuna maniera' ('whatever the reason
might have been, after having satisfied Tedaldo for some time, she suddenly decided to deny him any further pleasure, and she refused not
only to listen to any of his messages but under no circumstances would
she see him' [3.7.5; 202]). The multiple negatives in Italian suggest
the convoluted and perplexing nature of Madonna Ermellina's decision. Attempting to capture the complexity of the original Italian, we
could say that 'she wants nothing more then to deal with Tedaldo degli
Elisei.' Are we absolutely certain that she has refused him? Whatever her
protestations now, Madonna Ermellina will eventually reciprocate
Tedaldo's desire by the end of the story, so in retrospect we might well
wonder about how much real negative force those negatives had at the
outset.

Sicurano da Finale's revelation of himself as Zinevra, with its inclusion
of negatives that may or may not be superfluous, seems designed to alert
us to the slippage between a constructed gender identity (Sicurano,

whose voice and appearance are male) and an essential core (Zinevra, whose experience remains that of a woman even when she is performing the functions of a man). Using the term 'essential core,' I am cognizant of the debate about essentialism that has impassioned feminist critics largely on this side of the Atlantic; and I am also cognizant of the attempts over the last decade to think us out of the limitations that this debate has imposed on our thinking about what it means to be a woman or a man.[13] Zinevra's 'essential core' is hers and hers alone: in this particular case, that of a heterosexual woman with the particular qualities and life experiences she, as a fictional character, is said to possess. As the story demonstrates most manifestly, Madonna Zinevra remains faithful to her husband. But this revelation scene, with its portrayal of a character who returns to being a woman by letting go of the 'desire not to appear male,' suggests that another crucial articulation of fidelity is present here. Madonna Zinevra is faithful above all to herself, to being a woman even when she functions as a man in society.[14]

How should we translate 'quasi a un'ora la maschil voce e il più non volere maschio parere si partì'? The optimal English translation would reproduce the quavering uncertainty about whether that *non* has a negative value or whether it is pleonastic. I have not yet been able to figure out such a translation. Given that, I would opt for 'In an instant, masculine voice and the yearning not to be a man disappeared,' not because it is the only correct translation, but rather because it is a translation that communicates the story about Madonna Zinevra that we had not previously been able to hear.

This leads us to the next question: What does the story tell us about what it means for Madonna Zinevra to be a woman? To answer this, we need to take a closer look at the lengthy passage in which Bernabò is introduced, for it is here that he offers his description of his wife Zinevra as proof that she is not like the other women that his fellow merchants have described:

> Un solamente, il quale avea nome Bernabò Lomellino da Genova, disse il contrario, affermando sé di spezial grazia da Dio avere una donna per moglie la più compiuta di tutte quelle virtù che donna o ancora cavaliere in gran parte o donzello dee avere, che forse in Italia ne fosse un'altra: per ciò che ella era bella del corpo e giovane ancora assai e destra e atante della persona, né alcuna cosa era che a donna appartenesse, sì come di lavorare lavorii di seta e simili cose, che ella non facesse meglio che alcuna altra. Oltre a questo, niuno scudiere, o famigliare che dir vogliamo, diceva

trovarsi il quale meglio né più accortamente servisse a una tavola d'un
signore, che serviva ella, sì come colei che era costumatissima, savia e discreta molto. Appresso questo la commendò meglio saper cavalcare un cavallo, tenere uno uccello, leggere e scrivere e fare una ragione che se un
mercatante fosse; e da questo, dopo molte altre lode, pervenne a quello di
che quivi si ragionava, affermando con saramento niuna altra più onesta
né più casta potersene trovar di lei; per la qual cosa egli credeva certa-
mente che, se egli diece anni o sempre mai fuori di casa dimorasse, che
ella mai a così fatte novelle non intenderebbe con altro uomo.   (2.9.8–10)

Only one man, whose name was Bernabò Lomellin da Genoa, argued to
the contrary, declaring that as a special grace from God he possessed a lady
for his wife who was more richly endowed than any other woman in all of
Italy with all those virtues that a lady should possess, and even, to a great
extent those virtues that a knight or a squire should possess: she was physically beautiful, still very young, dexterous and handy with her hands –
there was no type of woman's work (such as working in silk and the like)
that she could not do better than anyone else. Besides this, he asserted that
it was impossible to find any servant or page who could better or more skill-
fully serve at a gentleman's table than she could, since she was most well
mannered, educated, and most discreet. Moreover, he praised her for her
ability to ride a horse, handle a falcon, read and write, and to keep
accounts better than any merchant; after singing many of her other praises,
he finally got around to the topic under discussion, declaring that he swore
you could not find a more honest or chaste woman than she, and for this
reason, he was firmly convinced that even if he stayed away from home for
ten years or forever, she would never agree to have anything to do with
another man.   (141–2)

To tell the truth, this passage, which reveals the represented thought of
Bernabò, is most curious. Readers appear to have taken it at face value,
with little regard for the sense of wonderment that the passage seems
designed to provoke. Can this be for real? We are supposed to believe
that his wife should be better endowed not only with the qualities that
other women possess, not only with the qualities that a merchant should
possess, but also with the qualities that to a great extent a noble knight
or knight-in-training should have?[15] We are supposed to believe that his
wife would never have anything to do with another man even if he
'stayed away from home for ten years or forever'? Is Bernabò not simply
delusional?

The passage is difficult to grasp because we cannot be entirely certain whether Bernabò is attesting to abilities that his wife has actually proven to have or whether he is attesting to potential that his wife could actualize if she were put into a different context, particularly an aristocratic one. In the beginning, Bernabò seems carried away by his own praise when he transports Zinevra from the mercantile world to the world of the feudal aristocracy by claiming that her virtues are ones that a woman 'or even a knight to a great extent or a knight-in-training must have' ('o ancora cavaliere in gran parte o donzello dee avere' [2.9.8; my translation]). The hyperbolic nature of this praise (her virtues are comparable even to those of a man of a higher class than she!) is rendered comical by the two qualifiers that offer weak restraint. The virtues are ones that a knight 'to a great extent' must have; and perhaps it would be better not to talk about a knight but about a young man in training to be a knight ('donzello'). A similar moment of comical confusion and restraint marks the next claim, namely, 'niuno scudiere, o famigliare che dir vogliamo, diceva trovarsi il quale meglio né più accortamente servisse a una tavola d'un signore, che serviva ella, sì come colei che era costumatissima, savia e discreta molto' ('he said that, with regard to her ability to serve, there was no squire [or servant, if we prefer this term] who could more attentively serve at the table of a lord than she, for she had all the qualities of a woman who was most well-mannered, wise, and discerning' (my translation). The sentence starts off with a comparison to a squire, but then backtracks, offering an attending member of a family's retinue (the 'famigliare' or servant) as a quasi-equivalent to a squire. The tone here is hard to pinpoint. The phrase may document Bernabò's casual shift from one designation to another: that is, does it really matter whether we compare Zinevra to a squire or to a more generic servant, since she will in any case emerge in a positive light? We might also read the phrase as tinged with a mild form of narrative distancing that comes from Filomena: that is, Bernabò compares Zinevra to young nobles who serve at table, but those of us who have a more precise sense of language might choose another term. Readers, however, must keep in mind that *famigliare* ('servant') is no straightforward synonym for *scudiero* ('squire'), even if the Zingarelli *Vocabolario della lingua italiana* tells us that *scudiero* can mean 'servitore,' on the grounds that Boccaccio's *Decameron* gives the phrase 'scudiere, o famigliar che dir vogliamo.'[16] Taking into account the class implications that emerge in this passage, we could transpose the situation into a different key, and propose the following statement as an analogue: 'she was able to wait on table as well as a butler or, in other words, a servant.' *Butler* and *servant* are not precise equivalents; a butler is a servant, yes, but not all servants are butlers. So with *scudiere* (squire) and *famigliare* (servant). *Scudiere* (like 'butler') is marked to indicate the class status of the master in these master–servant relationships.

Certainly this is not the only place in the story where Filomena indicates mild amusement at Bernabò's way with words. But it is only later, toward the end of the presentation of Bernabò among the merchants, that Filomena reports, in direct discourse, the line that is certain to make us raise an eyebrow or two. Nearing exasperation, Bernabò says, 'Io son mercatante e non fisofolo, e come mercatante risponderò' ('I am a merchant, not a phisolopher [*sic*] and it's as a merchant that I'll respond' [2.9.18; my translation]). Recent English translations of the *Decameron* (McWilliam, Musa/Bondanella, Waldman) translate 'fisolofo' as 'philosopher,' but once again, this term is marked for the degree of astuteness – or least the educational status – of the speaker. Throughout the initial portion of *Decameron* 2.9, Filomena has to walk a fine line, on the one hand, making us wonder whether Bernabò isn't a bit thick and, on the other, maintaining a high degree of sympathy for his character. As a result, she can reveal a malapropism such as this only toward the end of the scene, after we have already identified with him and come to be highly suspicious of Ambrogiuolo (whom she has permitted to speak at length, with the result that we can see the sophistry that characterizes his arguments about female inferiority).

Bernabò's praise nears its crescendo: 'la commendò meglio saper cavalcare un cavallo, tenere uno uccello, leggere e scrivere e fare una ragione che se un mercatante fosse' ('he praised her for her ability to ride a horse, handle a falcon, read and write, and to keep accounts better than any merchant' [2.9.10; 142]). As in the previous case (serving at the table of a gentleman), has Zinevra actually performed such activities or is she blessed simply by as yet unexercised potential? In what context could she have handled a falcon, for example? Once again, we cannot close our eyes to the rhetorical formulation, even if the English translations often encourage us to do precisely this. In the Italian original, it is not so clear that Bernabò is saying that his wife really knows in the absolute how to ride a horse and handle a falcon. The sentence would be better translated as 'he praised his wife for knowing better how to ride a horse, handle a bird, read, write, and keep accounts than if she were a merchant.' We can imagine that she might be able to read, write, and keep accounts better than if she were a merchant. But what precisely is one saying when, given the placement of the adverbial modifier, one is also claiming that 'she could ride a horse and handle a bird better than if she were a merchant'? The logic, here as elsewhere, is a bit hesitant, though the sentence allays our doubts when the claim ends on a firm note (that Zinevra is able to keep accounts better than if she were a merchant). It doesn't seem quite so odd that Zinevra might keep accounts better than a merchant; consequently, the reader engages in a kind of backcasting in order to make sense of other less likely claims that Bernabò makes.

Indeed, backcasting is important to the development of Zinevra's character as the story progresses. She is first seen, by Ambrogiuolo, as she sleeps. But already in this scene, even though Zinevra is not an active presence, we discover crucial information. Since Zinevra sleeps alone, flanked by a child (significantly, a girl), there is no male rival to Bernabò, at least as far as one can tell. Bernabò's claim that his wife is chaste seems to be borne out by the evidence. And indeed, one by one, all of Bernabò's claims – even the most apparently preposterous ones – will come to be borne out as Zinevra, threatened with death, transforms herself into Sicurano da Finale. It is almost as if Zinevra has grasped the details of her husband's description of her telepathically – or even more, as if in a dream. Her sartorial ability is confirmed as she converts her clothes and those of the male servant into ones more suitable for her purposes. Her ability to serve a noble is confirmed as she enters the service of the Catalan Senor En Cararh. From the Catalan, she eventually passes to the sultan, where she gives evidence of being able to assume (as Bernabò had claimed) responsibilities in the areas of custodianship, business management, and communication. While we never get proof that she can ride a horse or handle a falcon, we are told that Sicurano becomes one of the sultan's armed men (which would imply that Sicurano/Zinevra could ride a horse) and we are also treated to a vision of peregrine falcons passing from the Catalan to the sultan (a detail used, obviously, to imply that Sicurano/Zinevra might be responsible for handling them).

The backcasting appears impeccable. Even the name that Zinevra chooses for herself, Sicurano da Finale, has already been anticipated by Bernabò in his most defensive statement: 'E dico che io conosco ciò che tu di' potere avvenire alle stolte, nelle quali non è alcuna vergogna; ma quelle che savie sono hanno tanta sollecitudine dello onor loro, che elle diventano forti più che gli uomini, che di ciò non *si curano*, a guardarlo; e di queste così fatte è la mia' ('Let me say that I realize what you say might be the case among foolish women in whom there is no shame whatsoever, those women who are wise have so much concern for their honor that they become even stronger than men, who *care* very little for their own, in defending it' [2.9.18; 143; my emphasis]). Sicurano da Finale will prove to be among the men who *do* attempt to safeguard their honour (*di ciò si curano*), although clearly he is a particular case because in the final accounting he is not a man but a woman.[17]

When a narrator has a character switch gender identity, there are some curious things – we might well say queer things – that happen. This is particularly the case in languages that rely on grammatical gender. Already in *Decameron* 2.3, we saw this phenomenon, even if briefly. The abbot appears as a man to Alessandro and others in public, then reveals himself to be a woman when he is alone with Alessandro in the bedroom, then appears again briefly as a man who, in a speech to the pope, reveals himself to be a woman. In *Decameron* 2.3, that interval where the narrator must talk about a male character we now know to be female is quite brief (a mere two sentences!), allowing for the possibility that the narrator can simply refer to this character as 'the abbot' ('l'abate'), without having to substitute any pronouns that would reveal gender. *Decameron* 2.9, however, raises the issue of how to talk about a man we know to be a woman. A significant portion of the story (2.9.43–67) is dedicated to Sicurano da Finale, and here Filomena quite consistently speaks about Sicurano using masculine pronouns and adjectival endings. Significantly, the character becomes male not when Zinevra assumes the aspect of a seaman, not even when she approaches the Catalan En Cararh, but only when she enters into a relationship with En Cararh and assumes the name that will mark her as male: 'con lui s'acconciò per servidore e salissene sopra la nave faccendosi chiamare Sicuran da Finale' ('she arranged to be his manservant and boarded the ship under the name Sicurano da Finale' [2.9.43; my translation]).[18] This character will remain male until he reveals himself, in the presence of the sultan, to be Zinevra.

If we examine the English translations, we see that readers do not necessarily share the same conceptions about the gendered identity of Sicurano/Zinevra. G.H. McWilliam delays recognition of the maleness of this character, allowing maleness to emerge not upon receipt of the name Sicurano, but only after the sultan recognizes Sicurano's qualities. Moreover, following the key exchange between Ambrogiuolo and Sicurano that will raise questions about whether Sicurano's disguise might be solid, McWilliam lets the resolve and the determination of the woman *Zinevra* shine through, even though the Italian text does not clearly support this:

> Sicurano, udendo questo, prestamente comprese qual fosse la cagione dell'ira di Bernabò verso lei e manifestamente conobbe costui di tutto il suo male esser cagione; e seco pensò di non lasciarglielne portare impunità. (2.9.55)

> On hearing these words, Sicurano understood at once why Bernabò had been so enraged with her, and realized that this was the fellow who was responsible for all *her* woes. And *she* vowed to *herself* that he would not remain unpunished.[19]

Guido Waldman follows the Italian text when he makes the appearance of maleness coincide with the naming of Sicurano. Yet he too has Sicurano lapse back into Zinevra when Ambrogiuolo divulges key information, and what is more, he calls the reader's attention to this in a way that is in no way authorized by the Italian original: 'From this, Sicurano (that is, Ginevra) readily grasped the reason for Bernabò's bitterness against her; it was all too clear that this man was the author of all her troubles, and she made up her mind that he would not be allowed to escape punishment.'[20]

In defence of the English translators, of course, one would have to cite the phrase in which the gender identity of Sicurano appears shaky: 'Sicurano, udendo questo, prestamente comprese qual fosse la cagione dell'ira di Bernabò verso lei' ('Sicurano, hearing this, immediately saw the motive behind Bernabò's anger against her' [2.9.55; 149]).[21] The narrative, like Sicurano, is working hard to maintain the stability of an assumed gender identity. Even as he shows interest in the objects of female clothing and female accessories that Ambrogiuolo displays at the merchants' fair, Sicurano can banish concern about his gender identity precisely because he is able to articulate this potential rift between a traditional male gender identity and a less than traditional one. He has asked about objects that he recognizes (a belt, a purse). Ambrogiuolo laughs and replies that they are not for sale, though he would be glad to give them as a gift. This provokes a moment of doubt in Sicurano: Has his disguise been seen through? His response is to reaffirm his own identity: 'Tu ridi forse perché vedi me uom d'arme andar domandando di queste cose feminili' ('Perhaps you are laughing because you see a soldier asking for such womanly things?' [2.9.50; 148]).

Nevertheless, this particular moment of insistence, designed to stabilize a male identity, should give the reader of the *Decameron* pause. Although it is implied that Sicurano bears arms because he is charged with protecting the merchants, and although Sicurano points out that he is a 'man of arms' ('uom d'arme' [2.9.50]), Sicurano is never actually shown with weapons on his person. The invisibility of these arms is telling. When the prime worry is about the impenetrability of Sicurano's disguise, one can reaffirm the coherence of the character by reaffirming the identity of a male in a position of power and authority. This is what Sicurano does not only when he points out that he is a man of arms, but also when he speaks to Ambrogiuolo using informal address, especially given that Ambrogiuolo uses formal address with Sicurano. Still, it seems to me that the real concern is to make sure that Sicurano/Zinevra is never shown bearing arms. When Bernabò describes her as like a knight, a knight-in-training, and a squire, these figures are never doing any of the things that squires are really supposed to do, that is, bear arms. Rather, when Zinevra is compared to the knight, it is by means of metonymical relationship to aristocratic animals such as the horse and the falcon. When she is compared to a knight-in-training (*donzello* or *scudiere*), the activity remains limited to fine table service. This is the case even for the squire (*scudiere*), whose title in Italian would obviously link him with the management of arms, specifically the shield or *scudo*. Zinevra is being encoded as a woman even when she is a man. Women in the *Decameron* do not bear arms. Even Sicurano da Finale must in some measure respect this encoding as a woman, given that in the final analysis, despite his name, he is not securely a man.

What the story never tells us, of course, is whether Madonna Zinevra outfitted as a woman is as capable as Sicurano da Finale. The story encourages us to believe that she is. The decision to make her a citizen of Genoa seems strategic here. As we know from the city's surviving *commenda* (a kind of investment contract) from 1150 to 1216, Genoese women of the late twelfth and early thirteenth centuries engaged in a level of commercial and business activity that, at least by fourteenth-century Florentine standards, seems quite unusual.[22] It is true, as one historian of this period notes, that '[u]nfortunately, we do not know at the present time whether or not the women of Genoa sustained their participation in commercial investment during the years following the period of this study.'[23] If Genoese women's participation in the economy came to be limited, it might be that the *Decameron* presents a dated vision of what Genoese women were able to accomplish. On the other hand, could the fantasy of such a woman, selectively put into play in a fourteenth-century Florentine social and historical context, allow women to rise to the occasion, revealing women's many talents? Could a fictional woman such as Zinevra / Sicurano da Finale represent a viable exemplar in fourteenth-century Florence? Although we cannot be absolutely and finally certain, we might well imagine that she would.

Nevertheless, in the following two chapters, I shall ask the reader not to read selectively for the liberating possibilities that we may choose to find in individual characters and situations – a reading strategy that is available to us – but rather to consider what happens as the *Decameron* addresses the issue of women's language. In both of these chapters, I shall expand on what I have begun in this chapter on the *Decameron*'s cross-dressed women, first to show how the narrators of the *Decameron* construct the limits placed on women's uses of language, then to show how both Author and narrators construct the reader by means of a gendered use of figurative language.

chapter five

Women's Witty Words: Restrictions on Their Use

By the time the *Decameron* reaches its halfway point, it is patently evident that the ten storytellers are engaged in a communal project of constructing as well as describing the society they have left behind. During the open topic of Day 1, they have described the institutional and discursive challenges that beset them. They have offered tentative solutions to overcoming Fortune (Day 2) and to affirming the possibilities of individual agency and clever industriousness (Day 3). They have even begun to confront topics that come dangerously close to broaching news of the plague, as when, led by Filostrato, they confront unhappy love in Day 4. They have explored the pluses and minuses of social connectedness in Day 5. As Day 6 begins, they are about to confront the topic of witty remarks, a subject that promises to raise a thorny question: Who legitimately has the right to speak, and under what circumstances?

As a speech act, *Decameron* 6 has one clear perlocutionary force: to describe the day on which the narrators tell stories about witty remarks. Readers have always acknowledged that *Decameron* 6 is an indirect speech act, that beyond this first perlocutionary force there lie others: to show how the narrators reaffirm the 'magical' conception of language they had already begun to advance in Day 1;[1] to show how they attest to themselves as social beings and encourage group reflection on the roles they will have to assume if they return to Florence;[2] to draw attention to style over thematic content;[3] to explore the resonance between the frametale narrative and the stories.[4] In recent years, *Decameron* 6 has become a kind of lightning rod for readers of a feminist bent. For this, it seems, we may thank Madonna Filippa, who in *Decameron* 6.7, goes before a magistrate to argue on legal and biblical grounds that, although she is an adulteress, she should not be burned at the stake as the law requires.[5] Madonna Filippa's success has coloured the overall reading of Day 6, and not only in the United States. Some readers, especially those inclined to see Day 7 as an affirmation of new womanly virtues, have asserted that the women of Day 6 achieve power through language.[6] Barbara Zandrino, for example, reads Day 7 of the *Decameron* as the culmination of woman's triumph, 'celebrato da Boccaccio nella VI giornata con la rappresentazione esemplare di come le donne possano, a qualunque classe appartengano, dominare uomini ed eventi per mezzo del motto di spirito, di parole ingegnose, argute e concise' ('celebrated by Boccaccio on Day 6 of the *Decameron*, with the exemplary portrayal of how women, regardless of the class to which they belong, can dominate men and events by means of witty remarks, by means of clever, shrewd, and pithy words').[7]

This view of gender and language is lamentably disconnected from the contextual fabric of the Sixth Day. To recontextualize Madonna Filippa, and all the other women of *Decameron* 6 and 7 who wield rhetorical weaponry, let us first re-examine the opening episode of *Decameron* 6, to see how it poses questions about women's speech.

In the Introduction to Day 6 of the *Decameron*, the lower classes, represented by the servants Licisca and Tindaro, erupt into the world of the noble narrators. At first the cause of the uproar is unknown. Then it becomes clear that the origin is female garrulousness and perversity. Licisca attacks Tindaro, claiming that he has impertinently tried to speak before her; demanding the floor, she addresses herself to Elissa, the reigning queen of Day 6, and announces:

Madonna, costui mi vuol far conoscere la moglie di Sicofante e, né più né meno come si io con lei usata non fossi, mi vuol dare a vedere che la notte prima che Sicofante giacque con lei messer Mazza entrasse in Monte Nero per forza e con ispargimento di sangue; e io dico che non è vero, anzi v'entrò paceficamente e con gran piacer di quei d'entro. E è ben sì bestia costui, che egli si crede troppo bene che le giovani sieno sì sciocche, che elle stieno a perdere il tempo loro stando alla bada del padre e de' fratelli, che delle sette volte le sei soprastanno tre o quattro anni più che non debbono a maritarle. Frate, bene starebbono se elle s'indugiasser tanto! Alla fé di Cristo, ché debbo sapere quello che io mi dico quando io giuro: io non ho vicina che pulcella ne sia andata a marito, e anche delle maritate so io ben quante e quali beffe elle fanno a' mariti: e questo pecorone mi vuol fare conoscere le femine, come se io fossi nata ieri!   (6.Intro.8–10)

My lady, this fellow thinks he knows Sicofante's wife better than me, as if I had no idea of who she was, and he has the nerve to try to make me believe that the first night Sicofante slept with her, Messer Hammerhead took the Black Mountain by force and with some loss of blood; but that's not true and, on the contrary, I say he entered with ease and to the general delight of all the troops stationed there. This man is such an idiot, he thinks that girls are foolish enough to waste their opportunities waiting for their fathers or brothers, who six out of seven times take from three to four years longer than they should to marry them off. Brother, they would be in a fine state if they waited that long! I swear to Christ – and I don't swear like that if I don't know what I'm saying – I never had a neighbor who was a virgin when she got married, and as for the married women, I know all too well the many different kinds of tricks they play on their husbands. And this big knucklehead wants to teach me about women, as if I was born yesterday!   (381)

Licisca's outburst is startling, for in the world of the narrators, servants have moved in the background up until now, named only when Pampinea first gives them their assignments (1.Intro.98–101), and emerging as shadowy presences later only when they tend to household management. Likewise, in the stories of the first half of the *Decameron*, servants tend to be portrayed as nameless and compliant presences. From the time they first appeared on Day 2, servants in the stories have largely done the bidding of their masters and mistresses.[8] With Licisca, there emerges a maidservant who must be accounted for, both as 'servant' and as 'maiden.' Will the lower classes no longer remain hushed and orderly? Does Licisca speak not only for herself and for her consort, but also all women? Of these two questions, the more threatening for the group of storytellers is the second: is Licisca's discourse 'woman's discourse'?

The initial reaction of the women is to laugh so hard that 'tutti i denti si sarebbero loro potuti trarre' ('you could have pulled all their teeth out' [6.Intro.11; 381]). This image – almost as unsettling as Licisca's outburst – ought to be read not as a realistic detail but as a hermeneutic figure: the toothless mouth that reveals truth beneath falsehood, where in a move customary to Western metaphysical discourse, 'truth' turns out to be 'the truth about woman.'[9]

What is Licisca's revelation about woman? The first layer of this truth emerges as Elissa tries six times to impose silence on Licisca, to no avail. Just as 'six times out of seven,' according to the maidservant Licisca, men wait all too long to marry off their womenfolk, six times out of seven Elissa is unable to silence her. If silence is the figure for virginity, the truth is crystal clear in the very fact of Licisca's unchecked speech.

Furthermore, while framing her outburst as a vindication of the *truth* (she is right, Tindaro wrong, she knows and speaks, he attempts to convince her of what he claims to know), Licisca testifies to women's *deceitfulness*. Among her women neighbours, there are none who marry as virgins, and she knows how many married women persist in being unfaithful to their husbands. Licisca speaks the truth about women's lies. The model, familiar to us from Jacques Derrida's discussion of the hermeneutics that finds essence beneath appearance, is that of woman as 'twice castration: once as truth and once as untruth.'[10]

Curiously enough, Licisca, charged with speaking the truth about woman, mouths the truth that *men* in Boccaccian narratives speak about women. As Vittore Branca has stated in his note to this passage in the Mondadori edition of the *Decameron*, the kind of metaphorical language Licisca uses to describe a virgin's sexual initiation had been used by Boccaccio himself in the *Ninfale fiesolano* and will again be used by him in the *Corbaccio*.[11] In her choice of figurative language, Licisca appears aligned with Boccaccio, while in her statements about the premarital experiences of young girls, she falls into line with Panfilo and Dioneo, the narrators who, on Days 2 and 3 of the *Decameron*, had told of young maidens who had enjoyed premarital sexual experiences, and had used allusive figurative language (again originally supplied by men) in order to convey the details. And the collusion is reciprocal. Although we discover at the end of Licisca's long speech, reproduced above, that Elissa tries to interrupt her six times during it, nowhere are these interruptions evident. From the reader's point of view, Licisca maintains the floor, thanks to the male Author of the *Decameron*.

Still, the scene reveals women speakers who relinquish power as well as male speakers who secure it. Having heard Licisca's claims, Elissa, the queen of Day 6, declines to comment on the validity of them. Instead, she turns to Dioneo – the member of the group most clearly associated with sexual discourse, figurative language about sex, and the final word – and she says, 'Dioneo, questa è quistion da te: e per ciò farai, quando finite fieno le nostre novelle, che tu sopr'essa dei sentenzia finale' ('Dioneo, this is a question for you to settle, and so, when our storytelling is over, you shall pronounce the final judgment on this matter' [6.Intro.12; 382]). The tactical move may well be to isolate this disruptive voice by aligning it with the member of the group who speaks most like Licisca, and by keeping both their voices at a safe remove – spatial and temporal – from the world of storytelling. (Although the reader initially may assume that Elissa is delaying Dioneo's judgment of Licisca until the end of her reign, it certainly also seems possible that she is attempting to defer it until the end of the storytelling, which could be indefinitely postponed.)[12] But Dioneo maintains the disruptive factor. Like all the astute characters of the *Decameron*'s narrative world, he responds 'quickly' ('prestamente' [6.Intro.13; 382]) to the challenge before him. Refusing to defer his response, he announces that Licisca is right and Tindaro is an idiot. The Author of the *Decameron* permits Licisca's uninterrupted outburst; Dioneo, granted authority by Elissa, now places the stamp of approval on Licisca's assertion.

At this point, Elissa reasserts the authority that derives from her class status by imposing silence on Licisca, threatening her with a beating if she doesn't keep quiet, and sending both servants back to the kitchen. This singular combination of events – Elissa's refusal to judge Licisca's statements on sexuality, and her affirmation of her right to reinforce class distinctions – gives shape to the narrators' concerns during Day 6. Although their storytelling on Day 6 about witty remarks will presumably be free of the thematic restrictions (fortune, cleverness, love) that governed the previous four days, it will now become polarized around issues that Licisca has raised: gender and class, deceit and truthfulness.[13]

To Filomena, Licisca's mistress, Elissa offers the chance to right the situation by recognizing her as the first storyteller of Day 6. In this charged situation, Filomena elects to tell of a noble woman, Madonna Oretta, whose resourceful use of language stands to her credit.

A knight promises to take Madonna Oretta 'riding' by telling one of the finest tales in the world as they proceed on a journey. But, as Filomena notes, since the 'sword by his side was probably no more effective than his tongue was in telling stories' ('[al cavaliere] forse non stava meglio la spada allato che 'l novellar nella lingua' [6.1.9; 383]), the knight makes the journey excruciating by bungling his narrative. The gentle and gracious Madonna Oretta extricates herself from the situation by her deft use of figurative language: 'Messer, questo vostro cavallo ha troppo duro trotto, per che io vi priego che vi piaccia di pormi a piè' ('Sir, this horse of yours has too rough a trot, so I beg you, please, to set me down' [6.1.11; 383]).

Exploiting the foil of a knight incapable of telling his story, the novella highlights Madonna Oretta's ability to speak well. Her rhetorical ability is replicated in that of Filomena and of the group at large, a fact underlined not only by Madonna Oretta's upper-class status but also by the setting of the novella 'in contado, come noi siamo' ('in the country, as all of us are right now' [6.1.6; 383]).[14] It is in this spirit that the novella has often been read.[15] But the novella also prescribes the limits that a woman must respect if she criticizes a man of authority, even if he is of lower social stature than she. In short, Filomena illustrates how gender trumps class.[16]

Of supreme importance is the indirect manner of Madonna Oretta's speech. Since, in Filomena's eyes, the knight's rhetorical abilities are equivalent to his sexual prowess (as the metaphor of horseback-riding might have suggested in any case), Madonna Oretta must speak obliquely, for she may not risk appearing to castrate the man. She displaces fault onto the knight's horse (*cavallo*), and draws attention to this now guilty figure by preceding the noun with two modifiers ('*questo vostro* cavallo,' 'this horse of yours' [6.1.11; 383; emphasis mine]). She is properly humble and defers to the knight's pleasure ('vi priego che vi piaccia,' literally, 'I beg you that it be pleasing to you'), even to the point of allowing him to stay, metaphorically, on horseback while she continues, metaphorically, on foot ('a piè'). Underlining her discomfort with alliteration on the dental consonant *t* ('questo vostro cavallo ha troppo duro trotto'), she offers a softer and more pleasurable alternative with alliteration on *p* in her request for peace ('per che io vi priego che vi piaccia di pormi a piè'). She translates the harsh rhythm of his narrative into a prose characterized by uneven and awkward phrasings ('*questo vostro* cavallo ha *troppo* duro *trotto*'). Oretta does at the metadiegetic level what Filomena does at the diegetic level, when in her lengthy description of the knight's clumsy attempts to get his story going, she piles gerundial phrase on gerundial phrase for comic effect.[17]

I do not mean to suggest that indirectness is categorically reprehensible. As Deborah Tannen has shown, linguistic and rhetorical strategies must be evaluated in context.[18] We can not assume that blunt speech is preferable to indirect speech, nor should we assume that indirect speech is always the instrument of the less powerful. In fact, as I intend to demonstrate in my reading of *Decameron* 5.4 (see chapter 6), a male narrator like Filostrato shows how figurative language can be used to reinforce male power at the expense of women. In the case of Madonna Oretta, however, it is crucial that she does not use indirect speech, either to bruise the knight's ego or to emphasize her own superiority.

Indirectly, by drawing attention to Madonna Oretta's name, Filomena underscores the noblewoman's refusal to adopt an openly aggressive stance. Not only was Madonna Oretta the wife of Geri Spina, as Filomena observes, but she was the daughter of the marquis Obizzo Malaspina and Tobia *Spinola* (a fact that Filomena and her audience were likely to know). If names are the consequences of things, Oretta Malaspina promises to be a spiny lady on all fronts. Filomena is careful to prune her barbs.

Madonna Oretta stands in marked contrast to Licisca and her values. But Filomena also has several other objectives. She comments implicitly on the threat that Elissa, queen for Day 6, adopted in order to silence Licisca: *Decameron* 6.1 shows that one does not have to resort to threats of violence in order to hush someone. And Filomena offers a prominently oblique criticism of Pampinea's views.

Filomena's opening remarks set the stage:

> Giovani donne, come ne' lucidi sereni sono le stelle ornamento del cielo e nella primavera i fiori de' verdi prati e de' colli i rivestiti albuscelli, così de' laudevoli costumi e de' ragionamenti belli sono i leggiadri motti; li quali, per ciò che brievi sono, tanto stanno meglio alle donne che agli uomini quanto più alle donne che agli uomini il molto parlar si disdice. E' il vero che, qual si sia la cagione, o la malvagità del nostro ingegno o inimicizia singulare che a' nostri secoli sia portata da' cieli, oggi poche o non niuna donna rimasta ci è la qual ne sappia ne' tempi oportuni dire alcuno o, se detto l'è, intenderlo come si conviene: general vergogna di tutte noi.   (6.1. 2–3)

> Young ladies, just as on clear nights the stars decorate the heaven, and in the spring the flowers and budding shrubs adorn the green meadows and the hills, so, too, are good manners and polite conversation enhanced by witty remarks; and being brief, these remarks are even more suitable for women than for men, since it is less becoming in women than in men to speak at great length. The truth is, whatever the reason may be, whether it be our lack of intelligence or a singular enmity of the heavens to our times, today few, if any, women remain who know how to utter a witty remark at the opportune time or who understand one properly when it is delivered, and this is to the universal shame of every one of us.   (382)

In this passage, Filomena repeatedly echoes Pampinea's introduction to the novella about Mastro Alberto (1.10). Just in case her audience should fail to make the connection, Filomena reminds them that 'sopra questa materia assai da Pampinea fu detto' ('Pampinea has already spoken on this subject at some length' [6.1.4; 382–3]). Unlike Pampinea, Filomena does not paint a picture of women who make ostentatious and artless display of their bodies and their clothes, which she can then denigrate. Rather, she derides *all* women's inability to speak, attributing it to 'our lack of intelligence'; and even when she qualifies her statement by saying that perhaps the cause may lie in the 'enmity of the heavens to our times,' she avoids any attempt to delineate a time period in which women spoke better.[19] In her concluding exclamation, 'general vergogna di *tutte noi*' ('this is to the universal shame of *all of us women*' [my translation; my emphasis]), she makes it clear that all women are at fault, though some translators soften the blow by claiming that the defect belongs to all of us regardless of sex.[20]

When Filomena stresses that women ought to speak *briefly*, and observes shortly thereafter that Pampinea has spoken *at some length* about the matter, she is obviously adopting a mildly disparaging tone toward Pampinea. Nor does criticism of her companion does not stop here. Against the background of her sweeping attack on women, Filomena represents Madonna Oretta as superior to Madonna Malgherida of *Decameron* 1.10.

Madonna Oretta is 'una gentile e costumata donna e ben parlante' ('a noble, gracious, and well-spoken woman' [6.1.5; my translation]); Madonna Malgherida is 'una bellissima donna vedova' ('a most beautiful widow' [1.10.10; 56]) who is the object of Mastro Alberto's visual attentions, particularly because she has a 'vago e dilicato viso' ('pleasing and delicate face' [1.10.11; 56]). Madonna Oretta's merit, unlike that of Madonna Malgherida (and many of the women of the *Decameron*), is not determined by her physical appearance but by her character.

Moreover, when Madonna Oretta speaks well, Filomena enshrines her retort in direct discourse. Madonna Malgherida also uses 'assai belle e leggiadre parole' ('very polite and gracious words') to mock Mastro Alberto's love for her. But she speaks in concert with her female companions as if she were incapable of mocking him on her own.[21] Furthermore, Mastro Alberto's words are given more narrative weight, since Madonna Malgherida is permitted to speak in direct discourse only when she apologizes to him.

Perhaps predictably, the representation of men in the two stories stands in inverse relation to the portrayal of the women. Filomena manoeuvres Madonna Oretta's male companion into a position inferior to that of Mastro Alberto, the learned scholar who had put Madonna Malghcrida in hcr place. Of Madonna Oretta's interlocutor, we know very nearly nothing – only that he is a knight who does not tell his story well. Of Mastro Alberto, we are told that he is 'un grandissimo medico e di chiara fama quasi a tutto il mondo' ('a most distinguished physician, famous all over the world' [1.10.9; 56]), who is possessed of great nobility of spirit ('tanta fu la nobiltà del suo spirito' [1.10.10]). His striking comparison of himself to the leek dominates the novella, self-evident 'proof' that he is a forceful speaker, despite the fact that what he says is convoluted and counterintuitive.

Pampinea disparages women because they do not speak well. But the narrative evidence from her story suggests a different motive. It is not that Madonna Malgherida lacks the instruments to speak effectively; it is that she does not respect the rule of male superiority. As far as one can see, Madonna Malgherida communicates her meaning plainly, both when she is mocking Mastro Alberto and when she apologizes. So it is unclear what it means that she speaks 'badly,' but for the fact that she dared try humiliate a man; she treated him like dirt.[22] Madonna Oretta, in contrast, is accorded the recognition that she speaks well because she knows her place.

One could say that Filomena offers criticism in much the way that Madonna Oretta does: gently, obliquely. But more is at issue here. As she floats her criticism toward Elissa and Pampinea, Filomena reveals an underlying complication: when a woman speaks, she always risks infraction of a rule (the adherence to upper-class ideals in the case of both Licisca and Elissa, the requirement of brevity in the case of Pampinea, the obligation to preserve male authority in the case of Madonna Malgherida). Filomena, with her own statements and those of Madonna Oretta, attempts to cover all the bases.

When readers focus on what Madonna Oretta does well (i.e., speak persuasively), they overlook the limitations of what she does (i.e., speak only on the condition that she defer to male authority). In keeping with this point, a final observation remains.

Filomena's story establishes a woman reader of limited scope. Madonna Oretta's response to the knight's tale is somatic: 'a madonna Oretta, udendolo, spesse volte veniva un sudore e uno sfinimento di cuore, come se inferma fosse stata per terminare' ('As she listened to him, Madonna Oretta began to perspire profusely and every so often she felt her heart sink, as if she were ill and about to pass away' [6.1.10; 383]). In expressing her discomfort, she is not thinking about content.

She attends to external form (style, and the material stuff of which literature is made), but not to substance, informing spirit, or ideology.

How could we decide whether Madonna Oretta is a critical reader or not? Filomena skirts this kind of question, for she does not report the knight's story in direct discourse. Instead, she assures her audience that the tale was a very fine one before the knight began to tell it:

> [La novella] nel vero da sè era bellissima, ma egli or tre e quattro e sei volte replicando una medesima parola e ora indietro tornando e talvolta dicendo: 'Io non dissi bene' e spesso ne' nomi errando, un per un altro ponendone, fieramente la guastava. (6.1.9)

> [The story] in truth was in itself very good, but by repeating the same word three, four, or even six times, and then going back to the beginning to start the story all over again, and remarking from time to time, 'I'm not telling this very well, am I?' and frequently getting the names of the characters wrong and even mixing them up with one another, the knight managed to make a dreadful mess of it all. (383)

In order to convince her audience that a beautiful story has been ruined, Filomena shows how the knight's bumbling affects Madonna Oretta physically; her real body and her real symptoms stand as Filomena's 'proof.'

Madonna Oretta thus appears to be of a school that responds to obstructions in the production of meaning by assuming that a text is unreadable. She implicitly claims that the novella should conform to aesthetic ideals of unity and orderly development. But meaning is produced not only in what is easily readable and assimilable. It is also produced in tongue-tied silences, interruptions, and slips.[23]

So when is a narrator's rhetorical delivery so flawed that the audience is justified in turning a deaf ear to what he or she says? When the narrator is disparaging of his or her own style? When the plot is repetitive or does not conform to audience expectations? When the rhythms are disruptive and interfere with a smooth reading?[24] Perhaps. But before we dismiss a story, are we certain that these disruptive moments are not connected to larger textual strategies, and to the effects that the narrator wishes to achieve?[25]

We shall never know whether there might have been a better way to respond to the tongue-tied knight; nor shall we know whether, in another situation, Madonna Oretta might have shown her critical faculties to her best advantage. We can, however, imagine a different kind of reader, who would be attentive to the ways in which her own responses are shaped by the text.

In thinking about women's speech, we might ask, by way of comparison: When several members of the lower classes speak well on Day 6, would anyone ever suggest that the lower classes were gaining power through language? Hardly. Likewise, the discourse on woman in Day 6 is more complex, going beyond the ability of Oretta, Nonna, and Filippa to proffer well-turned words. Their rhetorical victories do not necessarily point to gains for women.

The *Decameron*'s female narrators are not at all concerned with reaffirming 'women on top' as a twentieth-century reader might understand this. Rather, their 'woman on top' is a chaste and honourable upper-class woman who uses language within the circumscribed limits. Filomena's Madonna Oretta speaks in a context that is outside and beyond sexuality. Lauretta extols the virtues of Nonna de' Pulci (6.3), who speaks in order to vindicate her honour. Unlike Licisca, these women are not forward, deceptive, or lustful. In fact, Nonna de' Pulci responds tit for tat to a *man* who has been fraudulent and lustful: Dego della Ratta, who paid counterfeit money for having lain with a kinswoman of the Florentine bishop. Furthermore, Lauretta is careful to stipulate that Nonna is permitted to respond sharply to a man – in public, no less – because he has unjustly called her womanly honour into question. The only character of the day who speaks like Licisca, as to form and sexualized content, is Brunetta, Chichibio's woman, who is safely esconced in the kitchen, the place of the lower classes.[26] Neifile, who tells this story, makes certain that all lower bodily appetites are located far from the world of her Florentine companions.

Only Filostrato takes issue with the view of women, speech, and sexuality that the female narrators espouse. In the latter half of Day 6, after several stories that deflect the focus from women, he presents a character who has much in common with the sexualized and deceptive women Licisca had portrayed. The outspoken Madonna Filippa is manifestly not like the well-spoken women that Filomena and Lauretta had depicted.

This novella too reinscribes the limits of what is available to women. Like many other novellas told by men in the *Decameron*, it allows that a woman could make significant gains in the realm of sexuality, and it suggests that a woman's sexuality is key to her intellectual and verbal triumphs. At several points in the story, one must wonder whether it is the wittiness of her remark that saves Madonna Filippa. The magistrate, see-ing her to be an extremely beautiful, well-mannered, and courageous woman, warns her that he cannot condemn her to the stake if she does not confess; and the townspeople also seem biased in her favour, given her qualities and her reputation. It doesn't seem that it would take an especially impressive statement to dissolve the case against her.

In a move that is vital to its larger message, the novella misrepresents the legal condition of women in late medieval Italy. Madonna Filippa's status as a legal subject without compare in the *Decameron* is simply an artful illusion. The following points deserve our full attention:

- The usual punishment for adultery in fourteenth-century Italy was not the stake, but rather a monetary penalty that could involve the woman's dowry.[27]
- In keeping with developments that derived from Roman law, men could also be accused of adultery.[28] But nothing is said of a criminal accusation against Lazzarino de' Guazzagliotri, Madonna Filippa's lover, as if to suggest that the legal system was intent only on prosecut-ing adulterous women. In fact, Lazzarino plays a very small role in the story.
- When Madonna Filippa presents her arguments before the magis-trate, she first claims that the statute against adulteresses is invalid because women had no say in the making of the law. She reaffirms a maxim common to medieval legal thought, namely, 'Quod omnes tangit ab omnibus approbari debet' ('What pertains to all must be approved by all'). But since women never had a say in the fourteenth-century jurisprudence, applying the maxim to them would have been as absurd as suggesting that it should be applied to slaves.[29]
- The story concludes as the people of Prato immediately change the statute. But given that the populace was not responsible for devising the statutes, legal provisions could hardly be modified on the spot.
- It is highly unlikely that a confirmed adulteress could return trium-phant to her home ('alla sua casa se ne tornò gloriosa' [6.7.19]), since this would have required a massive shift in the community's view of women's sexuality.[30]

Filostrato's story is a complicated speech act. By telling of a woman who is strong, independent, and forthright, Filostrato appeals to those who would like to see such qualities in women. If one such woman has existed, perhaps there could be more. At the same time, by projecting

Madonna Filippa into unreal historical conditions, Filostrato reassures those who would never approve of this brash and outspoken woman. If the conditions of the story are unreal, what is the likelihood that such an outlandish event could ever materialize?[31] The whole matter is quite puzzling. One is inclined to feel much like Madonna Filippa's husband Rinaldo, who leaves the courtroom 'confused by the whole mad affair' ('rimaso di così matta impresa confuso' [6.7.19; 398]).

This story illustrates the bind that readers of the *Decameron* frequently face. For almost every argument – particularly those regarding gender and power – there is a counter-argument. It seems nothing can be asserted with absolute certainty. But to adopt a laissez-faire approach to reading, to ignore the distinctions among the voices in debate, is tricky.

Throughout this chapter, in addressing the question of women's witty words on Day 6 of the *Decameron*, I have argued that the stories that ostensibly promote women's rhetorical triumphs also illustrate the limits placed on their speech and their critical faculties. These limits, as described by female narrators, are structurally very different from the limits described by Filostrato in his story of Madonna Filippa. The female narrators use women's speech to define what the honourable woman should be; Filostrato casts into doubt the very notion of woman's honour and effective speech. One might say that the restrictions on women like Madonna Oretta and Monna Nonna de' Pulci are internalized, and are therefore more easily transferable to medieval and early-modern women who could adopt them as exemplary. On the other hand, it might seem strange to talk about limits on Madonna Filippa, because she acknowledges none at all. The limits on her emerge not at the diegetic level, but in the moment when the reader acknowledges that legal and cultural practices in medieval Italy would have made Madonna Filippa an impossible reality. They are of a more institutional character, which explains why it is now possible to have such widely divergent responses to her character.

Madonna Filippa's arguments would have been considered specious in the fourteenth century. In the twentieth century, however, her argument for fuller representation under the law seems unproblematic. Participation in democratic decision-making has for some time been granted to people who did not always enjoy this right (women, blacks, youth aged 18 to 20), so when Madonna Filippa argues that the law must be approved by its subjects, we can easily imagine cases where we might ourselves advance such a defence. And when Madonna Filippa argues that she should be able to confer her sexual favours as she has seen best, her claim resonates with ideas about women's bodies and women's sexuality that have gained currency in Western culture since the 1960s. In effect, the wide divergence in readings of Madonna Filippa has been created by a fundamental shift in women's legal status, and in views of female sexuality. The story of Madonna Filippa depends, for its comic effect, on the parody of an established order. With the advent of historical changes that have given substance to what would have been unthinkable, it seems there are no limits on Madonna Filippa.

Should we proclaim Madonna Filippa exemplary, or should we accord praise instead to Madonna Oretta and Monna Nonna de' Pulci for their affirmations of the articulate and virtuous woman? Are we willing to approve of any transgression of limits, or any forms of restraint, no matter the other implications? How do we ourselves configure the forms and objectives of women's speech? The *Decameron* poses questions such as these, not because Boccaccio is interested in having the reader decide in favour of one of these characters rather than another (although I do believe that he had his own deeply rooted convictions about what sorts of moral behaviour were acceptable), but because he understands the importance of having us weigh the available alternatives and ask whether these alternatives are indeed the only ones available to us.

chapter six

Men, Women, and Figurative Language in the *Decameron*

As the narrators of the *Decameron* use figurative language, as they show the characters in their novellas using figurative language, they are performing gender and they are performing class. This is most markedly the case when figurative language is used to talk about sexual intercourse. As we shall see, the *Decameron* gives the impression that women will be on equal footing with men in these demonstrations of rhetorical power, but in the final analysis, the book empowers men, far more than women, to use figurative language about sexuality. This is one of the principal ways in which the *Decameron* consolidates male power.

At the end of Day 3, there takes place a particularly striking exchange between Neifile and Filostrato. As Neifile, queen of Day 3, places the laurel crown upon the head of Filostrato, whom she thus names her successor, she announces, 'Tosto ci avedremo se i' lupo saprà meglio guidar le pecore che le pecore abbiano i lupi guidati' ('Soon we shall see if the wolves know how to guide the sheep better than the sheep have guided the wolves' [3.Concl.1; 239]). The Author tells us that

Filostrato, udendo questo, disse ridendo: – Se mi fosse stato creduto, i lupi avrebbono alle pecore insegnato rimettere il diavolo in inferno non peggio che Rustico facesse a Alibech; e per ciò non ne chiamate lupi, dove voi state pecore non siete: tuttavia, secondo che conceduto mi fia, io reggerò il regno commesso. –

A cui Neifile rispose: – Odi, Filostrato: voi avreste, volendo a noi insegnare, potuto apparar senno come apparò Masetto da Lamporecchio dalle monache e riaver la favella a tale ora che l'ossa senza maestro avrebbono apparato a sufolare. –

Filostrato, conoscendo che falci si trovavan non meno che egli avesse strali, lasciato stare il motteggiare a darsi al governo del regno commesso ... (3.Concl.2–4)

Hearing this remark, Filostrato laughed and replied:
'If you had listened to me, the wolves would have taught the sheep to put the Devil back into Hell no worse than Rustico with Alibech; so you shouldn't call us wolves, for you have not acted like sheep; nonetheless, since you have entrusted the kingdom to me, I shall now begin my reign.'
To this Neifile replied:
'Listen, Filostrato, if you ever hoped to teach us anything, first you would need to be taught some sense, just as Masetto of Lamporecchio was taught by the nuns, and not regain the use of your speech until your bones rattled like a skeleton's.'
Recognizing that the ladies' sickles were as sharp as his arrows, Filostrato set aside his jesting and began to govern the kingdom entrusted to him ... (240)

Casting men and women as wolves and sheep who guide each other, Neifile allows for power to be shared even within a potentially hostile relationship. Picking up on this figurative language, Filostrato sends it in another direction, reminding us that figurative language about gender relations might lead from *words* about gender to sexual *deeds* – assuming, of course, that one were to believe him ('se mi fosse stato creduto,' or as Musa and Bondanella translate, 'if you had listened to me'). But when Filostrato tries to use Dioneo's story about Rustico and Alibech as leverage against the women, Neifile undercuts his position by citing his own story about Masetto da Lamporecchio. For any example there is a counter-example, for any argument there is a counter-argument, for every arrow there is a sickle.

Neifile is wielding her rhetorical power as a measure of female sexual power. This is clearly recognized in the text. Or is it? Examining this passage more closely, we see that the English translation introduces some features that tilt the scales in favour of women. Whereas the Italian has it that Filostrato recognizes that there were as many sickles as he had arrows ('falci si trovavan non meno che egli avesse strali'), the English translation explicitly grants possession of these sickles to women. Earlier too, the English translation establishes the women as hypothetical agents ('if you had believed me,' 'since you have entrusted the kingdom to me'), whereas the Italian maintains a more guarded stance by refusing to specify the agent ('se mi fosse stato creduto,' 'secondo che mi fia conceduto'). Moreover, because the English translation does not distinguish between second-person singulars and plurals, it does not capture fully the imbalances that are created by numbers. Note that Neifile begins by addressing her male interlocutor and telling him to listen ('*Odi*, Filostrato'), but her subsequent observation is addressed to all of the men ('if you all [*voi*] ever hoped to teach us anything, first you all [*voi*] would need to be taught some sense'). She then moves in for the kill by compressing the men into a single character, Masetto da Lamporecchio, who learned his lesson from multiple nuns.

Neifile's use of figurative language is strikingly like that of the marchioness of Monferrato (1.5), whom I discussed in chapter 2. Neifile launches the discussion by mapping the genders as animals, just as the marchioness casts women as chickens. These moves do not in themselves appear sexualized; they merely provide material that can be sexualized subsequently by a male interlocutor. Only when the king of France adds the roosters to the chickens, only when Filostrato maps the story of Rustico and Alibech onto the wolves and sheep (quite arbitrarily, we might note), does the language of these women take on a sexual cast. Granted, Neifile does now engage with this sexualized material by making reference to Masetto, but nothing she says refers very explicitly to the act of sexual intercourse. That is because figurative language about sexual intercourse remains the province of men in the *Decameron*.

Or is it the province of men and lower-class women? Licisca's outburst, which I discussed in chapter 5, would appear to be a clear-cut case where women are just as outspoken about sex as men. Let us take another look at the figurative language she employs:

Madonna, costui mi vuol far conoscere la moglie di Sicofante e, né più né meno come si io con lei usata non fossi, mi vuol dare a vedere che la notte prima che Sicofante giacque con lei messer Mazza entrasse in Monte Nero per forza e con ispargimento di sangue; e io dico che non è vero, anzi v'entrò paceficamente e con gran piacer di quei d'entro.   (6.Intro.8)

My lady, this fellow thinks he knows Sicofante's wife better than me, as if I had no idea of who she was, and he has the nerve to try to make me believe that the first night Sicofante slept with her, Messer Hammerhead took the Black Mountain by force and with some loss of blood; but that's not true and, on the contrary, I say he entered with ease and to the general delight of all the troops stationed there.   (381)

As we will remember, Licisca emerges the winner in this dispute, thanks to Dioneo. She proves most persuasive. But what about this figurative language that she uses? As I noted in the previous chapter, Licisca is mouthing opinions about women that are usually put forth by men in Boccaccio's narrative. Now I would ask: Is she the ultimate source of the figurative language about sexuality, or is it really Tindaro? Who is the original author of this metaphorical conceit? It is very difficult to tell because the Author of the *Decameron* uses indirect discourse to report the events.

As Millicent Marcus has argued, speaking about the tragic stories of Day 4, ultimately the language of the *Decameron* will be that of devils in hell and *papere* and nightingales, not of literal bleeding excised hearts. This rings true to me. There is one catch. This language is one that the women of the *Decameron* do not seem to own in the same degree.

Male narrators set the bottom line. They are the ones who use figurative language with an erotic charge. In *Decameron* 2.7, Panfilo introduces the first extended sexual metaphor when he has Alatiel (tutored by a senior male adviser, Antigono) explain how she spent many years in the service of 'San Cresci in Valcava' ('Saint Grow-big in the Hollow Valley'). Shortly thereafter, Dionco and Filostrato explore the concept of sex as work (wool-working in 2.10 and working the nuns' garden in 3.1). The religious theme returns as Panfilo represents sexual activity as 'riding the horse of St. Benedict or St. Giovanni Gualberto' (3.4) and Dioneo describes it as 'putting the devil back into hell' (3.10). In *Decameron* 5.4, Filostrato explores what it means to 'listen to the nightingale sing' and 'to capture the nightingale.' Dioneo offers figurative language for speaking about homosexual versus heterosexual relations (walking on dry vs. wet paths [5.10]). Filostrato and Panfilo show how rubbing concave objects can trope sexual activity (as in the scraping of the barrel in 7.2 and using the pestle and mortar in 8.2). Horses (introduced by Panfilo earlier) remain a preferred metaphor, as is evident from Filostrato's description of Parthian horses in 7.2 and Dioneo's novella about Donno Gianni who attempts to attach a tail to a mare (9.10). This latter story provides an easy passage between animal and agricultural husbandry, given that Dioneo also speaks of Donno Gianni using an appropriate tool for planting men and ensuring that the plants have vital liquid to take root. And in his famous last words about Griselda, poised between the apparent decency of vestimentary metaphor and the shock of female nudity, Dioneo asserts that Griselda, in response to Gualtieri's insane cruelty, might well have found another man to 'shake her fur' ('scuotere il pilliccione' [10.10.69]) in order to get a new dress.[1]

The women narrators of the *Decameron* rarely utilize figurative language to talk about the act of sexual intercourse. There appears but a single example where a female narrator has a female character use such figurative language,[2] and but a single example where a female narrator adopts such figurative language herself.[3] In both of these instances, the figurative language is not used, as it is in the discourse of the male narrators, to produce a sense of secret and illicit knowledge; rather, it is used in order to brand particular characters as excessive, confused, misdirected.

Some readers may object, of course, that other women characters in the *Decameron* do use figurative language. Should we not consider Alatiel, Bartolomea da Pisa, Alibech, Caterina (5.4), the wife of Pietro Vinciolo (5.10), and Madonna Belcolore (8.2)? Here, aside from the fact that each of these women appears in stories recounted by the male narrators, I would move several objections.

Certain women (the foreigners Alatiel and Alibech) are tutored in this figurative language by men, and indeed may not even be aware that their language could be figural or sexualized. Certainly Alibech believes she is naming things literally. As for Alatiel, whose language is given to her by Antigono, yes, it is true that we might imagine her, as Giorgio Bàrberi-Squarotti does, to be employing double entendres as only a woman who was expert in sexual matters and knowledgeable about both East and West could be.[4] Still, we should remember that when Alatiel spent years away from home, she never learned the language of any of her husbands or lovers. So why, at the end of the story, are we are supposed to believe that she has developed a high degree of foreign cultural literacy even if she did not develop any degree of linguistic competence? In this light, it strikes me that we could also imagine that Alatiel simply delivers a speech rehearsed in advance, whose sexual innuendoes are as unknown to her as the Western culture she purports to be describing.

Moreover, while male narrators can sometimes give women some marginal degree of control over figurative language about sexuality, key stories such as *Decameron* 5.4, the so-called novella of the nightingale, show how the *Decameron* makes eroticized figurative language a male prerogative.

In an expert and thought-provoking reading of tragic and comic stories in the *Decameron*, Millicent Marcus proposes that several of the most brutal tragedies are the result of the literalization of metaphor, and that Filostrato's tale of Ricciardo Manardi and Caterina da Valbona (*Decameron* 5.4) rewrites those tragic stories in order to show the beneficial consequences of embracing figurative exchanges.[5] Filostrato's tale is, in Marcus's words, 'an adventure in circumlocution,' where the young lovers succeed, first of all, because from the very beginning they share a figurative language ('dying' for love, suffering 'heat,' 'hearing the nightingale sing') that will allow them to circumvent protective parents and fulfil their desires.[6] Further helping to tip the scales away from death is Caterina's father, Messer Lizio, who rather than take offence, is open to accept and even himself to deploy the metaphors that the young lovers have offered. In the novella's most comic transposition of figures, Messer Lizio takes a veiled metaphor for sex ('making the nightingale sing') and extends and reshapes it so that it becomes, as Marcus notes, a 'conceit for marriage':[7] 'converrà che primieramente la sposi, sì che egli si troverà aver messo l'usignuolo nella gabbia sua e non nell'altrui' ('he will have to marry her first; thus he shall have put his nightingale into his own cage and not into anybody else's!' [5.4.38; 339]). Acceptance of figurative language shields Caterina, Ricciardo, and Messer Lizio from the tragedy that had befallen Ghismonda, Guiscardo, and Tancredi in *Decameron* 4.1.

A reading like Marcus's, which emphasizes the enormous difference that language can make, does much to explain why Filostrato's story is so striking and compelling.[8] No doubt, we are moved and reassured by the idea that the production and the manipulation of language is salutary. The tale further reinforces this by rendering the characters' dialogue very prominently, first as Caterina seeks to persuade her mother to let her sleep on the balcony (where she hopes to meet Ricciardo); then as Caterina's mother intercedes with her father; and finally, after the lovers are discovered *in flagrante delicto*, when Ricciardo pleas with Caterina's father to spare his life. One senses that the energy of life is conveyed in the possibility of continued expression. It is when silence falls that one suspects the worst.

Although I affirm the validity of Marcus's reading, which is most certainly supported by the novella, I believe that another reading of men, women, and figurative language in *Decameron* 5.4 – a reading in tension with Marcus's affirmation of the young lovers' active choice and expression – remains nestled here. If we read Filostrato's story with attention to the power relations formed around the use of figurative language, we see that the story isn't really very reassuring to readers – or at least not to readers of a feminist persuasion. As in several of his other stories, Filostrato keeps the control of social codes and of language in the hands of men, especially elder men. He presents a conflicted view of women: empowered on the one hand to express their sexuality (at least initially, and within certain bounds), but ultimately dispossessed of language.

The novella shows us that the creative use of language will make not a whit of difference in social relations if the status quo is significantly threatened. Ricciardo can fall in love with Caterina, even fiercely (*fieramente* [5.4.6]), and is not necessarily destined for a tragic end because the social configuration of the characters is different from the social configurations we see both in the tragic stories of *Decameron* 4 and the French and Provençal sources and analogues.[9] Caterina is unmarried (unlike the wives in the *Vida* of Guilhem de Cabestanh, in *Decameron* 4.9, and in Marie de France's 'Laüstic'), so her relationship with Ricciardo is potentially licit. Her parents are anxious to find a good match for her (as Tancredi was not in *Decameron* 4.1 and Lisabetta's brothers were not in 4.5). A male's overbearing feelings toward the young woman in his charge are avoided at least partly because a mother is present (as she was not in *Decameron* 4.1 or 4.5).[10] Finally, Guiscardo of *Decameron* 4.1 and Guilhem de Cabestanh of the Provençal narrative, though worthy and loving, do not have the wealth and nobility that make Ricciardo of a social standing at least equal to – if not better than – that of Caterina's family.

If we keep these social power relations in mind, we will be more likely to see that the free agency of the young lovers is a myth. Sexuality is hardly the arena where they (or we, for that matter) enjoy the greatest degree of choice. Their 'success,' if one wishes to call it that, is the result of the compatibility of the expression of their desires with that of the dominant ideology of their immediate family and community.

Encouraged to empathize with the young lovers seeking happiness in Day 5 of the *Decameron*, we may not want to see this inevitable fact. As long as we place ourselves as desiring subjects, we will interpret the events first through the eyes of Ricciardo (because the story begins with him, his desire for Caterina, and his plan for satisfying his desire), and then from the perspective of Caterina (because she seeks to persuade her mother that she needs to be on the balcony). These identifications will tend to remain steady as long as the novella keeps the reader focused on the tension-filled moments when the lovers might fail in their quest for love and life. Ricciardo suggests, with the unwittingness of a young lover accepting the dominant language of love, that he could die of his passion ('Caterina, io ti prego che tu non mi facci morire amando' [5.4.8]). He could die as he makes the dangerous ascent to the balcony in order to spend the night with Caterina. His near encounter with death is exposed in its full horror when Filostrato describes, with language certain to remind us of the throbbing excised hearts of earlier tragic tales, the moment of discovery and recognition: 'Quando Ricciardo il vide [messer Lizio], parve che gli fosse il cuore del corpo strappato' ('When Ricciardo saw him [Messer Lizio], he felt as if his heart were being ripped from his body' [5.4.42; 340]). Moments like these intensify our bond of empathetic identification with Caterina and Ricciardo, encouraging us to focus on their ability to overcome obstacles, and making us fear for them when they seem doomed.

The lovers avoid a tragic end, but not necessarily because they control figurative language. We cannot be entirely certain that we know what Caterina means when she says that she is hot at night and would be comforted by the song of the nightingale. Is she referring to the heat of her passion? Perhaps. Is she equating the nightingale with Ricciardo, rather than with a more general notion of amorous desire and fulfilment? This already seems less certain, especially since the situation of 'listening to the nightingale,' common in medieval love poetry from the twelfth century on, was 'identified with that long, or endless period when the lover is aware of his love, but still knows himself unable to reach it.'[11] Since Caterina's actual design is never revealed, we know solely what *we* think her language means. Only a few readers – and in my assessment, only those predisposed to spy erotic imagery at the least provocation – assume that Caterina is talking about her own burning passion when she complains of the heat; even readers aware that the nightingale is traditionally a poetic emblem of amorous desire are unlikely to think that the nightingale could be Ricciardo himself.[12] Many readers tend at this early point in the novella to see Caterina's statements as her mother does, that is, as exclamations of delight in the offerings of nature. Even when Ricciardo and Caterina meet on her father's balcony, and Filostrato states that 'piacer presono l'un dell'altro, molte volte faccendo cantar l'usignuolo' ('they took delight and pleasure in one another, and as they did, they made the nightingale sing time and time again' [5.4.29; 339]), it is not yet a given that the reader will take the nightingale to mean, as it clearly does after Messer Lizio arrives on the scene, Ricciardo's male member. In the context of a novella that has not yet turned bawdy, it seems more likely that 'they made the nightingale sing' would be the equivalent of phrases like 'there were fireworks' or 'the earth

shook,' stand-ins for the more explicit 'they had sex.' Although we piece
the puzzle together as the novella progresses, and see the full significance of early figurative language only retrospectively, we like to believe
that we have always been fully aware of what Caterina's language meant;
many readers tend even to affirm her control of her language because it
is unsettling to think that a speaker could wield figurative language without judging its full range and impact.

We ought to be reminded of the opaqueness of Caterina's language
by the presence of several other phrases that are likely to stump us.
Interceding for her daughter, Madonna Giacomina argues that Caterina
should be allowed to sleep on the balcony because 'I giovani son vaghi
delle cose simiglianti a loro' ('Young people like things that are like
themselves' [5.4.25; 338]). To what is she comparing the young people?
The nightingale? The cool nights? The phrase seems so peculiar that
Guido Waldman, in translating it, twists it so that it makes more sense,
rendering it as 'Those are the sorts of things that give pleasure to young-
sters.'[13] Likewise, when Messer Lizio responds to his wife's request by
saying, 'Che rusignuolo è questo a che ella vuol dormire? Io la farò
ancora adormentare al canto delle cicale' ('What is this nonsense about
being serenaded to sleep by a nightingale? I'll make her sleep to the
tune of the crickets [lit., cicadas] in broad daylight!' [5.4.23; 338]), what
does he mean to say? The sense of his statement is something like,
'She'll sleep when and how *I* want her to sleep!', with perhaps, I would
argue, a veiled threat (something like 'I could be truly unpleasant about
this if I wanted to be!' or 'I'll make her see stars in broad daylight!').
The point is not to decide on an exact translation of Messer Lizio's
grousing, but rather to remember that his figurative language permits
multiple translations. Between metaphorical language and its referent,
there is room for manoeuvring, and for misunderstanding. Not always
are we in control.

The figurative language of the novella resists us, but we resist thinking
that might be the case. Why? To the extent that they focus on meaning
as an end term rather than on the process by which meaning is constructed in a text, readers tend to forget about initial interpretive difficulties they may have encountered. In the case of *Decameron* 5.4, they
genuinely do not ever remember the time when they were not fully
aware of the way that words like 'heat' and 'nightingale' could become
sexually charged.

The novella privileges the moment of discovery, especially as it
returns insistently to the image of Messer Lizio drawing back the cur-

tain. When Messer Lizio first enters the balcony, he wishes to see how the nightingale allowed Caterina to sleep: 'E andato oltre pianamente *levò alto la sargia* della quale il letto era fasciato, e Ricciardo e lei vide ignudi e iscoperti dormire abbracciati' ('And walking out onto the balcony, *he lifted up the curtain* around the bed and saw Ricciardo and Caterina sleeping completely naked in each other's arms' [5.4.32; 339; emphasis mine]). This language of lifting the curtain, easily a metaphor itself for arriving at the meaning of a metaphor, is repeated when Lizio brings his wife Giacomina to see the scene for herself: 'giunti amenduni al letto e *levata la sargia*, potè manifestamente vedere madonna Giacomina come la figliuola avesse preso e tenesse l'usignuolo' ('when they both reached the bed and *lifted the curtain*, Madonna Giacomina saw for herself exactly how her daughter had managed to catch and hold on to the nightingale' [5.4.36; 339; emphasis mine]). The moment of lifting the curtain is so important that it is repeated yet a third time, when the lovers awaken, even though we are never given any indication that Caterina's parents would have let it down; so when Ricciardo wakes, realizes it is day, and calls out in distress to Caterina, Messer Lizio, '[having] raised the curtain' ('levata la sargia' [5.4.41; 340]), appears before them.

Since none of us really wants to believe that we could be duped (at least not for long) by someone else's crafty use of metaphoric language, we are likely to elect to be in the position of Messer Lizio, bourgeois mentality and all. (The novella even plays on our fears that we could be misled by our unconscious desires, and it offers us some encouragement to believe that Messer Lizio is cognizant of what both the lovers and he are doing even from the beginning. Why else should he lock the door to the balcony, for example? He cannot possibly fear that someone will enter the balcony from the inside.) As the novella steers the reader to shift subject position, it reinforces the idea that sexual activity is permissible only if it remains within the bounds of institutional authority.

Power, manifesting itself as control of discourse and of choice, moves into the hands of Messer Lizio. In a story where dialogue among the characters plays a very significant part, Messer Lizio is the last person to pronounce a long speech, threatening Ricciardo with death but giving him the option of contracting a marriage. Since Ricciardo is given no choice but to comply with Messer Lizio's will, it would seem that *his* ability to act, *his* power, is limited. But in fact, he shares in the elder man's power. His elegant and courteous speech[14] puts him on a par at least with the authoritative father, who, although he is a 'cavaliere' ('knight'

[5.4.4; 336]) and is certainly capable of solemn pronouncements (as in 5.4.43), has previously been heard to speak with less refined vocabulary and rhythms, most especially when he addresses his wife: 'Via, facciale-visi un letto tale quale egli vi cape' ('Fine, whatever, let her have a bed that fits out there' [5.4.26; my translation]) and 'Sù tosto, donna, lievati e vieni a vedere' ('Hurry on up, woman, get out of bed and come see' [5.4.33; my translation]). Tipping the balance in favour of Ricciar-do, of course, is the *Decameron*'s ironic commentary on the *Divine Comedy*'s presentation of Messer Lizio as a figure exemplary of a lost Golden Age of courtliness and disinterested benefaction. In the Terrace of Envy, Guido del Duca, lamenting the loss of that golden era, exclaims: 'Ov'è 'l buon Lizio e Arrigo Mainardi? / Pier Traversaro e Guido di Carpigna? / Oh Romagnuoli tornati in bastardi!' ('Where is the good Lizio and Arrigo Mainardi, Pier Traversaro and Guido di Carpigna? O men of Romagna turned to bastards!' [*Purgatorio* 14.97–9]).[15] The Lizio da Valbona of *Decameron* 5.4, however, would have some difficulty holding his own against the virtues of the historical personage acclaimed in the *Purgatorio* 14; he sometimes seems as if he emerged from the fabliau tradition instead. As for Ricciardo, his situation is different. While the narrator/ Author of the *Decameron* has evidently been inspired by the name 'Arrigo Mainardi' in *Purgatorio* 14.97, his claim to higher ideals is unsullied by a negative comparison to a character in Dante's poem. There is no historical record of a *Ricciardo* Manardi, and the Ricciardo of *Decameron* 5.4 appears to adhere to Guido del Duca's ideals in *Purgatorio* 14 (including, one gathers, the anxiety about bastardization of family lines).

The characters who recede as the men consolidate their institutional and discursive power are the women, who stand as mere witnesses to the men's agreement. Caterina, who may never have been especially conscious of the levels of figurative language that she manipulates, exercises ever-diminishing control of language. By the end of the story, it seems that she has just stumbled unwittingly upon the language that has ultimately functioned in her favour. When her father confronts her and Ricciardo, she lets go of the nightingale and of the possibility of speaking about it; she is reduced to tears and pleas. What she says is marked as less important than what the men say because it is reported in indirect discourse. She becomes ever less visible to us.

Meanwhile, Caterina's mother, Madonna Giacomina, falls short of the task of reading and speaking. Caterina's statements sail over her head, and she is never given the opportunity to play an active role in discovering the 'real meaning' of Caterina's language. In accord with medieval misogynist views of women as changeable, she is presented as unable to stay with any given opinion for very long. She changes her mind when a new (even if opposing) point of view is advanced. She does not respond at first to Caterina's request, but does so after Caterina complains insistently about the heat; later, she is quick to be angry with Ricciardo, but is silent after she sees her husband's reaction. Furthermore, although she was originally presented as a figure who could mediate between the young and the old, it is she who threatens to become the critical and punitive judge when she finds herself betrayed by Ricciardo: 'tenendosi forte di Ricciardo ingannata, volle gridare e dirgli villania' ('Feeling that she had been treacherously deceived by Ricciardo, the lady wanted to scream at him and to insult him' [5.4.37; 339]). This is, I think, a bid to make Messer Lizio look even more kind, compromising, merciful by comparison. Responsibility for any threat of unhappiness is shifted onto a woman (though we should note that screaming at Ricciardo and insulting him would be a far cry from tearing out his heart).

The novella strains at the end to make it look as if power is shared equally even if it is not. Consider the moment when the parents exit, leaving the young lovers alone: 'messer Lizio e la donna partendosi dissono. "Riposatevi oramai, ché forse maggior bisogno n'avete che di levarvi"' ('Messer Lizio and his wife left them, saying: "Now go back to sleep, for you probably need sleep more than you do getting up"' [5.4.47; 340]). What can it possibly mean that 'Messer Lizio and his wife' say this sentence? That they pronounce it in unison? The prospect seems quite absurd. More likely, the reader imagines Messer Lizio – who, after all, has been doing most of the talking since Madonna Giacomina fell silent – pronouncing the statement with Madonna Giacomina willing to go along with his views.[16]

Filostrato and Messer Lizio play with figurative language in the presence of women. They flaunt it. They dare the women to understand. Their goal is to control figurative language, to make it a matter of male rather than female prerogative. Filostrato makes figurative language about sexuality a point of contention as he describes the sleeping lovers, and tells his listeners that Caterina had hold of 'quella cosa che voi tra gli uomini più vi vergognate di nominare' ('that thing which you ladies are ashamed to name in the company of gentlemen' [5.4.30; 339]). It might appear that Filostrato acknowledges the ladies' sense of decorum when he refuses to name that thing upon which Caterina's hand rests. He is honourable, they are honourable, and indeed, what could the

problem with this be? But there is a problem because Filostrato's editorial comment is not as accommodating and gracious as that. In effect,
rather than recognizing the integrity of the ladies, he is obliquely accus-
ing them of engaging in duplicitous behaviour – of having one standard
of conduct and speech in public, another in private. He is cornering
them, so that their only legitimate option is denial of conspiracy and
renunciation of figurative language as furtive. The unstated consequence of such a renunciation is male control of figurative language,
male awareness of secrecy.

It seems that Filostrato has changed his tune since Day 4, so after he
finishes his story on Day 5, the women of the group laugh. Yet even if
they accept the humour, they might wish to be more discerning. The
fact that his story of Guiglielmo Rossiglione and Guiglielmo Guardastagno (*Decameron* 4.9) and his story of the nightingale (*Decameron* 5.4)
have different outcomes – tragic on the one hand, 'comic' on the other
– is of little relevance to the deep structure of the tales. Filostrato has
continued to narrate the same story about alliances among men, male
power, male mastery.

The Author's rubric to *Decameron* 5.4 highlights relations among men.
It reads: 'Ricciardo Manardi è trovato da messer Lizio da Valbona con la
figliuola, la quale egli sposa e col padre di lei rimane in buona pace'
('Ricciardo Manardi is found by Messer Lizio da Valbona with his
daughter, whom he marries, and he remains on good terms with her
father' [5.4.1; 336]).[17] The translator Guido Waldman, finding the
Author's rubrics unappealing to modern audiences, often takes the liberty of rewriting them.[18] His substitute rubric for this tale reads, 'Lizio's
daughter Caterina sleeps out on the balcony in the fresh air and listens
to the nightingale; how she catches one and what results.'[19] It is true
that Guido Waldman captures the story that *we might very much wish to
see*. He draws us into the tale with an enigmatic statement of the sort that
modern readers very much like. He emphasizes Caterina's agency; he
makes the novella a story about an enterprising young woman who gets
her man – alive. But Waldman's rubric is, as should be clear from my
argument above, a misrepresentation of what is really at issue in the
story. It is the Author's rubric that is on the mark, encouraging us to see
that the novella is ultimately not about a woman's agency, but about the
consolidation of power relations among men.

By the time Filostrato tells this tale, he has played enough of his cards
for readers to be able to see beyond surface messages (apparent philogyny) to the deeper message (concerns about male power, especially

among rivals). Awareness of this allows us to re-evaluate the 'philogyny' of other of Filostrato's novellas in which sexuality is at issue: Rinaldo d'Asti (2.2), Masetto da Lamporecchio (3.1), Madonna Filippa (6.7), Peronella (7.2). In almost all these novellas, the sexual encounters are presented as victories for the male rival: Rinaldo d'Asti returns home unscathed after an encounter with robbers and, more important, a one-night stand with a woman who took him in after her lover failed to appear that evening; Masetto da Lamporecchio successfully cuckolds Christ, and avoids having to shoulder the financial and emotional responsibilities of parenthood; and Peronella's lover Giannello achieves sexual satisfaction as he possesses her (but no attention is given to her sexual feelings).

On the one hand, a pro-woman message, on the other, a message about the supremacy of male relations. Filostrato, the sole narrator of the *Decameron* who speaks of his identity, his origins, and his future as a character (at the end of Day 3),[20] tells us that he is 'overcome by love,' just as the name imposed upon him would reveal. Telling us that he is masked, he dares the listener/reader to see who he really is. But what Filostrato tells us is not only that he is 'overcome by love.' To think so is to have missed the main point, which is that he is the bearer of an encrypted message. So we should not be surprised that in his novellas we find a 'cryptonomy' similar in structure to the one that Nicolas Abraham and Maria Torok identified for Freud's Wolf Man.[21]

For Freud, the Wolf Man's neurosis could be drawn back to a single decisive event in the Wolf Man's past: the primal scene or primal fantasy in which the Wolf Man had witnessed his parents engage in *coitus a tergo*.[22] Abraham and Torok, by contrast, privilege 'words' over 'events'; they read the dreams and the symptoms of the Wolf Man (material articulated in splintered fashion across Russian, German, and English) as a tongue-tied dialogue about the real or the fictional status of an event. According to Abraham and Torok, the Wolf Man found himself forced to state whether the event he witnessed was real or imagined, and could not in all good faith do so.[23]

Like Freud's Wolf Man, Filostrato 'is himself only when he creates himself as enigma.'[24] Of central importance in his cryptonomy is the nightingale. This bird (the *usignuolo* or *rusignuolo* of *Decameron* 5.4) stands in for the lover Ricciardo and his male member. Transposed into Italian as 'Rossiglione,' from the French *Roussillon* or *Rossillon* which is related to the Old French word for 'nightingale' (*rossignol*), it stands in also for the (by law) 'legitimate' husband in Filostrato's tale of

Guglielmo Rossiglione and Guglielmo Guardastagno (*Decameron* 4.9). Finally, as the transposition takes place on classical Latin terrain, the nightingale (*Philomela*) stands for Filomena, the woman of whom Filostrato is presumed to be enamoured.[25] Thus, the 'nightingale,' the name assigned to 'quella cosa che voi tra gli uomini più vi vergognate di nominare' ('that thing which you ladies are ashamed to name in the company of gentlemen' [5.4.30; 339]), also masks *that thing which Filostrato is incapable of speaking*. This is not, as some might be tempted to think, because 'nightingale' signifies the 'penis' as a name under censure. Rather, it is because the nightingale signifies a censored knot of subject positions: the puissance of the legitimate husband/father; the virility of the male rival who threatens the husband/father; and the woman who is the object of their desires.[26]

Listening to the nightingale is a form of listening to the crypt. The crypt displaces and fragments identity; so does the nightingale, the bearer of the silenced and encrypted message. The nightingale stands not only as the symbol of elusive amorous desire, but also of the identity (and ideology) that eludes us. Listening to the nightingale therefore reminds us, no matter how heartening the story about the pleasures of capturing that nightingale, that the reassurance about the identity of what we have caught is likely to be only temporary.

Thus far, I have focused mainly on how the *Decameron* places control of figurative language in the hands of men. At this juncture, we must also ask how the *Decameron* constructs the position of the woman reader/listener. Does the Author delimit her responses, and if so, how? How might we displace and reshape these boundaries?

Much of the work of constructing the implicit female reader of the *Decameron* is carried out as the Author represents the women's responses to stories in which figurative language is prominent. The pressure is on to recognize genital sexuality, but, reinforcing prescriptions about the language proper to women, the Author does not simply state that the women grasped the double entendres. Rather, over the course of the *Decameron*, the Author moves to subtly delimit the kinds of responses that will seem proper to women. Consequently, by the end, without ever having brought the matter very fully to the reader's attention, the Author encourages readers to construct their own (ideologically motivated) portraits of how women respond to erotic matters.

According to the Author of the *Decameron*, the women of the group offer complicated and intricate responses to stories of sexuality told by the men. The Author represents the women as conflicted in their response as early as Day 1, where the women blush and laugh reluctantly after Dioneo's story of the monk and the abbot (1.4). But it is after Panfilo's story of Alatiel – the first story to provide an allegory of sexual activity – that the Author intervenes with a commentary the reader is unlikely to have anticipated. He introduces a nagging doubt about the transparency of the women's responses:

> Sospirato fu molto dalle donne per li varii casi della bella donna: ma chi sa che cagione moveva que' sospiri? Forse v'eran di quelle che non meno per vaghezza di così spesse nozze che per pietà di colei sospiravano. Ma lasciando questo stare al presente, essendosi da loro riso per l'ultime parole da Panfilo dette e veggendo la reina in quelle la novella di lui esser finita, a Elissa rivolta impose che con una delle sue l'ordine seguitasse. (2.8.2)

> The ladies breathed many a sigh over the beautiful woman's amorous adventures; but who knows what caused their sighs. Perhaps some of them sighed no less because of their longing for such frequent embraces than because of their compassion for Alatiel. But setting this problem aside for the moment, after they had all had a good laugh over Panfilo's last words, which the Queen took to mean that his tale was completed, she turned to Elissa and asked her to continue the proceedings with a tale of her own. (127)

Although the Author has reported the reactions of the women and men, he has never up to now engaged in this sort of editorializing. Why should he change his tactic following this particular story? Because the story of Alatiel is the very first novella in the *Decameron* to offer an *allegory* for sexual activity (even if the development of a figurative mode of discourse is not intimately linked to the development of the plot as it is in later stories where figurative language dominates [e.g., 3.10, 5.4, 9.10]).

Designed to colour our response to the women, the passage creates an ambiguous origin and then undertakes to define it. The women sigh rather than providing a verbal response, thus leaving ample space for us to ponder what they might mean. Posing a rhetorical question, the Author insinuates that the true cause of those sighs is other than what we might think. He then further insinuates that *some* of the women *may* have sighed because they were thinking about Alatiel's frequent marriages rather than about her misfortunes. And lest we think that such an insinuation is inappropriate, he himself retreats quickly. This strategy is potentially double-edged. While it could reflect negatively on him, it also serves to suggest that he is decorous and even-handed toward women who are engaged in less than virtuous thoughts.

Beginning on Day 3, where the stories are concerned mainly with illicit sexuality, the Author pays special attention to the women's laughter. The women laugh nervously at Masetto da Lamporecchio (3.1); they laugh at Panfilo's tale of friar Puccio (3.4); they laugh after Dioneo's story of the devil in hell, for his words strike them as made for laughter (3.10). Note, however, that there is no laughter following any of the stories about illicit sexuality that the women themselves tell on Day 3. When the stories return to happier resolutions, laughter becomes the preferred response to stories where figurative language is central to the plot. The Author does not let us forget this, as his description of the women's laughter after the tale of the nightingale makes manifestly evident. They laugh and laugh:

> Aveva ciascuna donna, la novella dell'usignuolo ascoltando, tanto riso, che ancora, quantunque Filostrato ristato fosse di novellare, non perciò esse di ridere si potevano tenere. Ma pur, poi che alquanto ebbero riso, la reina disse ...   (5.5.2)

> Listening to the story of the nightingale, every woman there laughed so hard that even after Filostrato had ended his storytelling, they were unable to keep from laughing. Then, since they had laughed for a good while, the Queen said ...   (341)

Pointing out that people laugh in the *Decameron* ('nel *Decameron* si ride'), Giulio Savelli locates this laughter in the female and male narrators, in the characters of the novellas (granted, less frequently), and above all in the reader (whom he sees as laughing together with the narrators).[27] He asks us to direct our attention to the rhetorical strategies designed to provoke this laughter. Nevertheless, because Savelli does not take into account sexual difference as he evaluates laughter in the *Decameron*, he does not notice that the narrators are laughing primarily at the novellas told by men (which, as I have noted, highlight figurative language about sexuality). Laughter is registered in nineteen cases for the men and only ten or eleven for the women.[28] These numbers are particularly striking, given that the women outnumber the men seven to three.

In the middle section of the *Decameron*, this laughter, however asymmetrical, still seems without remarkable consequences. Later, however, it becomes clear that the rhetorical goal is to establish a parallel between the women of the group and the contemporary woman reader of the book, so that the laughter (with its attendant ideologies) can be reproduced.

Not only does the Author state when the group laughs, he notes that the group continues to laugh but for the intervention of the Day's ruler. Thus, after Fiammetta's tale of Scalza and the Baronci (6.6), the group laughs until Elissa commands Filostrato to begin. After Neifile's tale of Madonna Sismonda (7.8), the women cannot keep from laughing and talking, even though the king, Dioneo, commands them to be silent; finally, Dioneo tells Panfilo to begin the next story. Then the Author also imagines that this laughter might be projected forward in time. After Panfilo's story of the priest of Varlungo and Monna Belcolore (8.2), the Author comments that 'le donne aveano tanto riso che ancora ridono' ('the ladies laughed so much that they are still laughing'). By implication, we contemporary women readers also would laugh and continue to laugh unless someone stopped us.

I would now have us pause over three instances in which we find the women laughing at stories told by the male narrators. Here we can see how it is that the Author, by shading the description of the narrators' reactions, can both encourage readers to accept a gendered view of narratorial and readerly relations and at the same time refuse responsibility for this gendered view.

The first passage appears at the end of *Decameron* 7.2, Filostrato's tale of Peronella and the barrel. Peronella's lover is engaging in sex with her while she is leaning over a barrel containing her husband, who remains unaware of what is transpiring. Filostrato says, 'in quella guisa che negli ampi campi gli sfrenati cavalli e d'amor caldi le cavalle di Partia assaliscono, a effetto recò il giovinil desiderio' ('just as the unbridled stallions of Parthia mount the mares in the open meadows when they are hot with love, so he, too, satisfied his youthful lust' [7.2.34; 425]). The Author highlights the women's reaction to this specific phrase, noting, 'Non seppe sì Filostrato parlare obscuro delle cavalle partice, che l'avedute donne non ne ridessono, sembiante faccendo di rider d'altro' ('Filostrato's reference to the Parthian mares was not so veiled that the discerning ladies did not laugh over it, though they pretended to be amused by something else' [7.3.2; 425]).

The second passage appears in connection with Panfilo's novella about the priest of Varlungo and Monna Belcolore, a story in which the characters draw metaphors for sexuality from the realm of food grinding and processing (the man as windmill full of water, the man as pestle to the woman's mortar). At the novella's conclusion, the Author writes, 'Finita la novella di Panfilo, della quale le donne aveano tanto riso che ancora ridono, la reina a Elissa commise che seguitasse; la quale ancora ridendo incominciò ...' ('When Panfilo finished his story, at which the ladies laughed so hard that they must still be laughing at it now, the Queen ordered Elissa to continue; still laughing, she began ...' [8.3.2; 483]).

The third passage comes from the end of Day 9, after Dioneo has provided the last extended sexual metaphor in the *Decameron* (attaching a tail to a mare), in the story of Donno Gianni (9.10). The Author writes: 'Quanto di questa novella si ridesse, meglio dalle donne intesa che Dioneo non voleva, colei sel pensi che ancora ne riderà' ('How much the ladies laughed over this story, whose meaning was better grasped than Dioneo had intended, may be left to the imagination of that fair reader of mine who is still laughing over it' [9.Concl.1; 599]).

These three passages need to be read as a unit in order for us to understand their rhetorical effect in the *Decameron*. They serve above all to cement our perception of women's hermeneutic skills. Having already instituted a rift between how the women respond and what they may actually think, the Author now encourages the reader to believe that when the women are thinking at their most shrewdly clever, their interpretive skills are dedicated to decoding the obscene metaphors of the novellas told by men.

No matter that there is little textual justification for thinking that 'what the women actually think' centres on sex. The Author speculates that some of the women may have sighed over Alatiel's frequent marriages rather than her misadventures. He notes that the women laughed at Filostrato's metaphor of the Parthian horses but pretended to laugh at something else. He says that the women grasped Dioneo's meaning better than he intended. In no instance does the Author say that the women were thinking about sex. He projects that the women are hiding something and that they are transgressing a boundary determined by the male narrators. Then he allows the reader to fill in the blank. The Author – whose language is more complex than readers expect – shifts responsibility for these representations of women to the reader.

We should be struck, above all, by the instances where the English translations of the Author's statements prove imprecise, either because they fail to capture the full sense of the Italian text or because they add elements that can not be justified by the original Italian. The unevenness in translation reveals the impact of gender ideologies on our reading.

Here, for example, is the response to Dioneo's story of Donno Gianni, followed by a series of English translations:

> Quanto di questa novella si ridesse, meglio dalle donne intesa che Dioneo non voleva, colei sel pensi che ancora ne riderà.   (9.Concl.1)

> How much the ladies laughed over this story, whose meaning was better grasped than Dioneo had intended, may be left to the imagination of that fair reader of mine who is still laughing over it.   (trans. Musa and Bondanella, 599)[29]

> How the ladies laughed to hear this tale, whose meaning they had grasped more readily than Dioneo had intended, may be left to the imagination of those among my fair readers who are laughing at it still.   (trans. McWilliam)[30]

> Dioneo wished that the ladies in his audience were not quite so sharp – the laughter his story provoked in them will be clear enough to any woman who is yet to be amused by the recollection of it.   (trans. Waldman)[31]

> How much the company laughed at this story, which was better understood of the ladies than Dioneo willed, let her who shall yet laugh thereat imagine for herself.   (trans. Payne)[32]

This passage is fascinating for the way that it constructs the female reader. Although the laughter at this story might well be generic and ungendered (as indicated by the impersonal hypothetical construction 'quanto si ridesse'), most of these translators imagine only the women laughing, perhaps because the women have been singled out for having understood the story better than Dioneo would have liked. As the Author projects forward a future response to the story, allowing a woman who might still be laughing at the story to think to herself how much the group of Florentine narrators laughed, some translators reinforce the idea of a gracious female reading audience. Yet nowhere does the Author single out this woman who may laugh as 'fair' nor does he specify that she must be a 'reader.'

In order to grasp what it might mean that the women understood the story of Donno Gianni better than Dioneo would have liked, we need to have a more subtle understanding of this story, which, for all that it focuses on rude provincial life, is a complex narration that puts into play our ideological projections about reading and sexuality.

It would seem easy to read the novella as one of the stories that, like the story of the devil in hell (3.10) or Lidia and the pear tree (7.9), explores the power of language to shield against cognition of a sexual act. Or one might read it as like other relatively straightforward deceptions perpetrated by a member of the clergy who gets to have sex with the willing wife in large part because of the stupidity of the husband. But the novella portrays motivation with greater shadings.

By the time Donno Gianni gives in to the couple's request and sets about turning Gemmata into a horse, we can never be quite sure if the priest is a willing or reluctant participant. Many readers conclude that Donno Gianni has crafted the entire plan, allowing for contingencies that may or may not be realized, since he does after all warn Pietro in advance that he should say nothing, no matter what he should hear or see, and that he should pray to God that the tail gets attached well (9.10.15). But he has agreed to turn Gemmata into a horse only after being unable to make the couple desist and as he touches Gemmata in the course of his 'incantation,' his erection appears unexpectedly.[33] Moreover, Donno Gianni, unlike other carnally inclined members of the Decameronian clergy, does not take the opportunity to continue relations with Gemmata after the incantation is ruined by Pietro's verbal interference. In retrospect, one must wonder whether the desire for sex with a woman was ever a significant factor in the plan he conceived.

Not only does the novella raise questions about the degree to which Donno Gianni may have anticipated the final outcome, it also raises questions about the kind of sexuality that we believe to be in play. Indeed, if we are the slightest bit malicious as we read Donno Gianni's claim that he is able to turn his mare into a beautiful young woman and enjoy her when he wishes, we might well think he would be inclined to remain with more bestial pursuits, but for the fact that Gemmata and her husband have been so insistent.

Nor is wavering about sexual preference limited to this early moment in the novella, as we see if we consider the moment when Donno Gianni attempts to attach a tail to Gemmata. Dioneo tells us that 'niuna cosa restandogli a fare se non la coda, levata la camiscia e preso il pivuolo col quale egli piantava gli uomini e prestamente nel solco per ciò fatto messolo, disse: "E questa sia bella coda di cavalla"' ('with nothing left to do but the tail, he lifted his nightshirt and took out his tool for planting men, and quickly sticking it into the furrow for which it was made, he said: "And let this be the beautiful tail of a mare"' [9.10.18; 598]). The passage has garnered quite a bit of attention on account of the agricultural metaphors for the penis and the act of penetration. But while readers have been focused on the language Dioneo uses to describe Donno Gianni's equipment, they have largely ignored Gemmata – which means that they have ignored the language that Dioneo uses to describe where exactly Donno Gianni places his tool. The bumbling husband provides an insight. After crying out twice that he didn't want a tail – and provoking a rebuke from Donno Gianni, who had told him to remain quiet – Pietro complains, 'perché non diciavate voi a me: "Falla tu"? e anche l'appiccavate troppo bassa' ('Why didn't you ask me to do it? Besides, you stuck it on too low' [9.10.21; 599]).

What could Pietro mean when he says that Donno Gianni was putting the tail on too low? Is he simply revealing his knowledge of equine anatomy? Perhaps. But Pietro's cognitive abilities are limited. Even if he knows how horses are made (and therefore knows that the tail should have been placed higher up), he is willing to suspend disbelief and accept that horses can be made by magical incantation. Once again, if we read this statement with just the slightest bit of maliciousness, we might take it as proof that Pietro has not figured out that he could be having anything other than anal sex with his wife. In retrospect, it becomes clearer why the reproductive function of Donno Gianni's tool was emphasized. If he takes his tool for planting men and puts it into the furrow for which it was made – which implies, of course, that there is a furrow for which it was not made – it can only be because in a subsequent moment, we are asked to consider the alternative sexualities in play.

Thus, while many readers have taken the story to be about the rudimentary deception perpetrated by Donno Gianni, it is not at all likely that this is the point. Mario Baratto and Giorgio Bàrberi-Squarotti have been particularly attentive to the novella's exploration of a world of poverty, misery, and brute existence in which the concept of sexual pleasure is largely immaterial.[34] Moreover, as I noted above, the novella asks whether Donno Gianni might be having relations with the mare he 'turns into a woman,' what sort of sexual relations Pietro is having with his wife, whether Donno Gianni is desirous of sex with Gemmata or not. (Although Baratto and Bàrberi-Squarotti focus less on forms and manifestations of sexuality and more on the portrayal of the backward and impoverished world, I believe their analyses allow for a reading of the novella that puts normative heterosexuality into question.) The novella explores all of these questions about motivation and desire within a fictional world where there are complex and unexpected movements between human and animal, animal and plant, plant and inorganic matter.

With this in mind, let us now return to the Author's statement that the women understood this story better than Dioneo wanted them to. What does 'better' mean in this context? The possibilities would appear to be two:

1 The women (who are presumed to be unenlightened about sexuality) are able to decode the figurative language by matching signifiers (names for tools and for animal body parts) with signifieds (human genitalia).
2 The women get the subtleties of the novella (i.e., they understand the joke is more complicated, since it not only brings heterosexual desire to the fore but it makes the reader ask whether the fulfilment of heterosexual desire is even the point of the novella).

Traditionally, readers see the women's reaction as 'better' because they believe the women can now decode eroticized figurative language, not because they understand the women to be subtle readers of the novella. Giorgio Bàrberi-Squarotti is particularly interesting in this regard because he is one of the literary critics who, although he is exceedingly careful to provide a subtle and shaded reading of this novella, falls into the trap of attributing to the women the reading that is less complex, when in fact there is no absolute textual justification for doing so. Here is what he has to say about the women's reaction:

> La novella di donno Gianni è 'meglio dalle donne intesa che Dioneo non voleva': 'meglio,' cioè in un senso 'migliore,' almeno nella misura in cui la pura accettazione dell'osceno, elevato a unico significato della novella, significa che il racconto è stato dalle donne ricondotto all'ambito generale dell'esperienza comica del novellare all'interno del gruppo ... L'intento di Dioneo è esorcizzato dalle donne, la pretesa di esporre eventi 'insignificanti' e ingiudicati di un mondo ai limiti del primitivo è respinta, la vicenda di Donno Gianni e di Pietro da Tresanti si concentra tutta nel momento osceno, dimenticandone le premesse di miseria e di angustia del vivere, da cui esso nasce.[35]

> The novella of Donno Gianni is 'better understood by the women than Dioneo would have liked': 'better,' that is in a 'better' sense, at least in as much as the pure acceptance of the obscene, elevated to the sole meaning

of the novella, means that the women have brought the novella back to the
general arena of the group's experience of what is funny ... Dioneo's intent
is exorcised by the women, who reject his claim to show events of a world at
the limits of the primitive, events that are 'meaningless' and overlooked.
For them, the story of Donno Gianni and of Pietro da Tresanti is entirely
focused on the obscene moment, allowing them to forget the harsh, miser-
able life circumstances from which the story is born.

Such a critical perspective is aimed primarily at encoding the superior
position of the male reader. For all that the women may have understood better than Dioneo would have liked, they are still not on a par
with those predominantly male critics who know what a truly superior
reading would look like.

As I noted above, however, the textual justification for privileging the
male reader over the female reader here is a bit precarious. It depends
heavily upon the interpellation of readers as subjects. For these passages
in the *Decameron* appeal to us to define what a good reading is – and not
in the absolute, but according to a grading scale that is gendered.

I suspect that this text, like many others, is organized so that the
women readers are always in opposition to the male narrators and
Author, necessarily so. The message always reaches them, but in the
encoding of subject positions that the *Decameron* appears to encourage,
these women readers are not ever supposed to fully grasp the meaning.
That is because if women really get the joke – really, really get it – the
degree of pleasure wanes. The pleasure of the male narrator, the pleasure of the male Author, and the pleasure of the male reader depends
upon keeping the woman reader at least partially in the dark.

Of course, the very curious and compelling thing about this Boccaccian rhetorical strategy is that while it does assume the role of panderer
and of 'Galeotto' by subtly encouraging the reader to reaffirm genital
sexuality and also subtly encouraging a gender split among readers, it
also provides for the dismantling of these very interpretations. If, as
readers, we are so foolish and unguarded as to project our own gendered interpretations onto these passages, making them say things that
they do not explicitly say, who is at fault?

Thus, while the Author participates in delimiting the role of the
female reader and renders it more difficult for the female reader to
arrive at a critical reading, he also places the impetus for responsibility
and empowerment into the realm that is properly the reader's, be that
reader male or female.

chapter seven

Domestic Violence in the *Decameron*

To speak of domestic violence in a fourteenth-century Italian text like Boccaccio's *Decameron* is to position oneself on uncertain terrain. In our cultural imagination, domestic violence in the Middle Ages may seem like medieval misogyny, everywhere rampant. But the fact is that readers hesitate to consider the *Decameron* misogynistic and, in keeping with this, they have rarely chosen to see individual instances of violence against women in the *Decameron* as very significant to the reading of the work as a whole.

Furthermore, readers have tended to imagine domestic violence in the *Decameron* as very many people imagine domestic violence today: as instances of direct physical assault that remain for the most part confined to the lower classes.[1] Three examples immediately come to mind: Calandrino's merciless beating of his wife Tessa in *Decameron* 8.3; Tessa's violent retaliation against Calandrino in *Decameron* 9.5; and the wife beating by Giosefo in *Decameron* 9.9.[2] If we expand our notion of domestic violence – to include violence directed at an intimate partner (rather than just a spouse), physical abuse that is not effected 'directly,' and severe psychological abuse – we find a few more examples in the *Decameron*. Now we have moved beyond the circle of the less educated and less wealthy, to witness a scholar's cruelty toward a widow in 8.7,[3] a merchant's attempt to murder the wife he believes to be unfaithful to him in 2.9, and a lord's mistreatment of his humble and patient wife Griselda in 10.10. And if we include actual or implied threats of violence, we acquire even more examples: a father threatens his parturient daughter with death if she does not reveal the name of her lover (5.7), and Nastagio degli Onesti, in order to get his beloved to marry him, invites her to witness a scene of nightmarish cruelty against another woman (5.8).

These examples, all derived from Boccaccio's 'human comedy,' reveal a spectrum of violent behaviour that is more elaborate than the one presented by feminist scholars of medieval and early-modern Italy, since these scholars have tended to focus on women as the objects of male voyeurism, women who are raped, and women who are silenced.[4] In studying the *Decameron*, a text that powerfully embodies medieval and early-modern sensibilities and values, we gain further insight into the discourse about violence against women in Western culture. The *Decameron* allows us to reflect on our implicitly constructed narratives about domestic violence; it also illustrates the challenges that beset readers who are committed to political and ethical change.

As the *Decameron* begins, it seems hard to imagine a place for domestic violence. For the ten Florentines who flee to the countryside, the principal 'violence' is occasioned by the plague of 1348: this mysterious ill transforms bodies, brings death. The ten members of the group do not easily recall anything that would provoke memories of their own tragic experience. As a result, in the first third of their storytelling – much of which must conform to the conditions of a 'happy ending' – they avoid grim descriptions of violence and death.[5]

Women begin to die only on Day 4, when the topic is unhappy love. Unlike men, who meet death mainly because of their own crimes, or because of political and sexual strife, the women of Day 4 tend to die of natural causes (the wife of Filippo Balducci in the Author's novella), or by their own doing (Ghismunda in *Decameron* 4.1, Lisabetta da Messina in 4.5, Simona in 4.7, the wife of Guglielmo Rossiglione in 4.9). The violence that threatens men, actors in the world, does not threaten women directly. Rather, Day 4 represents women as the secondary victims of violence unleashed by sexual love. Tancredi does not kill his daughter Ghismunda – he kills her lover, and then Ghismunda takes her own life. The brothers of Lisabetta da Messina, having discovered their sister's relation with an employee of theirs, kill the employee; Lisabetta then allows herself to waste away. Simona dies only because she imitates her lover's fatal movements, as he rubbed sage leaves against his teeth. Guglielmo Rossiglione, having discovered his wife's adulterous affair, does not kill her. Rather, he kills her lover, who was his own best friend; then his wife lets herself fall out a window.

Only on Day 5, where the stories are dedicated to 'happy love,' does the threat of violence against women really begin to emerge. Men begin to use force or threatened force to get what they want from women.

Despite resistance from the woman he wants and opposition from other men, Cimone claims Ifigenia as his own in *Decameron* 5.1. A father draws his sword against his own daughter in *Decameron* 5.7. Nastagio degli Onesti threatens his beloved more shrewdly with a strange and terrifying dramatic representation, wherein a woman who refused her lover's advances is destined to suffer terrible mutilation at his hands (5.8). Whereas earlier stories downplayed the actual or threatened violence that women experienced at the hands of men,[6] on Day 5, violence against women comes to be foregrounded more insistently, and it turns more overtly graphic.

In the wake of a series of novellas where women seem empowered to speak out and exercise control over their lives (*Decameron* 6 and 7), many of the stories of Days 8 and 9 try to delimit the power that women might wield.[7] Not surprisingly, a number of these stories describe 'just retaliations' against women who have mistreated men, placed limits on them, or called their authority into question. The most striking examples of violence against women in the *Decameron*, all found in the final third of this work, are the response of male characters who perceive themselves as slighted (whether justifiably or not): Calandrino is certain that his wife is responsible for his having lost his invisibility (8.3); the scholar is determined to make the widow suffer in extreme weather just as he suffered for her (8.7); Talano d'Imole can count on fate to punish his wife's insubordinations (9.7); Giosefo responds with violence when his claim to absolute authority over his wife is in question (9.9); likewise, Gualtieri has to resort to extreme measures, since there is almost no humanly conceivable way for Griselda to prove her absolute submission to him (10.10). It seems hardly coincidental that violence against women emerges when the very possibility of women's empowerment does. The stories of the *Decameron* imply that if women gain power, their power must remain limited, by violent means if need be.

I would like to turn my attention now to the novella that strikes me as the most disturbingly violent and misogynistic in the *Decameron*: the story told on the Ninth Day by the queen for that day, Emilia. I have chosen *Decameron* 9.9 because I believe that the difficulties we encounter in reading it are representative of larger difficulties we have in reading accounts of domestic violence in medieval texts.

Prefacing her tale with a long sermon-like diatribe on women's imperfection and their necessary subservience to men, Emilia introduces Giosefo and Melisso who journey to ask Solomon for advice. To Melisso, who is unlucky in love, Solomon says quite simply, 'Ama' ('Love' [9.9.14; 593]). Melisso is dismissed, and Giosefo brought in. To Giosefo, who complains of having a recalcitrant and difficult wife, Solomon says, 'Va al Ponte all'Oca' ('Go to the Goose Bridge' [9.9.15; 593]). As the two men journey homeward, they happen upon a mule driver beating his animal in order to make it cross a bridge; although the men object, the mule driver insists that this is the only way to make the mule obey. Learning that this was the Goose Bridge, Giosefo then 'understands' that Solomon intended him to read the incident as an exemplum. Upon his return home, Giosefo stages a repetition of the scene for his friend Melisso: he asks his wife to prepare Melisso a dinner, which she prepares badly, and in response he beats her violently. She capitulates, becoming properly subservient and obedient, and both Melisso and Giosefo remain convinced that Solomon's advice, which they understood so badly at first, in fact worked wonders. The story ends here with Melisso returning to his homeland, where he tells a wise man what he learned from Solomon; and the wise man agreed that in fact Melisso, for all his prodigality, didn't really love anyone and would be much better off if he applied Solomon's advice to love. Emilia ends cursorily: 'Così fu gastigata la ritrosa, e il giovane amando fu amato' ('And so in such fashion was the shrew punished and the young man by loving was loved in return' [9.9.35; 596]).

Readers of this novella have found themselves at an impasse.[8] Some, shocked at its misogyny, condemn both the novella and its author. Others, attempting to preserve the view of Boccaccio as a pro-woman writer, claim flatly that the resolution of the novella is so unsatisfactory that Boccaccio must want us to accept the resolution as ironic. This suggests to me that the scene of violence has been considered fundamentally unreadable. It has elicited outrage or apology, rather than analysis.

Granted, it is not at all easy for readers of this novella to gain critical distance, since they never get grounded in a consistent point of view. The story begins as if it were about Melisso, but is dedicated mainly to Giosefo, only to return, in an unexpected way, to Melisso at the very end. Solomon himself is a strangely inconsistent adviser, speaking both in biblical language that seems straightforward ('Love') and in oracular pronouncements that invite contrary interpretations ('Go to the Goose Bridge'). Giosefo's wife seems to be the typical recalcitrant and obstinate wife of exemplum and fabliau, a wife who will not submit even after she is subjected to beatings and mutilation – but unlike those precedents, Giosefo's wife submits immediately to her husband after he beats her.[9]

Partly because the story binds together disparate and possibly contradictory subject positions, it is hard to know whether readers can legitimately use one character's perspective in order to critique that of another. Can we align ourselves with Solomon or Melisso in this novella in order to distance ourselves from Giosefo? It would appear not. Giosefo has aligned himself with Solomon, first of all; and Emilia takes care to end her story with a wise man who independently approves of Solomon's advice about love.

Throughout her novella, as in her introduction to it, Emilia's strategy is to provide universalizing statements no matter how partial or questionable the evidence. Strangely enough, the protagonists of her story use the evidence that violence is successful in order to reaffirm the wisdom of Solomon; it does not occur to them to question their interpretation of his pronouncements. Emilia offers her novella as an exemplum, but since she tells about a woman of the lower class – a woman who must prepare dinner, unlike the women of the upper and artisan classes who have servants – one wonders whether she means this novella as an exemplum for the upper-class woman as well.[10] Then, at the end of the novella, Melisso tells a wise man what he has learned from Solomon, but he appears to relate only the part of Solomon's advice that regards him specifically, since the wise man in his response repeats nothing about what Melisso might have learned from observing Giosefo and his wife. The wise man reaffirms the overall efficacy of Solomon's applied advice, but he seems to base his judgment on partial information.

These gaps and inconsistencies are no barrier to Emilia's universalizing statements. Hers is a layering of different texts apparently to be read differently by different readers, each of whom derives a partial lesson that, according to the narrator, reaffirms the coherence of the entire system.

Part of the project of any narrative, of course, is to construct a relation between the whole and its parts, to account for both unity and multiplicity. As Susan Lanser, author of 'Toward a Feminist Narratology,' phrases it, following Bahktin, 'in narrative there is no single voice.'[11] Showing how multi-layered texts address themselves simultaneously to different readers who hear quite different messages, Lanser argues for a more subtle and varied concept of voice and tone. She cites a nineteenth-century English letter in which a woman tells of her great happiness in marriage – then she invites us to read every other line. Embedded into this paean to domestic harmony is a story of terrible mistreatment in marriage. The letter is a quite remarkable example of how, though a surface text may appear straightforward, further investigation can show that it is rendered problematic by other voices. Lanser shows first that the audience is split in two: there are those who (like the husband) wish to hear the praise of marriage, and others who (like the narrator's secret correspondent) hear of her grim reality. But because Lanser does not see the world simply, she reminds us also that there is an audience that tries to make sense of both voices.

Lanser's feminist narratological approach can provide the first impulse for a rereading of Emilia's novella. Beginning with a narrative of apparent simplicity, Lanser locates at least one oppositional voice in it. Having recognized two mutually exclusive voices, she encourages the reader to find a third voice that could comprehend both the simple assertion and its oppositional counterpart. In the end, Lanser makes a crucial point: Surface simplicity can hide a profound complexity, which requires discriminating judgment.

Of course, we should apply Lanser's theoretical model with judicious modifications, because Emilia is *struggling* to present a unified point of view at all costs, even when there are multiple voices, even when the voices are partial. Already, at the surface level of Emilia's story, there is an organization of narrative material that requires discriminating judgment. What should we do when two or more voices are bound together in ways that resist being dismantled?

The answer – which sounds all too deceptively simple – is that we would have to exercise discrimination. Boccaccio was himself well aware of the imperative to articulate difference. Whether or not he saw this as a problem of gender difference, he would have acknowledged the importance of identifying differences and basing judgments on careful distinctions. How so?

Readers in the late Middle Ages prized the ability to make careful distinctions. When Dante has Thomas Aquinas – himself a master of discerning thought – identify Solomon as the brightest light among the wise souls in the Heaven of the Sun, it is because of Solomon's ability to distinguish true wisdom from arid abstractions. As Aquinas notes here, Solomon asks not for quantifiable scientific or philosophical information, but rather for the wisdom to rule well:[12]

> Ma perché paia ben ciò che non pare,
> pensa chi era, e la cagion che 'l mosse,
> quando fu detto 'Chiedi,' a dimandare.
> Non ho parlato sì, che tu non posse

ben veder ch'el fu re, che chiese senno
acciò che re sufficïente fosse;
   non per sapere il numero in che enno
li motor di qua su, o se *necesse*
con contingente mai *necesse* fenno;
   non *si est dare primum motum esse,*
o se del mezzo cerchio far si puote
trïangol sì ch'un retto non avesse.

(Paradiso 13.91–102)[13]

But, in order to make evident that which is still concealed, think about who he was, and what motivated him when he was told 'Ask.' I have not spoken in such a way that you would not be able to see plainly that he was a king, who asked for wisdom so that he might be a king worthy to the task – not to know the number of mover spirits here above, or if *necesse* with a contingent ever made *necesse*; or *si est dare primum motum esse*; or if, in a semicircle, a triangle can be drawn so that it has no right angle.

This exemplary figure should inspire earthly beings to greater caution and prudence:

E questo ti sia sempre piombo a' piedi,
per farti mover lento com' uom lasso
e al sì e al no che tu non vedi:
   Ché quelli è tra li stolti bene a basso,
che sanza distinzione afferma e nega
ne l'un così come ne l'altro passo;
   perch' elli 'ncontra che più volte piega
l'oppinïon corrente in falsa parte,
e poi l'affetto l'intelletto lega.
   Vie più che 'ndarno da riva si parte,
perché non torna tal qual e' si move,
chi pesca per lo vero e non ha l'arte.
   E di ciò sono al mondo aperte prove
Parmenide, Melisso e Brisso e molti,
li quali andaro e non sapëan dove ...

(Paradiso 13.112–26)

And let this be like lead on your feet, so that you would move slowly, like a weary man, to the pros and the cons that you do not understand. Right down low among the fools is anyone who indiscriminately affirms and denies, whatever the case may be. Such a person finds that often the precipitous opinion inclines to the wrong side, and then emotion hinders the intellect. People who fish for the truth but don't know what they are doing leave the shore worse than in vain, since they do not return the same as when they set out. Parmenides, Melissus, and Bryson, and many others stand as open proofs of this to the world: they started out, but they had no idea where they were going. (My translation)

Dante is reshaping for his own audience the biblical passage in which God recognizes Solomon's great wisdom. In 3 Kings 3:5, God appears to Solomon in a nighttime dream and states that he will give Solomon whatever he asks for ('postula quod vis ut dem tibi').[14] After a long and courteous introduction, in which he humbly acknowledges his own limitations, Solomon asks for the wisdom to rule properly:

dabis ergo servo tuo cor docile
ut iudicare possit populum tuum et discernere inter malum et bonum
quis enim potest iudicare populum istum populum tuum hunc multum

(3 Kings 3:9–10)

Give your servant an understanding heart
so that he can judge your people, and distinguish between evil and good.
For who can judge these people, your people who are so many?

God, highly pleased with Solomon, responds:

quia postulasti verbum hoc et non petisti tibi dies multos
nec divitias aut animam inimicorum tuorum
sed postulasti tibi sapientiam ad discernendum iudicium
ecce feci tibi secundum sermones tuos
et dedi tibi cor sapiens et intellegens
in tantum ut nullus ante te similis tui fuerit
nec post te surrecturus sit

(3 Kings 3:11–12)

Because you asked for this, and you did not ask for long life,
or riches, or the lives of your enemies,
but you asked for the wisdom to exercise discerning judgment,
I have done as you have requested,

and I have given you a wise and understanding heart.
Before you there has never been anyone like you,
nor after you will anyone like you come forth.

If we look again at Emilia's novella about Solomon's advice with the biblical and Dantesque passages in mind,[15] we must read Giosefo's request for knowledge as absolutely preposterous. Giosefo can in no way compare to the biblical Solomon, who thought of the larger good; nor is he in any way like the Dantesque Solomon, who put forth a commendable request for what we might call a 'methodology' over 'mere facts.' Giosefo is blatantly self-serving as he asks for information directed at a very isolated and specific concern, how to control his obstinate wife. Even Melisso's request should strike us as questionable. Melisso requests a benefit to himself ('How may I be loved?') and receives a generic answer, which, as it happens, he applies to his own advantage.

Lest I be misunderstood, I hasten to clarify. I find fault in Giosefo and Melisso not because they focus on the personal rather than the political, not because they fail to consider what the Bible calls 'these people, your people who are so many,' but rather because they do not focus on anything but themselves and the immediate benefits they could derive from Solomon. Swept up by their own egotistical desires, Giosefo and Melisso can provide only a sad distortion of a larger question: How might we best recognize virtuous love and strive to make it a reality in our lives?

By the end of the story, one has the distinct impression that Giosefo and Melisso have learned nothing more than they knew before. Unable to make important distinctions, they uncritically embrace the 'lesson' of the Goose Bridge and treat a woman as if she were a creature who deserved to be beaten.[16] Women are not animals, of course, but the lesson that Giosefo and Melisso should have learned (and that we should learn) goes beyond this. Violence is not morally or ethically acceptable simply because it helps one to achieve one's stated goal.

In reflecting on the prudential wisdom of authority figures, the Bible, Dante, and Boccaccio all reaffirm that not all forms of knowledge, not all attempts to better one's human condition, are equally valid. Both the Bible and Dante exhort us very explicitly to strive for the practical wisdom that leads to improved social and political communities. Boccaccio is not an author to engage in any sort of explicit persuasion, but this does not mean that we cannot derive a lesson from the story that he chooses to put in the mouth of Emilia on Day 9. This is a story about a misguided interpretation of Solomon's advice; it reveals the perpetrators of violence against women to be indiscriminate readers and thinkers. The recalls of biblical and Dantesque passages invite us to distance ourselves both from the logic of the abusive man (Giosefo) and from the logic of the narrator who accepts and justifies violence against women (Emilia). Furthermore, whether or not this was his intent, Boccaccio encourages us to be as concerned about the life of the couple, the smallest unit of community, as we are about the life of entire peoples.

In my discussion of *Decameron* 9.9 thus far, I have focused on something we could call 'reading misogyny against the grain.' This is the approach that Millicent Marcus adopted in her reading of misogyny in *Decameron* 8.7. It requires that we place misogynist discourse into a larger context where its claims can be evaluated more carefully and seen to be insufficient. As a reading strategy, it owes a great deal to Dantean narrative techniques and to the kinds of ironic readings Dante encourages us to adopt, especially when we listen to the stories of the characters who populate his *Inferno*.

Such a reading has tremendous merit, and I see it as the crucial first step in a feminist reading of the story about the Goose Bridge. But in order to gain more insight into the workings of misogynistic narratives, we need to move our line of inquiry to another plane. By what rhetorical means do misogynists try to disable any critique from their opponents? In other words, after we characterize the 'offensive rhetoric' of misogynistic discourse, what can we say about its 'defensive rhetoric'?[17]

To answer this, we would have to think about how the narrators construct their stories in favour of, or in objection to, women's increasing freedom. On Day 9 of the *Decameron*, as Emilia and another narrator, Pampinea, argue against the more liberal view of woman that Filomena has asserted, they marshal narrative language from Filomena's story, on Day 5, about Nastagio degli Onesti. This is particularly evident in Pampinea's story, where Margherita is disfigured by a wolf because she refuses to acknowledge the authority of her husband, Talano d'Imole, who has told her that according to a dream he had, she would be disfigured by a beast if she entered the woods. Recalcitrant being that she is, she defies him, only to be attacked and mutilated. The prophetic nature of Talano's 'vision' has been tested and reaffirmed. The message would appear to be: Remember, Filomena, that if Nastagio's 'vision' had been tested, it too would have been reaffirmed. In order to avoid violence, woman must comply with male desire.

Emilia attempts an even more daring use of Filomena's narrative.

First, in the description of the scene at the Goose Bridge, Emilia produces a calque of the scene that Filomena described in *Decameron* 5.8, the story of Nastagio degli Onesti. In a forest outside Ravenna, Nastagio sees a knight who is violent and cruel to a naked and dishevelled woman; he feels sorry for her and attempts to intervene; but the knight stops him, explaining that he and the lady must enact this scene of violence every Friday; Nastagio then changes his mind about this scene, and decides to use it in order to frighten his lady love into capitulating to his desires, and accepting his offer of marriage. Likewise, in the encounter at the Goose Bridge, Giosefo and Melisso try to intervene when they see the mule driver beating his mule, and the mule driver stops them, explaining that violence is the only solution. Thus far, Emilia is treating Filomena's narrative material much as Pampinea did earlier. Once again, the message is: Violence works. But Emilia does not stop here. As she concludes her story, she recalls Nastagio once again, this time more obliquely. Emilia has Melisso learn a lesson that the prodigal Nastagio never learned – namely, to find love not through expenditure of material goods but by dint of expressions of love.

What is the logic behind Emilia's two references to Filomena's tale of Nastagio degli Onesti? In order to shore up her own narrative authority, Emilia carries out a pre-emptive strike. She tries to occupy positions that Filomena cannot attack; she tries to ensure that Filomena has no way to respond. If Filomena does so, *she* will look incoherent: she will inevitably be arguing against a position that she herself took earlier. If she attacks Giosefo, she must acknowledge that she is attacking Nastagio. If she attacks Melisso, she must acknowledge that she should have ended her own story about Nastagio differently.

Previously, when we examined Emilia's claim that violence is authorized and effective, we saw the fault lines in her 'offensive rhetoric.' Now, as we consider Emilia's 'defensive rhetoric,' we can see it is directed at subverting the authority of anyone who might disagree with her (specifically Filomena). In effect, Emilia implies that the opponents of female inferiority and subservience have no ground to stand on – or, rather, that the ground on which they stand is no different from the ground on which she stands.

In Emilia's introduction, this becomes most evident as she argues for violence as a sweeping solution. She admits in advance that not all women will agree with the remedy that she proposes for female wilfulness, but then she lumps all women together as she quotes the proverb 'Buon cavallo e mal cavallo vuole sprone, e buona femina e mala femina vuol bastone' ('Both good and bad horses require the spur, just as both good and bad women require the stick' [9.9.7; 592]). Then again, she appears momentarily to concede, just before she tries to consolidate her own position: 'Le quali parole chi volesse sollazzevolemente interpretare, di leggier si concederebbe da tutte così esser vero; ma pur vogliendole moralmente intendere, dico che è da concedere' ('Anyone who sees the humor in these words will readily agree that they are true; but I say that they are also admissible if they are considered in their moral sense' [9.9.8; 592]).

Whether we think about the issue in the joking sexual terms to which Emilia alludes, or in serious 'moral' terms that she herself espouses, we remain stuck in a system that limits the choices women can make: women have the right to choose between the kinds of sticks that would maintain social order. Were we to read this through the lens offered us by radical thinkers such as Andrea Dworkin and Catherine MacKinnon, we might think that Emilia's statement proves that sex is but another form of violent control. But Emilia's formulation is a bit stickier: Women might be willing to entertain the idea of figurative 'rods,' even if they don't like the literal instruments of painful control that Emilia argues for. And once they have accepted any sticks at all, how could they deny the admissibility of sticks in the 'moral' sense?

Emilia does, however, offer us the very means by which to undo the oppressive logic she argues for: reading and interpretation. She does not merely maintain the moral validity of her solution; she allows that the proverb might have a contested interpretation, and she argues for her interpretation as an interpretation. What she means by a 'moral' interpretation might be less than clear. In context, it seems that Emilia offers her moral reading as a more serious enterprise than the jocular sexual reading. But the moral reading was, in the Middle Ages, one of the kinds of reading demanded by the fourfold interpretation of scripture, according to literal, allegorical, moral (tropological), and anagogical significance.[18] To find the 'moral' or 'tropological' sense of the text was to find its proper application to one's life as a Christian. Precisely because Emilia is a narrator who remains unaware of the gaps in her thinking, we must exercise great care when we try to find the moral sense of her story, when we think about its application to our own lives.

I have argued that a judicious reading of Emilia's story can offer us insight into the rhetorical justifications for violence against women, and into the kinds of defensive mystifications that make it difficult for us to perceive the issues clearly. Having recognized some of the strategies that reinforce the 'legitimacy' of violence against women, we may well wish to reflect on some of the strategies that could displace the discourse of violence. The strategies of resistance are multiple, and they are always dependent on context, but principal among them would be: Refuse the notion of women's essential inferiority and necessary subservience, even when it is asserted by women. Refuse universalizing claims that are based on incomplete information. Unravel and complicate the notion of women's 'complicity' in violence. Recognize perpetrators as accountable. And, above all, reframe the choices that women have. It is women's choices about their own lives, after all, that the perpetrators of domestic violence try to limit, and it is women's choices that the process of reading and rethinking can put into play again.

Conclusion

Over the time that I have written this book and presented portions of it at scholarly conferences, I have continued to sense in sectors of my public a certain anxiety about the usefulness of gender as an analytic category.[1] The concern, as regards the *Decameron*, seems to be that to focus on gender may detract from Boccaccio's singular contribution. If we attend to gender and sexual difference, can we still read the *Decameron* as offering what Franco Fido calls a 'luminoso progetto di civiltà' ('a brilliant outline of civilization')?[2] Would we still be able to maintain that both men and women can work together toward the common goal of noble, honest living? Will we still be able to assert that human expression, elevated by a masterful authorial style, can be used to reflect on the human condition and to prepare us to confront the challenges of living and dying well?

The fear also seems to be that to talk about gender is to talk about only one half of humanity (women) and to arrive at conclusions that regard only that half of humanity. And that to focus on gender is to turn divisive, to resort to pointless polemics and polarizations, that is to say, to dwell on what might well be a less noble aspect of humanity. And that there is such a fundamental rift that we not only cannot communicate using the same terms but we cannot share a common project, cannot live together, cannot construct a society together.

Yet, as I have sought to demonstrate, it is the reading unwilling to consider how sexual difference is articulated in the *Decameron* that gives us an incomplete view of the book's cultural project. All too often the readings that have claimed universality have focused only on the male half of humanity. Even if championing woman, they have remained largely unconcerned with the ways that the presumed benefits to woman are compromised. Moreover, they fail to see that the view of gender relations that they offer us remains untouched by the nuances, the distancings, and the cautionary notes that the *Decameron* offers.

These sorts of readings have often been carried out under the general rubric of a 'unified reading' that helps us to understand the *Decameron* not as a series of largely unrelated narratives, but as a cultural project of impressive scope and enduring value.[3] Although there are variations among these readings, they tend to reaffirm the basic lineaments as offered by Franco Fido: from the confusion of *Decameron* 1 and from the reflections on the role of fortune and clever industriousness in *Decameron* 2 and 3 to the reaffirmation of man's reason, his linguistic abilities, and his magnanimity. Within the arc of the last seven days of the *Decameron*, Fido sees a movement from the celebration of love, the strongest of human passions, to the reaffirmation on Days 6 and 7 of the powers that are specifically human (intelligence, verbal expression, and wit), to the clever tricks of Days 8 and 9, concluding with the generosity and magnificence that crowns the storytelling on Day 10.

I feel a degree of solidarity with authors who propose a unified reading, since they focus, as do I, on the sustained rhetorical project of the *Decameron*. But I suspect that their response to my reading would hardly be reciprocal. In looking to the scholarly work that Fido cites as representative of the unified reading, I could not help but be struck by the fact that it was all carried out by Italian males working within Italian critical traditions: Sapegno, Bosco, Petronio, Billanovich, Branca, Battaglia, Di Pino, Ramat, Neri, Getto, Padoan (and presumably Fido as well, since he sends his book forth from Bologna, Italy). I must admit that, in my own mind, I had remembered Fido as far more open to the work on Boccaccio that had been done on this side of the ocean, particularly by women scholars. Returning to his book, I discovered why I had remembered him as a champion of the women who have preceded me. In a move that I would call supremely Boccaccian, Fido dedicates his book to the Other, namely, to North American exponents of Boccaccio criticism among whom women figure so prominently. As Fido takes care to point out – thus securing his own position as a surrogate for the Author of the *Decameron* – Boccaccio would have appreciated such a group for the role that well-spoken women have played in it. Equally important: Fido dedicates his book to precisely those scholars with whom he notes he has not always been in agreement. The qualified dedication, combined with the identification of the Italian proponents of the unified reading, suggests that the readings emerging from this side of the Atlantic, however diverse among themselves, present a challenge to the unified reading as it has been conceived so far.

I would counter that when we think about a unified reading of the *Decameron*, we cannot void out its nuances and complexities. We must take a more accurate view of the *Decameron*'s rhetorical goals and its rhetorical strategies. And when we introduce awareness of sexual difference into our reading of the *Decameron*, we are immediately confronted with obstacles to some of the most reassuring unified readings of this work. It becomes more difficult to speak about human responses to an unpropitious world without realizing that these responses are affected by gender, class, and estate. It becomes more difficult to assert the *Decameron*'s unconditionally pro-woman stance.[4] It becomes considerably more of a challenge to read the *Decameron* in edifying fashion, citing as proof that it begins with the most evil of men (ser Cepparello) and ends with the most virtuous of women (Griselda).[5] Above all, it becomes risky to make totalizing claims about what Boccaccio is saying.

In the course of inviting readers to witness – and participate in – the *Decameron*'s vibrant debate about the issues, my book offers several stories of its own. It would be well to review them within the forum provided by this conclusion.

First of all, I have described a *Decameron* that both polarizes sexual difference and moves away from clear polarizations of male and female. The early chapters of this book (chapters 2 and 3 in particular) are intended to reveal the polemics around sexual difference in the *Decameron*, whether these are organized around the polarization of Fiammetta and Dioneo or, more generally, around the tensions between female and male narrators. This issue emerges also in chapter 6, dedicated to men, women, and figurative language in the *Decameron*. As I take care to point out particularly at the conclusions to chapters 2 and 3, we must remember that these are rhetorical choices and they do not necessarily represent the historical tensions between real fourteenth-century women and men. In fact, one of the very curious rhetorical effects of the *Decameron* is this: although the early part of the storytelling seems particularly marked for gender (hence, my analysis of chapter 3 shows the most marked difference in Days 2 and 3), subsequent stories attempt to diffuse these differences, making it considerably more difficult for the reader to distinguish between female and male points of view. This too is part of the *Decameron*'s rhetorical effect: to show, I believe, how female voices are increasingly aligned with what we perceive to be a non-gendered, universal view. By doing this, the *Decameron* places us in a position where we have

to weigh the relative effects of emphasizing or de-emphasizing oppositional sexual differences.[6] This is, once again, a balancing act. No matter
what choice the reader makes, she always risks that it will be a controversial choice. Has she emphasized too much or too little the voices that
emerge along gender and sexual lines? Has she assigned the appropriate
value to universal characteristics and to historical specificities?

All readers of the *Decameron* must measure its double pull, toward and
against unity, on multiple fronts. Seeking to define this double pull,
Franco Fido has offered the label 'il regime delle simmetrie imperfette.' Perhaps what is most curious is that readers who are most
concerned to see progress toward edification in the *Decameron* are also
most concerned to shore this up by maintaining what they see as the
Decameron's pro-woman – or at least not-misogynist – positioning. Giorgio Padoan, for example, sees no particular political ideology in the
Decameron, but he insists that it is incontrovertible that the *Decameron* is a
paean to Love, written to benefit women in love.[7] It appears that such
readers can allow for imperfect symmetries, provided that these not
include sex and gender. To allow for sexual and gender asymmetries
would mean to put the current conception of power and social organization into question.

Second, I believe that the *Decameron* reveals the limits placed upon
women who would choose to speak out and to claim for themselves lib-
erties (expressive, sexual, vocational) that are not always considered
within the purview of women. Thus, in chapter 4, I have shown that the
Decameron's stories about the cross-dressed women are not necessarily
about unsettling the patriarchal order in the ways in which readers
often take them to be – although it is true that there remain other
impulses to question the construction of gender and the construction of
truth in a patriarchal society. In chapter 5, I have focused less on the way
in which women's witty words are evidence of their empowerment and
more on the way in which the power of women's witty words is heavily
circumscribed. Especially in my reading of the tale of the nightingale
(*Decameron* 5.4) contained in chapter 6, I have argued that although
many readers believe that figurative language is equally the province of
men and women, a closer examination of the evidence reveals that figurative language in the *Decameron* is used as a 'wedge' to establish gendered subject positions. In my final chapter, on domestic violence in the
Decameron, I am concerned to show how the representations of violence
against women in this work do indeed suggest that women's empowerment and the spectre of violence are intertwined.

Still, in stating that the *Decameron* makes known the limits placed on women who dare to seek empowerment, I would add that we cannot assume that this knowledge is unqualifiedly prescriptive, nor can we assume that responsibility for these limits lies with any single authorial figure, be it a single narrator (or cluster of narrators), the fictional Author of the *Decameron*, or Giovanni Boccaccio himself. In narratives like the *Decameron*, the relationship between prescriptive and descriptive assertions is necessarily both fluid and dynamic; readers of the *Decameron* over the centuries also bear significant responsibility for what has come to been defined as prescriptive. Indeed, one of the things that strikes me as most fascinating about the *Decameron*, as I have read it here, is that it allows us to see how the foreclosure of possibilities available to women can exist without any deliberate volitional program. Multiple narrative and readerly contributions have to intersect in order to produce a rhetorical and/or political outcome. Thus, multiple contributions from multiple subjects with presumably independent agendas, combined with factors that could be purely casual or random, can produce a 'text' that no individual authorial subject could have produced.

As for Giovanni Boccaccio and his fictional Author of the *Decameron*, I see them engaged always in an elaborate two-step. What these authorial figures seem to give with one hand, they seem to take away with the other. The result is that when we attempt to nail them down to any specific position, we find ourselves revealing more about ourselves than about them.

Throughout, I read the storytelling of the *Decameron* as an ongoing ambitious project in the construction of social reality, impressive for its wide-ranging scope, for its engaging and jocular treatment of the weighty issues that touch the lives of women and men, and for its complex representation of moral and ethical questions, for its masterful innovation of the narrative forms, and for its subtle sense of the poetic possibilities in language. The social reality the *Decameron* offers us is not always, as Franco Fido would have it, 'luminoso,' luminous, bright, and reassuring. It is in many places murky and chaotic. The *Decameron* refuses to offer unquestionable guarantees that the good in human nature will triumph. It continues to remind us that the strategies we employ to respond to unpropitious events and the strategies we employ to bring about social change are not always uncompromisingly admirable. It asserts that questions of an ethical nature are not resolved easily and that there are, in many cases, multiple truths in tension with each other rather than a single truth.

Writing this book on the *Decameron* has convinced me of how much more remains to be done in order to gain a more accurate understanding of this work. I organized my inquiry into the *Decameron* principally around the question of sexual difference and I would defend this choice both because I think most readers would agree that sexual difference is key to the *Decameron*'s articulation of meaning and because, along with Luce Irigaray, I believe that gender and sexual difference remain the issues that our own epoch must work through. So much more remains to be done, however. We need more work within the area of gender, feminist, and sexuality studies on the *Decameron*. As literary scholars are wont to note, this work must be carried out within literary and textual frameworks so that we continue to refine our notion of how the *Decameron* is in dialogue with textual – and specifically literary – traditions. But we also need more work that would reveal how the language of the *Decameron* is deeply imbued in and constitutive of fourteenth-century social reality.[8] This work requires substantial input from disciplines such as history, anthropology, economics, and legal studies. Just as the issue of sexual difference within the *Decameron* has long been assumed to be 'obvious' – with the result that the actual complexities and nuances of sexual difference have gone unnoticed – so too historical context has gone wanting, perhaps because so many readers have seen the storytelling of the *Decameron* as an event that takes place at the margins of history.[9] With more such information about social and historical context, we would have a keener sense of how the *Decameron* positions itself in the tension between classes – an issue that I believe is key and which I have been able to touch upon here only in relation to the question of sexual difference.[10] More information about social and historical context would also help us to see how the *Decameron* positions itself between actual and possible (fantastic and utopian) worlds.[11]

Finally, and perhaps most important: in tandem with the work that is scholarly and research oriented, there must be work of an imaginative and creative sort. This work involves us in an ongoing dialogue with works like the *Decameron*; it looks toward the future. As I have attempted to show here – in part as I have revealed the implicit dialogue among the narrators, in part as I have revealed the questions that the novellas of the *Decameron* evoke obliquely – the *Decameron* calls on us to respond to the questions it poses with our own retellings and rewritings.[12] It exhorts us to ask whether the questions that it asks about social life – and the questions we ask about our own social life – are the best and most appropriate questions. It shows us that narration, even when it happens in moments of detachment from the hum of daily activity, is crucial to our attempts to understand ourselves and our communities. It shows us that narration can be a shared rhetorical project with no single identifiable author; and when this common rhetorical project is launched, not all the rhetorical strategies employed will emerge with equal force. This is where a different sort of reader – a discriminating reader able to evaluate the effectiveness and the limitations of these rhetorical strategies – emerges as vital. With all these considerations in play, and relying on the insights of this discriminating reader, the *Decameron* asks us, above all, to shape our own brilliant outline of civilization.

Notes

Introduction

1 I use 'Author' to refer not to Giovanni Boccaccio, the historical author of the *Decameron*, but to the implied Author of the *Decameron*, who is a fictional construct. This is consistent with the usage of the term 'Autore' in Italian scholarly writings about this work.

2 Many of the questions to which I allude in this opening paragraph are ones that I have confronted in 'Writing (Not Drawing) a Blank,' in Jonathan Monroe, ed., *Local Knowledges, Local Practices: Writing in the Disciplines at Cornell* (Pittsburgh: University of Pittsburgh Press, 2003). This essay may be of particular interest to those readers who wish to know how these questions about the *Decameron* play out in the writing classroom.

3 Victoria Kirkham, *The Sign of Reason in Boccaccio's Fiction* (Florence: Olschki, 1993), 118.

4 *Epistole*, 22.19–24, quoted in Kirkham, *The Sign of Reason*, 118–19.

5 Kirkham, *The Sign of Reason*, 118.

6 Ibid., 117.

7 Ibid., 127.

8 This point is reiterated also by F. Regina Psaki in 'Women in the *Decameron*,' in James H. McGregor, ed., *Approaches to Teaching Boccaccio's 'Decameron'* (New York: Modern Language Association of America, 2000), 79–86.

9 These kinds of questions led to my studied assessment of the picture in my entry on 'Giovanni Boccaccio (1313–1374),' in Rinaldina Russell, ed., *The Feminist Encyclopedia of Italian Literature* (Westport, Conn.: Greenwood Press, 1997) 30–3.

10 *Boccaccio and Feminist Criticism* is edited by F. Regina Psaki and Thomas C.

Stillinger; the volume is expected to be published by the *Annali d'Italianistica* book series 'Studi e testi.'

11 The English translation of Branca is mine.

12 Some readers may well object that Branca did not select this photograph and therefore one should not discuss the photograph in relation to Branca's newspaper article, but I would politely disagree. Throughout this book, I am interested in the way that the work of multiple agents, all with presumably independent agendas, can intersect to create a meaningful pattern; moreover, I am interested in the effect of factors that could be random. While Branca should not be held responsible for the photograph that accompanies his article – no more than Bocccaccio can be held responsible for the visual representations of textual moments from the *Decameron* – it can be enlightening to consider the way that text and image, in tandem, create meaning.

13 Millicent J. Marcus, 'Misogyny As Misreading: A Gloss on *Decameron* VIII, 7,' *Stanford Italian Review* 4 (1984): 23–40.

14 Obviously, my language here evokes *Woman Defamed and Woman Defended: An Anthology of Medieval Texts*, ed. Alcuin Blamires with Karen Pratt and C.W. Marx (Oxford: Clarendon Press, 1992).

15 The most lucid and articulate theorist of sexed thought is the philosopher Adriana Cavarero; see her 'Per una teoria della differenza sessuale,' in *Diotima: Il pensiero della differenza sessuale* (Milan: La Tartaruga, 1987), 41–79. For an overview of Italian feminist thought generally, and of the idea of sexed thought in specific, see Franco Restaino and Adriana Cavarero, *Le filosofie femministe* (Turin: Paravia Scriptorium, 1999), 101–10.

Chapter 1: Woman as Witness

1 For an overview of the history of the source criticism on the *Decameron*'s description of the plague, see Joseph E. Germano, 'La fonte letteraria della peste decameroniana: Per una storia della critica delle fonti,' *Italian Quarterly* 27 (1986): 21–30. For the identification of Paulus Diaconus as the principal source, see Vittore Branca, 'Un modello medievale per l'introduzione,' in *Boccaccio medievale*, 7th ed. (Florence: Sansoni, 1990), 381–7.

2 The English translation is from Paul the Deacon, *History of the Langobards*, trans. William Dudley Foulke (Philadelphia: University of Pennsylvania [Department of History], 1907), 56–8. In one case, I have modified Foulke's translation; where he rendered 'Fugiebant filii' as 'Sons fled,' I have corrected this to 'Children fled' so as to communicate the force of the masculine generic. For the Latin text, see *Pauli Historia Langobardorum* (Hannover: Impensis Bibliopolii Hahniani, 1878).

3 This in contrast to what Vittore Branca says about Boccaccio's development of the 'particolari sui bubboni e sulle bestie ecc.' ('the details about the buboes and the beasts etc.') to which Boccaccio paid most attention (*Boccaccio medievale*, 386 note).

4 By fixing its attention on the rupture of boundaries, the *Decameron* recognizes the Black Death as an event that qualifies as a historical trauma. My discussion of trauma and the crisis of witnessing has been influenced by the contemporary reflections on this subject, most notably, Shoshana Felman and Dori M. Laub, MD, *Testimony: Crises of Witnessing in Literature, Psychoanalysis, and History* (New York: Routledge, 1992). In addition, it was James N. Rizzo who first sensitized me to issue of trauma in Boccaccio's *Decameron*, in part through his contributions to my seminar on Boccaccio, in part through his unpublished senior honours thesis, 'An Essay on Subjectivity and Trauma' (Cornell University, 1995).

5 Marchione di Coppo Stefani's description of the plague, which imitates the *Decameron*'s, provides the 'lectio facilior' of the situation, by levelling the gender relations. In his *Cronaca fiorentina* (written late 1370s and early 1380s), and found in vol. 30 of *Rerum Italicarum Scriptores*, ed. Niccolò Rodolico (Città di Castello: S. Lapi, 1903), we read at rubric 634: 'Lo figliuolo abbandonava il padre, lo marito la moglie, la moglie il marito, l'uno fratello l'altro, l'una sirocchia l'altra' ('Child abandoned the father, husband the wife, wife the husband, one brother the other, one sister the other' [230]).

6 In retrospect, even the *Decameron*'s earlier description of the buboes seems portentous. Paulus Diaconus had said they were the size of a nut or date; in the *Decameron*, they are said to be the size of an apple or an egg. Obviously the buboes of 1348 are bigger, consistent with the representation of the Black Death as more threatening. But 'apple' and 'egg' may have been selected for their ability to evoke human sexuality.

7 See *The Black Death: The Impact of the Fourteenth-Century Plague*, ed. Daniel Williman (Binghamton, NY: Medieval and Renaissance Texts and Studies, 1982), 39–64, esp. 47.

8 *The Holy Bible: Douay Version*, trans. from Latin Vulgate (Douay, AD 1609; Rheims, AD 1582), preface by Cardinal Archbishop of Westminster (1956; repr. London: Catholic Truth Society, 1963).

9 For this observation, I am indebted to Giancarlo Lombardi, 'Boccaccio e Camus,' unpub. paper written for a seminar on Boccaccio at Cornell University in the fall of 1991.

10 On voyeurism in Boccaccio, see Michel David, 'Boccaccio pornoscopo?' in *Medioevo e Rinascimento veneto. Con altri studi in onore di Lino Lazzarini*, 2 vols. (Padua: Antenore, 1979), 1: 215–42.

11 Joy Hambuechen Potter, 'Woman in the *Decameron*,' in Gian Paolo Biasin et al., eds, *Studies in the Italian Renaissance: Essays in Memory of Arnolfo B. Ferruolo* (Naples: Società Editrice Napoletana, 1985), 90.

12 Neifile will continue to articulate this view, particularly in her first stories, about Abraham the Jew (1.2) and Martellino (2.1).

13 Presumably, the proposal is that the entire group leave Florence, men and women together, although the reader must keep in mind that the author of the *Decameron* never reports exactly what Pampinea says to the men when 'loro la lor disposizione fé manifesta e pregogli per parte di tutte che con puro e fratellevole animo a tener lor compagnia si dovessero disporre' ('[she] outlined their plan to them, and begged them, in everyone's name, to keep them company in the spirit of pure and brotherly affection' [1.Intro. 87; 17]).

14 Here I have corrected Musa and Bondanella's translation, which reads, 'Pampinea, who had driven away her sad thoughts in the same way' (18).

15 The reader who fears that *uom* (man) is unquestionably generic here would do well to consult the Accademia della Crusca's *Concordanze del 'Decameron,'* ed. Alfredo Barbina (Florence: Giunti, 1969), in order to review the instances of *uomo* that precede 1.Intro.98. At least up until this point in the *Decameron*, Boccaccio is particularly attentive to sexual difference in the Preface and Introduction to the work, and he is likely to specify *uomini e donne* or *uomini and femine* (men and women) when he means that. This does not mean that the instance of *ogn'uom* in 1.Intro.98 does not have the force of a masculine generic; rather, I wish to emphasize that this phrase, coming as it does after a series of instances where Boccaccio does draw sexual distinctions, might wander into the zone of ambiguous meaning.

16 Likewise, Joy Hambuechen Potter writes that 'even though women function well as rulers in the *cornice*, it is a man who sets the tone, insisting that the world of the plague be forgotten, and a man who makes the decision to return to Florence, just as men tell the first and the last of the hundred stories' ('Woman in the *Decameron*,' 91).

17 See David Wallace, *Giovanni Boccaccio: 'Decameron'* (Cambridge: Cambridge University Press, 1993), 23.

18 In proposing to read the *Decameron* as, among other things, an extended dialogue about gender issues, I am resisting the tendency of some readers to think that gender is an isolated issue that emerges in certain privileged stories. Even if the tensions between the men and the women of the *brigata* (as well as between the gender ideologies of the stories and the gender ideologies of the Author) have not yet received a full–length treatment, I would note that some other scholars have offered views that coincide with my own.

The *Decameron* is built on the tension between a woman's desire to separate from the disintegrating community in order to ensure self-preservation and the desire of the young men, for whom the company of women is key. In *Contraddizioni nel 'Decameron'* (Milan: Guanda, 1983), 17–19, Cesare De Michelis notes this, not in order to explore the problem of gender, but to observe that there is in the *Decameron* a contradiction regarding the central role of woman, as well as a tension between masculine and feminine ideological positions, represented by Panfilo (who leads the group back to Florence) and Pampinea (who leads them away).

Chapter 2: Fiammetta v. Dioneo

1 Janet Levarie Smarr, *Boccaccio and Fiammetta: The Narrator as Lover* (Urbana: University of Illinois Press, 1986), 181.
2 Ibid., 174–92.
3 Ibid., 182.
4 See Robert Hollander and Courtney Cahill, 'Day Ten of the *Decameron*: The Myth of Order,' in Robert Hollander, *Boccaccio's Dante and the Shaping Force of Satire* (Ann Arbor: University of Michigan Press, 1997), 109–68, esp. 109–14.
5 See, e.g., Susanne L. Wofford, 'The Social Aesthetics of Rape: Closural Violence in Boccaccio and Botticelli,' in David Quint et al., eds, *Creative Imitation: New Essays on Renaissance Literature in Honor of Thomas M. Greene* (Binghamton: State University of New York Press, 1992), 189–238; Mihoko Suzuki, 'Gender, Power, and the Female Reader: Boccaccio's *Decameron* and Marguerite de Navarre's *Heptameron*,' *Comparative Literature Studies* 30 (1993): 231–52; and Ray Fleming, 'Happy Endings? Resisting Women and the Economy of Love in Day Five of Boccaccio's *Decameron*,' *Italica* 70 (1993): 30–45.
6 Focusing on the hermeneutic crisis depicted in Day 1 of the *Decameron* and on the power of words to transform reality, readers have called attention to the progressive superimposition of differing semantic codes, which allow a signifier to slip from one code to another and produce unexpected signifieds that remap the directions we might give to any given narration. See Guido Almansi, 'Literature and Falsehood,' in *The Writer As Liar: Narrative Technique in the 'Decameron'* (London: Routledge and Kegan Paul, 1975), 19–62; Franco Fido, 'Vita morte e miracoli di San Ciappelletto: Risarcimenti di una semiosi imperfetta,' in *Il regime delle simmetrie imperfette: Studi sul 'Decameron'* (Milan: Franco Angeli, 1988), 45–63; Giovanni Getto, 'Struttura e linguaggio nella novella di Ser Ciappelletto,' in *Vita di forme e forme di vita nel 'Decameron',* 4th rev. ed. (Turin: Petrini, 1986), 34–77; Millicent J. Marcus, 'Pseudo-Saints and Storytellers: the Tale of Ser Ciappelletto,' in *An Allegory of*

Form: Literary Self-Consciousness in the 'Decameron' (Saratoga, Calif.: Anma Libri, 1979), 11–26; Giuseppe Mazzotta, *The World at Play in Boccaccio's 'Decameron'* (Princeton: Princeton University Press, 1986), 58–63; and Joy Hambuechen Potter, *Five Frames for the 'Decameron': Communication and Social Systems in the 'Cornice'* (Princeton: Princeton University Press, 1982), 50–2, 60–1.

In a study published recently (which strangely enough, avoids citation of all the studies mentioned above), Michelangelo Picone argues that Day 1 of the *Decameron* is the narrators' response to the questions about the function of literature that the Author had posed in the Introduction. See his 'Lettura macrotestuale della prima giornata del *Decameron*,' in Tatiana Crivelli, ed., *'Feconde venner le carte': Studi in onore di Ottavio Besomi*, 2 vols. (Bellinzona: Casagrande, 1997), 1: 107–22.

7 The distinction is made by J.L. Austin in *How to Do Things with Words*, ed. J.O. Urmson and Marina Sbisà, 2nd ed. (1975; reprt. Cambridge, Mass.: Harvard University Press, 1997).

8 Georges Güntert has shown that the exchange between the Saladin and Melchisedech depends, among other things, on their ability to distinguish manifest from underlying messages, and on their ability to establish a readerly pact. See his 'Premessa ermeneutica: La parabola dei tre anelli (*Decameron* I, 3),' chap. 3 of *Tre premesse e una dichiarazione d'amore: Vademecum per il lettore del 'Decameron'* (Modena: Mucchi, 1997), 77–106, and esp. 105.

9 In 'Faith's Fiction: A Gloss on the Tale of Melchisedech (*Decameron* I, 3),' *Canadian Journal of Italian Studies* 2 (1978–9): 40–55, Millicent Marcus argues that this novella offers us a paradigm for the ideal reader; she sees the sultan as 'a model for the reading public at large, making his change from hostile to receptive paradigmatic of the response that Boccaccio would elicit from his own readership' (51).

10 Ibid., 52.

11 Ibid., 49.

12 Letterio Di Francia has studied this novella in relation to its sources, in 'La IV novella del *Decameron* e le sue fonti,' in *A Vittorio Cian, i suoi scolari dell'Università di Pisa* (Pisa: Mariotti, 1909), 63–9. And of course A.C. Lee discusses the novella in *The 'Decameron': Its Sources and Analogues* (reprt. London: David Nutt, 1909; New York: Haskell House Publishers, 1972).

Readers of *Decameron* 1.4 have tended to focus on issues other than the sources. Bernard N. Schilling discusses this novella in light of the Rule of Saint Benedict; see 'The Fat Abbot,' in *The Comic Spirit: Boccaccio to Thomas Mann* (Detroit: Wayne State University Press, 1965), 21–42. For a representative structuralist reading, see Angelo Marchese, 'Strutture narrative della I giornata del *Decameron*,' in *Metodi e prove strutturali* (Milan: Principato, 1974), 248–53. Guido Almansi first provided a detailed reading of the combinatory logic of this tale; see his 'Lettura della quarta novella del *Decameron*,' *Strumenti critici* 4 (1970): 308–17, republished in *L'estetica dell'osceno* (Turin: Einaudi, 1974), 131–42. Almansi also discusses this novella in *The Writer As Liar: Narrative Technique in the 'Decameron'* (London: Routledge and Kegan Paul, 1975), 63–6 and 69–76. Christopher Kleinhenz offers a stylistic analysis in 'Stylistic Gravity: Language and Prose Rhythms in the *Decameron* I, 4,' *The Humanities Association Review* 26 (1975): 289–99. Mario Baratto reads the novella as an affirmation of nature over reason; see *Realtà e stile nel 'Decameron*,' 2nd ed. (Rome: Editori Riuniti, 1993), 230–4.

13 Lee, *The 'Decameron': Its Sources and Analogues*, 15. Obliged to identify a possible source for Dioneo's novella, Lee opts for the far less explicit story from the *Novellino*.

14 Almansi, *The Writer As Liar*, 65.

15 The quoted language is from Almansi, *The Writer As Liar*, 75; but the argument is found on pages 69–76.

16 Without commenting on the peculiarity of the discursive choices, Almansi writes that the girl is 'whittled down to a single conventional notation concerning her physical appearance ('strikingly beautiful') and a psychological detail after the Abbot's advances ('the girl, who was not exactly made of iron or of flint, fell in very readily for the Abbot's wishes')' (*The Writer As Liar*, 69).

17 Ibid., 69.

18 For the text of novella 54 of the *Novellino*, see *Il Novellino: Testo critico, introduzione e note*, ed. Guido Favati (Genoa: Fratelli Bozzi, 1970), 243–4.

19 For the text of the fabliau, see vol. 6 of *Nouveau recueil complet des fabliaux (NRCF)*, ed. Willem Noomen (Assen: Van Gorcum, 1991), 193–205.

20 Jean-Paul Sartre, *Being and Nothingness: An Essay on Phenomenological Ontology* (1943), trans. Hazel E. Barnes (London: Methuen, 1957), 252–302.

21 Here I am holding to Elizabeth Grosz's careful and precise distinctions between Freud's concept of scopophilia, Sartre's notion of 'the look,' and Lacan's account of the gaze. See her entry on 'Voyeurism/Exhibitionism/The Gaze,' in *Feminism and Psychoanalysis: A Critical Dictionary*, ed. Elizabeth Wright (Oxford: Basil Blackwell, 1992), 447–50.

22 Musa and Bondanella translate 'she might well be the wife or the daughter of some person of importance' (40). I have corrected their translation of *tale femina* here.

23 Some readers, engrossed in the theoretical questions I have posed above, may wish to believe that questions about representation and character (questions that belong to the Imaginary order), compared to questions about

desire, pleasure, and subjectivity (questions of the Symbolic order), are inconsequential. What, such readers may ask, can we possibly know about the truly important questions if we are merely concerned with representations of women's beauty and morality? To such readers, anxious to get to questions of high theory, I would respond that anyone seeking to understand the rhetorical design of a text must ask how certain utterances, generated as a measured and intelligent critical response to other utterances, can produce a discourse whose weight is more or less than the sum of its parts. This requires that we examine the *relation* between the Imaginary and Symbolic orders. It is not a question of deciding between them.

24 Here I have corrected Musa and Bondanella's translation, since they mistranslate 'accomandandolo ella a Dio' as 'he commended her to God.'

25 Shoshana Felman discusses such failures in terms of frameworks offered by Jacques Lacan and J.L. Austin; see *The Literary Speech Act: Don Juan with J.L. Austin, or Seduction in Two Languages,* trans. Catherine Porter (Ithaca: Cornell University Press, 1983), esp. 82–5.

26 Ibid., 84.

27 Dioneo's spatial mapping of sexual difference in *Decameron* 1.4 is a traditional one, of course, relying on narratives that position man as subject, woman as object. Teresa de Lauretis critiques this narrative paradigm in her chapter on 'Desire in Narrative,' in *Alice doesn't: Feminism, Semiotics, Cinema* (Bloomington: Indiana University Press, 1984). *Decameron* 1.5 cannot entirely undo this paradigm; it acknowledges the dominance of this constitutive paradigm, and suggests ways to call the paradigm into question.

28 In *Metodi e prove strutturali* (246–7), Angelo Marchese has shown how *Decameron* 1.5 and 1.9 share the same deep syntactic structure, which is: XA + YB $\rightarrow$ Ya $\rightarrow$ X – A. For *Decameron* 1.5, Marchese assigns the following values to these variables: X = the king of France; Y = the marchioness of Monferrato, A = (male) sensuality; B = (female) honour; a = modify the situation with actions and words. And for *Decameron* 1.10, the values are: X = the widow; Y = master Alberto; A = (womanly) foolishness; B = (male) wisdom; a = modify the situation with a witty remark. But not only does Marchese remain blind to the fact that the novellas do not share the same ideology, he uses his commentary to shore up male pride and justify male failings. About *Decameron* 1.5, he remarks, 'Anche in questo caso l'intelligenza acuta ed elegante, congiunta a uno squisito senso di cortesia ... hanno la prevalenza sul motivo occasionale della sensualità (*ma forse diremmo meglio della galanteria*), un altro vizio dei "grandi" che viene amabilmente riprovato' ('In this case too, a keen and elegant intelligence, joined to an exquisite sense of courtliness ... prevail against the causal motive of sensuality (but perhaps we would

be better to call it galantry), another vice of the "greats" that comes to be reprimanded lovingly' (246; translation mine). About *Decameron* 1.10, he writes, '[L]a struttura semantica del racconto è rivolta più a sottolineare la pochezza della vedova, intenzionata a burlarsi di maestro Alberto, che a riprovare lo scusabilissimo vizio del suo amore senile' ('the semantic structure of the story is aimed more at emphasizing the shallowness of the widow, intent upon mocking master Alberto, than at criticizing the very forgivable vice of his senile love' (247; translation mine).

29 Judith Butler, *Exciteable Speech: A Politics of the Performative* (New York: Routledge, 1997), 87.

30 Ibid., 87–8.

31 Ibid., 47.

32 Ibid., 50.

33 R. Howard Bloch, *Medieval Misogyny and the Invention of Western Romantic Love* (Chicago: University of Chicago Press, 1991), 47.

34 Almansi has noted that Fiammetta complicates the narratives of Day 2 by rendering them far more complex in their investigations of moral issues (*The Writer As Liar*, 125–6). For the argument that Fiammetta complicates the storytelling on Day 1 of the *Decameron*, see the discussion earlier in this chapter. I would add that this pivotal position tends to fall to Fiammetta, who most often tells her stories at the centre of a Day, in the fifth or sixth position.

35 In 'L'evoluzione dell'intreccio: Bouvin e Andreuccio,' *Filologia e critica* 1 (1976): 5–14, Luciano Rossi has compared 'Boivin de Provins' with the novella of Andreuccio da Perugia, arguing that Boccaccio certainly knew this fabliau. Analysing the two narratives in light of Propp's *Morphology of the Folktale*, Rossi shows how the narratives diverge in plot development; he also finds that Boccaccio opens up many narrative possibilities as he renounces the double identity of the male character (11). My reading diverges from Rossi's, as he fails to see that gender affects Proppian categories in ways that we cannot afford to ignore.

36 See 'Boivin de Provins,' 21–5: 'Et vint en la rue aus putains, / Tout droit devant l'ostel Mabile, / Qui plus savoit barat et guile / Que fame nule qui i fust. / Iluec s'assist desus un fust ...,' and compare 127–30: ' – "Je ai non Fouchier de la Brouce. / Mes vous samblez ma niece douce / Plus que nule fame qui *fust!*" / Cele se pasme sor le *fust.*'

37 My argument is consonant with Howard Bloch's assertion that '[a]mong the fabliaux that stage their own production none is more significant than "De Boivin de Provins"'; see R. Howard Bloch, *The Scandal of the Fabliaux* (Chicago: University of Chicago Press, 1986), 96.

38 In an alternate text of the fabliau, printed in *The French Fabliau: B.N. MS.*

837, ed. and trans. Raymond Eichmann and John DuVal, 2 vols. (New York: Garland, 1984–5), 1: 62–79, the audience is treated to another version of the story come full circle. When Boivin leaves the site of his mischief, we watch him divest himself of his aliases and become the Boivin we first met. As he leaves Mabile's house, he is still the 'peasant' that Mabile believed him to be (39, 41). Then, as he tells his story to the magistrate, his verbal and sexual prowess emerge; he is 'Sir Fouchier' (43). He becomes 'Sir Boivin' (50) at the very end, when he is about to depart, and the amused magistrate compensates him.

39 In creating the first female voyeur of Italian literature, a figure that will inspire Tasso's Armida, Fiammetta is revising earlier episodes of voyeurism in the *Decameron* (1.1, 1.4), both of which involve male voyeurs. One might claim that technically, the first female voyeur of the *Decameron* is the princess of England, disguised as an abbot, who studies Alessandro and his manners most carefully (2.3.20–4). I think, however, that a solid case can be made for continuing to think of this as an instance of 'male' voyeurism.

40 Giovanni Getto, 'La composizione della novella di Andreuccio,' in *Vita di forme e forme di vita nel 'Decameron,'* 4th rev. ed. (Turin: Petrini, 1986), 94; translation mine. Florindo Cerreta also sees Andreuccio's education as highly successful; see 'La novella di Andreuccio: Problemi di unità e d'interpretazione,' *Italica* 47 (1970): 255–64. Gregory Lucente even mobilizes various details that could call into question the success of Andreuccio's journey to knowledge, and then wilfully reads them in an optimistic key; see 'The Fortunate Fall of Andreuccio da Perugia,' *Forum Italicum* 10 (1976): 323–44. For Lucente, Andreuccio wandering about with his ring is ready to face both chance and men because he is armed with 'the emblem of knowledge on his finger' (337); Andreuccio, though wandering through the streets, is said to have 'at last caught up with the rest of us in the world of 'mondana virtù,' with 'those who know' (340). Lucente also reassures us that 'it is without further preoccupation that we may watch as he departs Napoli' (340). But as I argue immediately below, such a reading depends heavily on denial.

41 Mazzotta points at a similar conclusion, based on evidence that is extratextual rather than textual: 'Andreuccio wins, but we are asked to extend the trajectory and realize that this all may happen all over again because even as he is at the top of the wheel, he is always on its shifty curve' (*The World at Play in Boccaccio's 'Decameron,'* 210). If we actually read to the end of the story, as I argue we should, we will see that one need not extend the trajectory of the novella to see the provisional nature of Andreuccio's victory.

42 Marcus, who is discussing Alatiel as 'author of her destiny,' begins by drawing an analogy between Alatiel and the Sicilian prostitute ('By rewriting her past,

as did Ser Ciappelletto and Andreuccio's Sicilian prostitute, Alatiel literally becomes the author of her destiny, bringing about the happy ending so unwarranted by her "real" adventures on the stormy Mediterranean Sea' [*An Allegory of Form*, 43]). Then, probably because the Sicilian prostitute is not the principal protagonist of *Decameron* 2.5, Marcus shifts her focus to Andreuccio ('Despite the equivocal morality of the Andreuccios and the Alatiels of Day II, it is they who will prevail in the world of the *Decameron*, and not the Beritolas and the Arrighettos who passively await fortune's next blow and invite their own extinction' [ibid.]).

43 Relevant in this regard is the work of Gary Cestaro, who has explored the power of the word in *Decameron* 2.2. See his 'Rinaldo d'Asti: Drama of the Signifié.' *Carte italiane* 7 (1985–6): 14–27.

44 This expansion of narrative and social roles strikes me as the origin of the more complex exploration of ethics and morality that Almansi has seen in the second half of *Decameron* 2 (*The Writer As Liar*, 125–6).

45 As illustration of this, I would cite the difficulty experienced by an anonymous reader of the manuscript of my 'How (thanks to a woman) Andreuccio da Perugia became such a loser, and how (also thanks to a woman) reading could have become a more complicated affair,' *Romance Languages Annual* (1999): 302–7, who objected that 'Fiammetta is seen to raise the issue [of critical reading], which then is shown not to have any ramifications for the subsequent stories of Day 2. This totally undermines the force of Fiammetta's lesson for the reader.' This reader understood my point: that part of the message of Fiammetta's story falls on deaf ears. What the reader has failed to grasp, however, is that we cannot read these muted moments of the *Decameron* as indicative of failure. Rather, it is our responsibility as readers to try to understand why certain messages rather than others have been muted. In brief, I believe that it is easy to read *Decameron* 2.5 in an 'imaginary' key, where men and women engage in sex wars. It is more faithful to the text – but certainly harder – to read this novella in a 'symbolic' mode, and to see in it an extended reflection about language and interpretation.

46 Marilyn Migiel, 'Beyond Seduction: A Reading of the Tale of Alibech and Rustico (*Decameron* III, 10),' *Italica* 75 (1997): 161–77.

47 See Wayne C. Booth, *The Rhetoric of Fiction* (Chicago: University of Chicago Press, 1961), 9–16.

48 Vittore Branca justly recalls Andreuccio in his notes to the Mondadori edition of the *Decameron*, but does not pursue the implications of the connection between the two tales.

49 To tell the truth, the story of Andreuccio da Perugia seems already to be pressing forward into the group's consciousness in *Decameron* 8.9, when

Lauretta tells of Maestro Simone's fall into excrement (recalling Andreuccio's fall into a latrine), and when Bruno and Buffalmacco invent names for
an imagined beauty destined for Maestro Simone (recalling madonna
Fiordaliso's representation of herself as a 'cavalleressa' in 2.5). In this
regard, Victoria Kirkham has pointed out the possible connection between
'cavalleressa' in 2.5 and the related invented names of *Decameron* 8.9.

50 Dioneo notes of the beautiful women of Palermo that they would be considered noble and honourable by anyone who did not know them ('da chi non
le conosce, sarebbono e son tenute grandi e onestissime donne' [8.10.7]),
and thus recalls Andreuccio's firm belief that madonna Fiordaliso is a great
lady ('fermamente credette lei dovere essere non men che gran donna'
[2.5.17]).

51 There is something peculiarly akin to Dioneo in Fiammetta, since she herself
has to adopt a rhetorical stance similar to his when she brings her audience
to condone illicit behaviour. It is significant, however, that while we can say
that there is something of Dioneo in Fiammetta, we would not be able to say
the reverse (i.e., that there is something of Fiammetta in Dioneo).

52 Booth, *The Rhetoric of Fiction*, 15.

Chapter 3: Boccaccio's Sexed Thought

1 Thomas G. Bergin, *Boccaccio* (New York: Viking, 1981), 289–90.
2 Aldo Scaglione, *Nature and Love in the Middle Ages* (Berkeley: University of
California Press, 1963), 73.
3 This is the subject of Millicent J. Marcus's essay 'An Allegory of Two Gardens:
The Tale of Madonna Dianora (*Decameron* X, 5),' *Forum Italicum* 14 (1980):
162–74.
4 Dario Fo, *Manuale minimo dell'attore*, ed. Franca Rame, new ed. (Turin:
Einaudi, 1997 [1987]), 300. For the English translation, see Dario Fo, *The
Tricks of the Trade*, trans. Joe Farrell, ed. with notes by Stuart Hood (London:
Methuen, 1991), 196–7.
5 The phrase I quote from Filomena then reappears verbatim in the Author's
rubric at the start of Day 2 (2.Intro.1).
   We might choose to understand the masculine pronouns *infestato* and
riuscito as masculine generics. This is what Mark Musa and Peter Bondanella
do when they translate: 'people who after a series of misfortunes attain a
state of unexpected happiness' (62). But as we know, the masculine generic
is not reliably and fully inclusive. The evidence that use of the masculine
generic has promoted an androcentric view, to the detriment of women, is
mounting. See Mykol C. Hamilton, Barbara Hunter, and Shannon Stuart-

Smith, 'Jury Instructions Worded in the Masculine Generic: Can a Woman Claim Self-defense When "He" Is Threatened? (1992),' in Camille Roman, Suzanne Juhasz, and Cristanne Miller, eds, *The Women and Language Debate: A Sourcebook* (New Brunswick, NJ: Rutgers University Press, 1994), 340–7; Mykol C. Hamilton, 'Using Masculine Generics: Does Generic "He" Increase Male Bias in the User's Imagery?' *Sex Roles* 19 (1988): 785–99; and Jeannette Silveria, 'Generic Masculine Words and Thinking,' in Cheris Kramarae, ed., *The Voices and Words of Women and Men* (Oxford: Pergamon Press, 1980), 165–78.

6 Millicent J. Marcus, 'Spinning the Wheel of Fortune: The Tales of Andreuccio (II, 5), Beritola (II, 6) and Alatiel (II, 7),' chap. 2 of *An Allegory of Form: Literary Self-consciousness in the 'Decameron'* (Saratoga, Calif.: Anma Libri, 1979), 28.

7 See, e.g., Thomas M. Greene, 'Forms of Accommodation in the *Decameron*,' *Italica* 45 (1968): 297–312.

8 In some cases (as with Martellino in 2.1 and Andreuccio in 2.5), they are threatened with loss of bodily integrity; but in both cases, these protagonists emerge intact.

9 It is important to note that the widowed count of Antwerp, wrongly accused of sexual assault in *Decameron* 2.8, loses his home but not his two children, who prove to be crucial in the design to return their father to his original fortunate state. The count's misfortune is therefore categorically different from the misfortunes of Madama Beritola, Alatiel, and Zinevra, who lose all their family members, even if only temporarily.

10 See Penelope Doob, *Nebuchadnezzar's Children: Conventions of Madness in Middle English Literature* (New Haven: Yale University Press, 1974).

11 In an essay originally published in Italian in 1974, Cesare Segre draws attention to the insistent references to Alatiel as 'thing' (*cosa*); see his 'Comical Structure in the Tale of Alatiel,' in *Structures and Time: Narration, Poetry, Models*, trans. John Meddemmen (Chicago: University of Chicago Press, 1979), 129. In *An Allegory of Form*, Millicent Marcus elaborates: 'Two things conspire to rob Alatiel of her humanity and reduce her to the level of mere ornament: first, her suitors do not know who she is, and second, they share no medium of communication with her' (41).

12 Dioneo's argumentation is sophistic but some readers have accepted it; see, for example, Teodolinda Barolini, '"Le parole son femmine e i fatti sono maschi": Toward a Sexual Poetics of the *Decameron* (*Decameron* II 10),' *Studi sul Boccaccio* 21 (1993): 175–97. One might think at first that this is because Barolini's work does not engage feminist issues, but then we find that even a feminist reader like Jane Gallop mistakenly conflates sex with the acquisition

of knowledge and power; see Gallop, *Feminist Accused of Sexual Harassment* (Durham: Duke University Press, 1997).

13 The phrase 'total surrender to the erotic instinct' is Scaglione's, from *Nature and Love in the Middle Ages*, 73.

14 See Howard C. Cole, 'Dramatic Interplay in the *Decameron*: Boccaccio, Neifile, and Giletta di Nerbona,' *MLN* 90 (1975): 38–57; Marga Cottino-Jones, *Order from Chaos: Social and Aesthetic Harmonies in Boccaccio's 'Decameron'* (Washington: University Press of America, 1982), 61; and David Wallace, *Giovanni Boccaccio: 'Decameron'* (Cambridge: Cambridge University Press, 1993), 41–2.

15 When a stable-hand sneaks into the queen's bed in *Decameron* 3.2, she is convinced it is her husband; indeed, as Pampinea would have it, the queen is never enlightened on this matter. Later, in *Decameron* 3.6, a jealous Catella thinks she has tricked her husband into participating in an illicit encounter, when in fact she has just had sex with Ricciardo, who has turned the tables on her. Catella does find out, but when she threatens to reveal all, Ricciardo calls attention to the fact that if his word is pitted against hers, he is sure to be believed.

16 Wallace, *Giovanni Boccaccio: 'Decameron,'* 41–2.

17 Ibid., 42.

18 Ibid., 43.

19 Ibid., 44.

20 Ibid., 45.

21 Ibid., 47.

22 As the bibliography on Day 3 amply demonstrates, critics have devoted their attention mainly to the first and last stories, both told by men.

23 The formal aspects of Day 7 encourage this homogeneous view. Cesare Segre, for example, has underscored the remarkable compactness of thematic and structural aspects on this day of the *Decameron*, which reinforces what he calls a 'unified outlook.' See Segre, 'Funzioni, opposizioni e simmetrie nella Giornata VII del *Decameron*,' *Studi sul Boccaccio* (1971): 81–108; this essay has been translated into English as 'Functions, Oppositions, and Symmetries in Day VII of the *Decameron*,' in *Structures and Time: Narration, Poetry, Models*, trans. John Meddemmen (Chicago: University of Chicago Press, 1979), 94–120.

24 Giovanni Getto, 'Le novelle dello scambio di illusione e realtà,' in *Vita di forme e forme di vita nel 'Decameron*,' 4th rev. ed. (Turin: Petrini, 1986), 165–88.

25 Barbara Zandrino, 'La luna per lo sole (VII Giornata),' in Giorgio Bàrberi-Squarotti, ed., *Prospettive sul 'Decameron'* (Turin: Tirrenia, 1989), 113–30.

26 David Wallace, 'Seventh Day: Controlling Domestic Space,' in *Giovanni Boccaccio: 'Decameron,'* 77–84.
27 Unfortunately, even readers attentive to gender in the *Decameron* have
   tended to downplay the importance of class. Barbara Zandrino, for example,
   has noted that in Day 6, no matter what their class, women outwit men. She
   writes, 'Il trionfo femminile, celebrato da Boccaccio nella VI giornata con la
   rappresentazione esemplare di come le donne possano, a qualunque classe
   appartengano, dominare uomini ed eventi per mezzo del motto di spirito, di
   parole ingegnose, argute e concise ... raggiunge l'apoteosi nel progetto di
   Dioneo, nella raffigurazione di una donna che è l'esatto contrario di quella
   proposta dalle prediche di Gilberto da Tournai' ('Boccaccio celebrates the
   triumph of women on Day 6 of the *Decameron*, where he provides an exemplary representation of how women, whatever their class background, can
   dominate men and situations by means of witty remarks, clever, sharp, and
   terse words ... This reaches its culmination in Dioneo's project, with the portrayal of a woman who is the exact opposite of the woman put forth in the
   sermons of Gilbert of Tournai' [in 'La luna per lo sole (VII Giornata),'
   115]). But I would maintain that the narrators of the *Decameron* are highly
   class conscious.
28 'Gianni Lotteringhi ode di notte toccar l'uscio suo; desta la moglie, e ella gli
   fa accredere che egli è la fantasima; vanno a incantare con una orazione, e il
   picchiare si rimane' ('Gianni Lotteringhi hears a knock at his door during
   the night; he awakens his wife, and she makes him believe it is a ghost; they
   go and exorcise the ghost with a prayer, and the knocking stops' [7.1.1;
   417]); 'Frate Rinaldo si giace colla comare; truovalo il marito in camera con
   lei' ('Brother Rinaldo lies with the mother of his godchild ... her husband
   discovers him in her bedroom' [7.3.1; 425]); 'Tofano chiude una notte fuor
   di casa la moglie' ('One night, Tofano locks his wife out of the house' [7.4.1;
   430]); 'Un geloso in forma di prete confessa la moglie' ('A jealous husband
   disguised as a priest hears his wife's confession' [7.5.1; 434]); 'Lodovico dis-
   cuopre a madonna Beatrice l'amore il quale egli le porta: la qual manda
   Egano suo marito in un giardino in forma di sé e con Lodovico si giace; il
   quale poi levatosi va e bastona Egano nel giardino' ('Lodovico reveals to
   Madonna Beatrice the love he bears for her, whereupon she sends her husband Egano into a garden disguised as herself while she lies with Lodovico;
   then, afterward, Lodovico gets out of bed, goes into the garden, and gives
   Egano a beating' [7.7.1; 445]); 'Un diviene geloso della moglie, e ella, legan-
   dosi uno spago al dito la notte, sente il suo amante venire a lei' ('A man
   becomes jealous of his wife, and she ties a string to her toe during the night,
   so that she will know that her lover has come to visit her' [7.8.1; 451]).

29 See Maria Gabriella Stassi, 'Amore e "industria": III Giornata,' in Giorgio
Bàrberi-Squarotti, ed., *Prospettive sul 'Decameron'* (Turin: Tirrenia, 1989), 39–
58. Stassi encourages us to see the limits of the system throughout; on the
subject of the limitations placed on women, she writes, 'Le donne, in so-
stanza, alla fine vincono, ma più come complici involontarie e passive di un
intrigo condotto dagli uomini, che come eroine della storia' ('Women do
win in the end, but more as passive and involuntary accomplices of an
intrigue organized by men than as heroines of the story' [43]).

30 I explore this more fully in chapter 5, 'Women's Witty Words: Restrictions on
Their Use,' and chapter 6, 'Men, Women, and Figurative Language in the
Decameron.'

31 On this point, see chapter 7, 'Domestic Violence in the *Decameron.*'

32 Carol Gilligan, *In a Different Voice: Psychological Theory and Women's Development*
(Cambridge, Mass.: Harvard University Press, 1982).

33 The quotation from Virginia Woolf is taken from *A Room of One's Own* (New
York: Harcourt, Brace and World, 1929), 76, and is cited by Gilligan on p. 16
of *In a Different Voice.*

34 See the detailed summary and critique of Gilligan's position in Lawrence
Kohlberg, Charles Levine, and Alexandra Hewer, *Moral Stages: A Current Formulation and a Response to Critics* (Basel: Karger, 1983), 121–41.

35 See Kohlberg, Levine, and Hewer, *Moral Stages,* 121, where, in reviewing
Gilligan's *In a Different Voice,* the authors write: 'The general thesis of this
book, with which we are in partial agreement, is that the influential theories
of personality development for the most part have been created by males
and reflect greater insight or understanding into male personality development than into female personality development.'

Chapter 4: To Transvest Not to Trangress

1 The term 'wager story' has been applied by Gaston Paris, 'Le Cycle de la
Gageure,' *Romania* 32 (1903): 481–551. Texts of wager stories can be found
in Gerbert de Montreuil, *Roman de la violette ou de Gerard de Nevers* (Paris:
Champion, 1928); *Le Roman du Roi Flore et de la belle Jeanne. Due novelle antiche
anteriori al 'Decameron' del Boccaccio che servirono d'argomento a due bellissime isto-
rie contenute in esso in divin libro* (Genoa: n.p., 1859); also in Guido Almansi,
Il ciclo della scommessa: Dal 'Decameron' al 'Cymbeline' di Shakespeare (Rome:
Bulzoni, 1976), 81–90.

2 In 'Il travestimento nel *Decameron*: Orizzonti e limiti di una rigenerazione,'
Studi sul Boccaccio 17 (1988): 205, Monica Donaggio argues that this is most
obviously the case with Madonna Zinevra of *Decameron* 2.9. In Donaggio's

view, a comparison of Madonna Zinevra with women in other 'wager stories' – the wife of Gerard de Nevers in *Le Roman de la violette*, Jeanne in *Le Roman du Roi Flore e de la belle Jeanne*, and the wife in an anonymous Italian novella – will prove Madonna Zinevra's singularity. According to Donaggio, Zinevra alone acts with masculine vigour. The wife of Gerard de Nevers is too passive and it is her husband who disguises himself, as a jongleur, in order to discover the truth; although Jeanne disguises herself as a man in order to survive, it is her husband who discovers that the accusation against her is false and it is her husband who kills her accuser in a duel; finally, the wife in the anonymous novella, though again disguised as a man, is saved because she is a tearful beauty who draws the attention of a man who can rescue her.

    I find Donaggio's assessment troubling, however, because it is too categorical in its assessment of female protagonists as either active or passive. Moreover, Donaggio does not always render faithfully the roles that men and women assume in these texts. Her essay seems motivated, as many source studies are, by the desire to privilege the text that is its chief focus. But more is going on in these wager stories than meets the eye. In all of them, as in Pampinea's story about Alessandro and the princess of England (as well as in its source in the legend of Saint Eugenia), narrators adopt a variety of strategies as they proclaim truth, vilify falsehood, and show how men and women are conditioned by the positions that gender roles require them to assume. In all of these stories – including the story of Madonna Zinevra – the assertiveness of honourable and worthy female protagonists is muted.

3 *Decameron* 2.3 has received scant critical attention; only a handful of scholars have analysed this novella in order to highlight Boccaccio's views on Fortune and his reworking of sources. Guido Pugliese attempts to re-evaluate the story as a unified artistic effort on Boccaccio's part; see his '*Decameron* II, 3: Un caso di contingenza causale,' *Esperienze letterarie* 5:4 (1980): 29–41. Without entering into the debate about the artistic merits of *Decameron* II, 3, Ruggero Stefanini examines the genealogy of this novella and its conception of fortune in his 'La leggenda di Sant'Eugenia e la novella d'Alessandro (*Dec.* II, 3): L'esibizione apologetica del seno nella tradizione narrativa, con un "excursus" sulla "fortuna" nell'opera di Boccaccio,' *Romance Philology* 33 (1980): 338–410. Giuseppe Mazzotta reads the novella against the backdrop of Dante's views on Fortune; see *The World at Play in Boccaccio's "Decameron"* (Princeton: Princeton University Press, 1986), 83–6.

4 One might argue that in *Decameron* 2.5 it would be a requirement that the audience distance itself from the female protagonist too. I would say, however, that given the tendency in the *Decameron* to privilege clever industrious-

ness over honour and morality, the Sicilian prostitute proves to be a likeable character, whom the listeners follow with a certain tolerance.

5 See the on-line *Encyclopedia Britannica* at www.britannica.com, s.v. 'Cornwall, Duchy of': 'The duchy (the oldest in England) was created by royal charter on March 7, 1337, by Edward III for his eldest son, Edward the Black Prince, and for such of his heirs as would become kings of England. Henry VI expressly declared that the monarch's first-begotten son at the time of his birth was to be duke of Cornwall; thus, ever since, the eldest living son has become duke automatically at birth or whenever he becomes heir apparent.'

6 Giovanni Boccaccio, *Decameron*, trans. Guido Waldman (Oxford: Oxford University Press, 1993), 81.

7 Musa and Bondanella translate 'postogli in mano uno anello' as 'she placed a ring on his finger' (78). It is more likely, however, that the princess places the ring into Alessandro's hand so that he can place it on her finger. The giving of the ring was not reciprocal in this period; rather, the ring was given by the husband to the wife. (See Christiane Klapisch-Zuber, 'Zacharias, or the Ousted Father: Nuptial Rites in Tuscany between Giotto and the Council of Trent,' in *Women, Family, and Ritual in Renaissance Italy*, trans. Lydia G. Cochrane [Chicago: University of Chicago Press, 1985], 183, 185–7.) And while Vittore Branca and others are certainly correct in noting that the Italian 'gli si fece sposare,' literally 'she had him marry her,' means that she made him give her his solemn promise that he would marry her (see Branca's note in the Mondadori edition), fourteenth-century marriage practices had it that the indication of consent to marry – even in private and without the necessary banns or witnesses – was sufficient to constitute a valid marriage. See James A. Brundage, *Law, Sex, and Christian Society in Medieval Europe* (Chicago: University of Chicago Press, 1987), particularly on covert marriages in the late twelfth century (see 333–6), the early thirteenth century (see 362–4), and the later thirteenth and early fourteenth centuries (see 440–3).

8 Giovanni Boccaccio, *The Decameron*, trans. G.H. McWilliam, 2nd ed. (New York: Penguin, 1995), 89.

9 Monica Bardi has noted that Zinevra's proposed solution (that the servant produce her clothes as evidence that she is dead) has a subtext in the story of Joseph and his brothers in Genesis 37, where Joseph's brothers produce Joseph's bloodied garments as proof that he has been killed by a wild beast. See her 'Il volto enigmatico della fortuna: II Giornata,' in Giorgio Bàrberi-Squarotti, ed., *Prospettive sul 'Decameron'* (Turin: Tirrenia, 1989), 25–38, and in particular 27. We could take this argument just a bit farther, however, and

note that there is also a subtext in the story of Joseph for Ambrogiuolo's use of clothing in order to prove that he has had a sexual encounter with Zinevra. While Joseph is in the service of Potiphar in Egypt, Potiphar's wife attempts to seduce him. She pulls on his garment, but he manages to flee, leaving his garment in her hand. She then produces the garment as proof that Joseph had attempted to assault her sexually. In Genesis 37, both instances involve the production of clothing by others in order to define Joseph's existence and character, or lack thereof. In the case of *Decameron* 2.9, another strategy is at work, since Ambrogiuolo first uses Zinevra's clothing to make the claim that she is a dishonourable woman, but then Zinevra emerges as an active agent in the construction of her own story when she proposes to the servant that he use her clothing to make the claim that she no longer exists.

10 Franca Brambilla Ageno, 'Errori d'autore nel *Decameron?' Studi sul Boccaccio* 8 (1974): 127–36, esp. 129–30. Brambilla Ageno refers us to the article in which she proposed her emendation of the text, that is, in *Giornale storico della letteratura italiana* 131 (1954): 242.

11 See Giovanni Boccaccio, *Decameron*, ed. Vittore Branca (Milan: Mondadori, 1985), 970.

12 Indeed, this might be far more consistent with fourteenth-century norms for the construction of gender identity, given that the prohibitions on female cross-dressing were quite rigid. For an overview of female homosexuality in the medieval and Renaissance period, see Mary-Michelle DeCoste, '*Vano amore*: Representations of Women Desiring Women in Italian Renaissance Literature' (unpub. PhD dissertation, Cornell University, 2000).

13 In 'The Essence of the Triangle, or Taking the Risk of Essentialism Seriously: Feminist Theory in Italy, the U.S., and Britain,' *differences* 1 (1989): 3–58, Teresa de Lauretis lays out the risks of essentialism, while at the same time showing how feminism, in order to remain feminism, must hold to the notion of essential and originary difference. Increasingly, feminist theorists have tried to go beyond the sex/gender distinction and to move us beyond the dilemmas created by a too constructivist position. Luce Irigaray, in *Sexes and Genealogies*, trans. Gillian C. Gill (New York: Columbia University Press, 1993), moves sometimes to use the term 'sex' where Hegel and others have used 'gender,' on the grounds that 'gender in grammar expresses the reality of the two sexes in a very diverse and unequal way' (127n). She states that she uses the word sex 'in regard to male and female persons and not just to male and female genital organs' (128n). Likewise, Luisa Muraro holds to this position in *L'ordine simbolico della madre* (Rome: Editori Riuniti, 1992), 131–2.

Eve Kosofsky Sedgwick, *Epistemology of the Closet* (Berkeley: University of California Press, 1990), offers the alternative terms 'minoritizing' and 'universalizing' as an alternative to 'essentialist/constructivist' that would allow us to 'minimize [our] reliance on any particular account of the origin of sexual preference and identity in individuals' (40–1). Toril Moi, in *What Is a Woman? And Other Essays* (Oxford: Oxford University Press, 1999), relies on a strong and perceptive rereading of Simone de Beauvoir's *The Second Sex* in order to rethink the relation between one's body and one's subjectivity (for this especially important point, see p. 82).

14 Nancy F. Partner makes a similar observation about Heloise's fidelity to her interior self; see her 'No Sex, No Gender,' in Partner, ed., *Studying Medieval Women* (Cambridge, Mass.: Medieval Academy of America, 1993), 117–41.

15 See 'L'educazione del cavaliere,' in Luigi Gianoli, *Il cavallo e l'uomo. Il cavallo nella storia antica, nel medioevo e nel rinascimento. Le scuole, le Olimpiadi, la didattica, il galoppo, il trotto, il polo, la caccia, le razze* (Milan: Longanesi, 1967).

16 Nicola Zingarelli, *Lo Zingarelli 2003: Vocabolario della lingua italiana*, 12th ed. (Bologna: Zanichelli, 2002).

17 Of interest is Aldo Busi's alternate interpretation of the name Sicurano, evident from the title he grants to *Decameron* 2.9: 'Così fan tutte, ma Sicurano no di sicuro.' See Giovanni Boccaccio and Aldo Busi, *Decamerone da un italiano all'altro*, 2 vols. (Milan: Rizzoli, 1990–1).

18 The adjectival forms clearly indicate that we are still to conceive of this character as a woman even though she has 'transformed *her*self into a sea*man*' ('*trasformatasi* in marinar*o*' [2.9.42; my translation; emphasis mine]) and even though she is dressed as a man and recognized as such during a conversation with the Catalan ('Col quale entrat*a* in parole,' '*She* began to speak with him' [2.9.43; my translation; emphasis mine]).

19 Boccaccio, *Decameron*, trans. McWilliam, 175; emphasis mine.

20 Ibid., 154–5.

21 Aldo Busi avoids the troublesome point in this sentence by eliminating it: 'Sicurano comprese subito qual era stata l'origine della rabbia di Bernabò e capì di essere davanti a colui che era la causa di tutto il suo male.' See Boccaccio and Busi, *Decamerone da un italiano all'altro*, 1: 182.

22 Mark Angelos, 'Urban Women, Investment, and the Commercial Revolution of the Middle Ages,' in Linda E. Mitchell, ed., *Women in Medieval Western European Culture* (New York: Garland, 1999), 257–72, esp. 263. According to Angelos, a study of 4000 Genoese *commenda* from 1150 to 1216 showed that women constituted one-quarter of the total number of investors.

23 Ibid., 269.

Chapter 5: Women's Witty Words: Restrictions on Their Use

1 Partly because of these thematic echoes, partly because of the structural symmetries between Day 1 and Day 6, readers have seen these two days as mirror reflections of each other. See Pamela D. Stewart, 'La novella di Madonna Oretta e le due parti del *Decameron*,' *Yearbook of Italian Studies* (1973–5): 27–40, and Cok Van der Woort, 'Convergenze e divaricazioni tra la Prima e la Sesta Giornata del *Decameron*,' *Studi sul Boccaccio* 11 (1979): 207–41.

2 This attention to Florentine associational ties originates in Giovanni Getto, 'Culto della forma e civiltà fiorentina nella sesta giornata,' in *Vita di forme e forme di vita nel 'Decameron*,' 4th rev. ed. (Turin: Petrini, 1986), 140–64, and is continued in David Wallace, 'Sixth Day: Florentine Society and Associational Form,' in *Giovanni Boccaccio: 'Decameron'* (Cambridge: Cambridge University Press, 1993), 67–77.

3 Gian Mario Veneziano, 'La cornice a teatro: VI Giornata,' in Giorgio Bàrberi-Squarotti, ed., *Prospettive sul 'Decameron'* (Turin: Tirrenia, 1989).

4 According to Veneziano, the emphasis on style over thematics in the subject matter of Day 6 leads to a particular emphasis on the mirroring effect set up between the frametale narrative and the novellas of Day 6; see 'La cornice a teatro: VI Giornata,' in *Prospettive sul 'Decameron*.'

5 Readers on the lookout for proto-feminism in the *Decameron* are partial to Madonna Filippa. Thomas G. Bergin singles her out, 'the saucy Filippa of Pisa,' as a 'true spokeswoman of "women's lib"' (see his Introduction to Giovanni Boccaccio's *Decameron*, trans. Mark Musa and Peter Bondanella [New York: Mentor, 1982], xxix).

Victoria Kirkham properly calls these misguided proto-feminist efforts to task, but then seems inclined to assign blame to Madonna Filippa rather than leaving responsibility with readers, where it properly belongs. In *The Sign of Reason in Boccaccio's Fiction*, 127 note, Kirkham writes: 'Filippa is usually admired for clever eloquence by Italianists, and she has even been cited as a pioneer of feminism ("una vera eroina boccacciana", "espressione di cortesia borghese", "una donna moderna") as in *Dieci novelle dal "Decameron" di Giovanni Boccaccio*, trans. and comm. C. Bura and M.A. Morettini, Perugia, Editrice Grafica Perugia, 1980, p. 108.' According to Kirkham, Madonna Filippa 'gets a deserved debunking by a student of canon law,' namely Kenneth Pennington, 'A Note to *Decameron* VI 7: The Wit of Madonna Filippa,' *Speculum* 52 (1977): 902–5.

6 See Barbara Zandrino, 'La luna per lo sole (VII Giornata),' in Giorgio Bàrberi-Squarotti, ed., *Prospettive sul 'Decameron'* (Turin: Tirrenia, 1989),

113–30, and Nicolò Mineo, 'La sesta giornata del *Decameron* o del potere delle donne,' *Rivista europea di letteratura italiana* 3 (1994): 49–68.

7 Zandrino, 'La luna per lo sole (VII Giornata),' 115.

8 See *Decameron* 2.2, 2.5, 2.9, 3.6, 4.5, 4.6, 4.9, and 4.10. There is a single exception: in Panfilo's novella of Alatiel, Antioco, Osbech's servant and the only one of Alatiel's male companions to know her language, falls in love with the young woman (2.7.80).

9 On this hermeneutic figure, see Barbara Spackman, '*Inter musam e ursam moritur*: Folengo and the Gaping "Other" Mouth,' in Marilyn Migiel and Juliana Schiesari, eds., *Refiguring Woman: Perspectives on Gender and the Italian Renaissance* (Ithaca: Cornell University Press, 1991), 19–34, esp. 22–3 and 33–4.

10 Jacques Derrida, *Eperons: Les styles de Nietzsche / Spurs: Nietzsche's Styles*, trans. Barbara Harlow (Chicago: University of Chicago Press, 1979), 97; quoted also by Spackman (see note 9), 23 note.

11 See Giovanni Boccaccio, *Ninfale fiesolano*, ed. Armando Balduino, in vol. 3 of Vittore Branca, ed., *Tutte le opere di Giovanni Boccaccio* 10 vols. in 11 (Milan: Mondadori, 1964–98), octaves 244–5, where Africo rapes the nymph Mensola: 'Per la contesa che facean si desta / tal che prima dormia malinconoso, / e, con superbia rizzando la cresta, / cominciò a picchiar l'uscio furioso; / e tanto dentro vi diè della testa, / ch'egli entrò dentro, non già con riposo, / ma con battaglia grande ed urlamento / e forse che di sangue spargimento.

'Ma poi che messer Mazzone ebbe avuto / Monteficalli, e nel castello entrato, / fu lietamente dentro ricevuto / da que' che prima l'avean contastato;/ma poi che molto si fu dibattuto,/per la terra lasciare in buono stato,/ per pietà lagrimò, e del castello / uscì poi fuor, umìl più ch'un agnello.'

For the English translation, see Giovanni Boccaccio, *The Nymphs of Fiesole*, trans. Joseph Tusiani (Rutherford, NJ: Fairleigh Dickinson University Press, 1971), octaves 244–5: 'Throughout this lively struggle in the pool, / someone who until now had sadly slept / lifted his head with soon-awakened pride, / and started knocking, wrathful, on the door. / With such a rage he pushed his head inside / that not with peace he entered but with war: / indeed, a roaring battle, fierce and loud, / with even, perhaps, the shedding of some blood.

'But when at last Sir Stock had won Black Hill / and stepped into the castle joyously, / the foe that had resisted his advance / welcomed and greeted him with great content. / Finally, having labored long and hard / to leave the conquered post in perfect peace, / he shed a pitying tear, and left the castle / meek as a lamb, and wholly dumb and docile.'

Although there are several passages in the *Corbaccio* in which the spirit offers heavily veiled descriptions of sexual intercourse, the one closest to the statements in the *Decameron* and the *Ninfale fiesolano* is found in *Corbaccio* 230ff. (not 411ff. as Branca's note to the Mondadori edition states): 'sono ottime sensali a fare che messer Mazza rientri in Vallebruna, donde dopo molte lagrime era stato cacciato fuori' ('they are excellent madams and go-betweens for enablng Master Shaft to reenter the Obscure Valley from which he had been chased after many tears'). See Giovanni Boccaccio, *Corbaccio*, ed. Giorgio Padoan, in vol. 5, tome 2 of Vittore Branca, ed., *Tutte le opere di Giovanni Boccaccio*, 10 vols. in 11 (Milan: Mondadori, 1964–98); and for the English translation, Giovanni Boccaccio, *The Corbaccio, or The Labyrinth of Love*, trans. and ed. Anthony K. Cassell, rev. ed. (Binghamton, NY: Medieval and Renaissance Texts and Studies, 1993), 42.

12 If I am right, Elissa's move has a counterpart in modern parliamentary procedure, where it is possible to kill a motion, in effect, by moving to postpone indefinitely. The same result can be achieved by more surreptitious means (ones actually unfaithful to parliamentary procedure), whereby a motion is tabled and then never again brought before the body. See *Robert's Rules of Order, Newly Revised (1990 edition)* (Glenview, Ill.: Scott, Foresman & Co., 1990), especially 'Postpone Indefinitely,' 123–7.

13 Veneziano is the proponent of the argument that Day 6 is unusual in its focus on style rather than thematics; see 'La cornice a teatro: VI Giornata,' 98.

14 Many readers have commented on this play of mirrored reflections. See Getto, 'Culto della forma e civiltà fiorentina nella sesta giornata,' in *Vita di forme e forme di vita nel 'Decameron,'* 140–64, and Franco Fido, 'Architettura,' in Renzo Bragantini and Pier Massimo Forni, eds., *Lessico critico decameroniano* (Turin: Bollati Boringhieri, 1995), 30.

15 Giovanni Getto sees this first witty remark, and the others that follow it, as the 'simbolo riassuntivo di un intero costume, di tutta una visione della vita,' 'a symbol that summarizes an entire code of conduct, a comprehensive vision of life' (*Vita di forme*, 143). For Victoria Kirkham, Madonna Oretta offers an example of the beautiful speech that reveals man's excellence of character; in this, Kirkham likens her to Tito (*Decameron* 10.8) and to the frame narrators themselves (*The Sign of Reason in Boccaccio's Fiction* [Florence: Olschki, 1993], 182–4, 196). According to Mario Baratto, the novella functions, by antiphrasis, to exalt fine narrative technique; portraying the knight as failed narrator, Baratto focuses mainly on Filomena (and Boccaccio behind her) as the expert narrator of the tale, and portrays Madonna Oretta more as ideal audience than as ideal speaker (*Realtà e stile nel 'Decameron,'* 2nd ed. [Rome: Editori Riuniti, 1993], 75–6).

16 David Wallace, who is representative in this regard, sets the story of

Madonna Oretta against the 'counter-exemplum' of Licisca's outburst at the
beginning of Day 6; he does so in order to try to demonstrate that Filomena's story is about gender rather than social class: 'The problem for Oretta
here, if she is to bring about a courteous imposition of silence ("un cortese
impor di silenzio," 4) is not primarily one of social class: she is the man's
social peer, and probably his superior since the historical Oretta Malaspina
was the daughter of a marquis. The problem here is gender. A woman cannot cut short a knight's lengthy and inept narration without cutting at his
exercise of manhood' (*Giovanni Boccaccio: 'Decameron,'* 69).

17 On the superb narrative technique of this passage, which Mario Baratto calls
a 'perfetta traduzione stilistica di una mancanza di stile' (a 'perfect stylistic
translation of a failure of style'), see *Realtà e stile,* 75.

18 Deborah Tannen, 'The Relativity of Linguistic Strategies: Rethinking Power
and Solidarity in Gender and Dominance,' chap. 1 of *Gender and Discourse*
(Oxford: Oxford University Press, 1994), 19–52.

19 Compare Pampinea, who had drawn the distinction between 'women of the
past' [*(le) passate*] and 'modern' women (*le moderne*) (1.10.5).

20 Musa and Bondanella's English translation fails to communicate this important point as it relies on the ungendered 'every one of us.'

21 For this interpretation of the women's group effort, I am indebted to Shira
Goldwyn. Her observation leads me to question why it is that at the end of
Decameron 1.10, Mastro Alberto takes his leave of Madonna Malgherida along
with his companions, who are mentioned for the very first time in the story
only here, as they leave and the novella is about to end: 'Il maestro, levatosi
co' suoi compagni, ringraziò la donna; e con festa da lei preso commiato, si
partì' ('The doctor, rising along with his companions, thanked the lady,
cheerfully took his leave of her, and departed' [1.10.20; my translation;
emphasis mine]). Musa and Bondanella mistranslate this passage, thinking
that the doctor rises 'from the company of the ladies'; evidently, they are
confused by the fact that the doctor's companions appear so late in the story
(see *Decameron,* trans. Musa and Bondanella, 58).

22 Pampinea calls attention to this humiliation of man by playing on the folk
etymology of *homo-humo* ('man-earth'). Madonna Malgherida and her companions mock Mastro Alberto repeatedly, upon observing 'uno *umo,* così
antico d'anni e di senno, inamorato' ('a man so old in years and rich in wisdom fall in love' [1.10.12; 57]).

23 This is the basic premise behind the 'cryptonomic analysis' of Nicolas Abraham and Maria Torok, which allows obstacles to understanding to be con-
verted into readable entities, once they have been reframed within the verbal
situation that they themselves conceal. See Nicolas Abraham and Maria

Torok, *The Wolf Man's Magic Word: A Cryptonomy*, trans. Nicholas Rand, foreword by Jacques Derrida (Minneapolis: University of Minnesota Press, 1986).
As Nicholas Rand notes of this method, 'Cryptonomy is a critical instrument
that permits us to pinpoint areas of silence in works of literature as well as
in the oeuvre of human life, and grant them potential of expression, that is,
the possibility of untying their tongue'; see his 'Translator's Introduction,'
lxvi.

24 It won't be long before we see minor stylistic quirks. In the novella of Nonna
de' Pulci (6.3), repeated internal rhymes (homoteleuton) on *donna, monna,*
and *nonna* make the prose quite choppy. See such phrasings as 'il vescovo
vide una giovane la quale questa pistolenzia presente ci ha tolta *donna,* il cui
nome fu *monna Nonna* de' *Pulci,* cugina di messere Alesso *Rinucci* e cui voi
tutte doveste conoscere' (6.3.8). This stylistic lapse does not undermine the
novella's message. But we would do well to ask ourselves how many such
lapses it would take to do so.

25 Disruptive rhythms and homoteleutons play a major part in the story of
Chichibio (6.4), as Marga Cottino-Jones has shown ('The Hiccuping Rhythm
of Chichibio's Adventure: A Comic Farce,' in *An Anatomy of Boccaccio's Style*
[Naples: Cymba, 1968], 83–96). In this story, of course, the effects of rhythm
and sound are linked to the comic lower-class character.

26 When Chichibio refuses to give her a leg of the crane he is preparing, she
responds, 'In fé di Dio, se tu non la mi dai, tu non avrai mai da me cosa che
ti piaccia' ('I swear to God, if you don't give it to me, you'll never get what
you want from me again!' [6.4.9; 390]).

27 See Pennington, 'A Note to *Decameron* 6.7,' 902–3.

28 See Lynn Marie Laufenberg, 'Women, Crime, and Criminal Law in Fourteenth-century Florence' (unpub. PhD dissertation, Cornell University,
2000). Especially relevant is chapter 3, 'Women and Criminal Cases in the
Court of the Podestà.'

29 On the maxim *Quod omnes tangit,* see Pennington, 'A Note to *Decameron* 6.7,'
903–4.

30 Indeed, if the immediate audience is any indication, views of what is shocking have not changed that much since the first day. Here is the women's
reported reaction to Filostrato's tale: 'La novella da Filostrato raccontata
prima con un poco di vergogna punse li cuori delle donne ascoltanti, e con
onesto rossore ne' lor visi apparito ne dieder segno; e poi, l'una l'altra
guardando, appena dal ridere potendosi abstenere, soghignando quella
ascoltarono' ('As the ladies were listening to the story Filostrato was telling,
at first their hearts were touched by a slight sense of shame, made evident by
a blush of modesty which appeared on their cheeks, but then, starting to

exchange glances with each other, they could hardly keep themselves from laughing, as they listened to the rest of the tale with half-concealed smiles' [6.8.2; 398]). As the Italian text shows, they repeat almost exactly their reaction to the very first novella that treated really shocking subject matter, Dioneo's tale of the monk and the abbot (1.4): 'La novella da Dioneo raccontata prima con un poco di vergogna punse i cuori delle donne ascoltanti e con onesto rossore nel loro viso apparito ne diede segno; e poi quella, l'una l'altra guardando, appena del rider potendosi abstenere, soghignando ascoltarono' ('At first, the story told by Dioneo pricked the hearts of the ladies who were listening with a bit of embarrassment, which was made evident by the modest blushes on their faces; but then, as they looked at each other, they could hardly keep from laughing, and they smiled as they listened' [1.5.2; 42]).

31 The novella exercises such a powerful fascination, however, that it is the unusual reader who now recognizes that the events of this story could take place only in a fantastic and imaginary world. In *Narrative Intellection in the 'Decameron'* (Iowa City: University of Iowa Press, 1975), Stavros Deligiorgis wrote that '[n]either the woman's defense before the judge nor the change in the law books that comes as a result of her defense are conceivable in a society other than the one that the narrator sets up' (141). Several years later, Pennington asserted, 'All of Boccaccio's critics have seen that her arguments would never have convinced the real podestà of Prato. Boccaccio never intended that they should' ('A Note to *Decameron* 6.7,' 905). But such comments on the contrived aspects of the novella appear to be ever rarer. One of the very few in recent years is from Francesco Bruni, who states, 'Qui Boccaccio mima le procedure della vita giudiziaria e legislativa del Comune, ma proiettandole su uno spazio fantastico.' 'Here Boccaccio reproduces the judicial and legislative procedures of the Comune, but projects them onto an imaginary, fantastic space' (*Boccaccio: L'invenzione della letteratura mezzana* [Bologna: Il Mulino, 1990], 264; my translation).

Chapter 6: Men, Women, and Figurative Language in the *Decameron*

1 Nor should we forget Filippo Balducci's renaming of women as geese that peck in a way his son would not understand (4.Introduction) and the Author's collection of sexually charged terms in the Conclusion to the *Decameron*.

2 In *Decameron* 3.6, Fiammetta has Catella use a barrage of mixed metaphors when she berates the man she believes to be her husband for his sexual misdeeds: "ma lodato sia Idio, che il tuo campo, non l'altrui, hai lavorato, come

tu ti credevi. Non maraviglia che stanotte tu non mi ti appressasti! tu aspet-
tavi di scaricare le some altrove e volevi giugnere molto fresco cavaliere alla
battaglia: ma lodato sia Idio e il mio avvedimento, l'acqua è pur corsa alla
ingiù come ella doveva!' ('But, praise be to God, it was your own field you
were plowing and not someone else's, as you thought! No wonder you didn't
come near me last night! You were waiting to unload yourself somewhere
else, and you wanted to arrive fresh as a knight entering the battlefield; but
thank God and my wits that the water ended up flowing in the right direction!' [3.6.37; 199–200]). Catella's figurative language is the imprint of emotional excess, rendered also in the length of her speech, her threats of
violence, and her repeated invocations of God.

3 In *Decameron* 4.2, Pampinea moves between the language of riding and the
language of flying in order to describe Frate Alberto's exploits with women.
Having prepared the listener for Frate Alberto's imminent transformation
into the Angel Gabriel, she goes on to note that, 'pensando che cavaliere, e
non agnolo, esser gli convenia la notte, con confetti e altre buone cose
s'incominciò a confortare, acciò che di leggiere non fosse da caval gittato'
('thinking more about getting in the saddle than of being an angel that
evening, [he] began to fortify himself with confections and other delicacies
so that he would not easily be thrown from his horse' [4.2.30; 263]). Later,
when he meets with Madonna Lisetta, Pampinea tells us that 'molte volte la
notte volò senza ali' ('He flew many times that night without his wings'
[4.2.32; 264]). Once again, the figurative language serves principally as an
indication of the character's miscalculation, especially since the impulse to
mix metaphors is very strong. Although he appears to be a successful in his
transformation as knight and angel, for he excels both at riding and flying
with Madonna Lisetta, his shortcomings become painfully clear when he
really needs to escape Madonna Lisetta's brothers-in-law, who are in angry
pursuit of him.

4 Giorgio Bàrberi-Squarotti, 'L'orazione di Alatiel,' in *Il potere della parola: Studi
sul 'Decameron'* (Naples: Federico & Ardia, 1989), esp. 91–6.

5 Millicent Marcus, 'Tragedy as Trespass: The Tale of Tancredi and Ghismonda (IV, 1),' chap. 3 of *An Allegory of Form: Literary Self-consciousness in the
'Decameron'* (Saratoga, Calif.: Anma Libri, 1979), 44–63.

6 Ibid., 56.

7 Ibid., 58.

8 As Mario Baratto notes, 'La V, 4 resta singolare, si potrebbe dire unica, nel
Decameron, per il tema che la occupa interamente e ne guida lo stile narra-
tivo' ('Novella 5.4 remains exceptional – indeed, one of a kind – in the
Decameron on account of the theme that occupies it entirely and directs its

narrative style.' *Realtà e stile nel 'Decameron,'* 2nd ed. [Rome: Editori Riuniti, 1993], 257).

9 See the *Vida* of Guilhem de Cabestanh, the *Roman du Chatelain de Couci*, and Marie de France's 'Laüstic.'

10 Comparing *Decameron* 5.4 with 4.1, Marcus notes, 'Though Caterina is also an only child born in her father's dotage, the active presence of the mother in the story defuses the incestuous possibilities which govern Ghismonda's fate' (*An Allegory of Form*, 56).

11 See Thomas Alan Shippey, 'Listening to the Nightingale,' *Comparative Literature* 22 (1970): 51.

12 Indeed, as Shippey has argued, the effectiveness of *Decameron* 5.4 depends on the reader noticing that Caterina's use of the courtly phrase 'listening to the nightingale' (a traditional representation of the longing of the frustrated lover) is incongruent with her situation as a lover who achieves sexual fulfilment (ibid., 52 note).

Louise O. Vasvari, in *'L'usignuolo in gabbia*: Popular Tradition and Pornographic Parody in the *Decameron,' Forum Italicum* 28:2 (1994): 224–51, argues, on the basis of what she calls 'pornithology,' that the reader should equate the nightingale with the male genitalia because birds are in general an eroticized metaphor in Italian and Latin. But it seems revealing that Vasvari can cite no instances aside from *Decameron* 5.4 in which the nightingale per se (as opposed to the cock, the blackbird, or the sparrow, for example) is used as a metaphor for the penis.

13 Giovanni Boccaccio, *Decameron*, trans. Guido Waldman (Oxford: Oxford University Press, 1993), 342.

14 Vittore Branca points out in the notes to his edition of the *Decameron* that Ricciardo's earlier impassioned plea to Caterina is articulated as a sequence of four hendecasyllables; see also *Boccaccio medievale e nuovi studi sul 'Decameron,'* 7th ed. (Florence: Sansoni: 1990), 70.

15 Italian text and English translation are taken from Dante Alighieri, *The Divine Comedy*, trans., with commentary, Charles S. Singleton, 6 vols. (Princeton: Princeton University Press, 1977).

16 It is also possible that since the command to 'rest' is a coded invitation to engage in further sexual activity, putting this sentence in the mouth of 'both parents' shields us from the shock value that the statement would have if it were put into the mouth of a woman.

17 In the opening section of his novella, Filostrato even leads his listener to believe that perhaps the main source of interest (even erotic interest) might be between the men. Introducing Ricciardo, Filostrato says, 'Ora usava molto nella casa di messer Lizio e molto con lui si riteneva' ('Now there

often came to the house of Messer Lizio, who spent considerable time with him' [5.4.6; my translation]), only later to reveal that the subject of this sentence, 'un giovane bello e fresco della persona' ('a handsome and winning young man' [5.4.6; my translation]) is a match for the beautiful and attractive daughter of Messer Lizio.

18 Waldman explains: 'Readers today, whatever their susceptibilities, usually take it amiss if a publisher or reviewer gives away the tale's ending before they have started reading it. I have therefore in certain cases rewritten the story's *heading* to preserve the element of surprise' (Boccaccio, *Decameron*, trans. Waldman, xxxiii).

19 Ibid., 340.

20 See Roberto Fedi, 'Il "regno" di Filostrato: Natura e struttura della Giornata IV del *Decameron*,' *MLN* 102 (1987): 43.

21 Nicolas Abraham and Maria Torok, *The Wolf Man's Magic Word: A Cryptonomy*, trans. Nicholas Rand, foreword by Jacques Derrida (Minneapolis: University of Minnesota Press, 1986).

22 Sigmund Freud, 'From the History of an Infantile Neurosis (1918 [1914]),' in *The Standard Edition of the Complete Psychological Works*, trans. James Strachey, 24 vols. (London: Hogarth Press, 1966–74), 17: 1–123.

23 See Rand, 'Translator's Introduction' to *The Wolf Man's Magic Word*, lviii. In general, Rand identifies the difference between the two readings of the Wolf Man as follows: Freud's theory of the primal scene or fantasy allowed for a coherently organized narrative that does not fully grasp the 'unreadability' of the Wolf Man; Abraham and Torok's theory provides insight into the Wolf Man's 'life poem' because they are able to see that the Wolf Man's dreams and symptoms are organized around mutually exclusive assertions.

24 Ibid., lix.

25 See Ovid, *Metamorphoses* 6.668 where however, we are never told what birds Procne and Philomela are turned into. In the Latin tradition (where there seemed to be confusion about which sister was which bird), Procne and Philomela come to refer to the swallow (*hirundo*) and the nightingale (*luscinia, lusciniola*) respectively.

26 Only on Days 4 and 5 do we see how important the nightingale, as a figure with an encrypted message, has become; but in retrospect, one suspects that as early as Day 2 Filostrato may have anticipated the importance he will ascribe to names on Day 4 (especially *Guiglielmo Rossiglione* and *Guiglielmo Guardastagno*, when he notes that the encounter between the lady and Rinaldo d'Asti takes place at *Castel Guiglielmo* (2.2.1, 2.2.13, 2.2.14, 2.2.15).

27 Giulio Savelli, 'Riso,' in Renzo Bragantini and Pier Massimo Forni, eds, *Lessico critico decameroniano* (Turin: Bollati Boringhieri, 1995), 344.

28 There is some equivocation about the responses to the women's stories because it is not absolutely clear whether the women laugh at Neifile's story of Cecco (9.4). At the beginning of 9.5, the Author reports, 'senza troppo riderne o parlarne passatasene la brigata' ('the group disposed of it without much laughter or comment' [9.5.2; 574]).

29 Giovanni Boccaccio, *The Decameron*, trans. Mark Musa and Peter Bondanella (New York: Mentor, 1982), 599.

30 Giovanni Boccaccio, *Decameron*, trans. G.H. McWilliam, 2nd rev. ed. (New York: Penguin Books, 1995), 698.

31 Giovanni Boccaccio, *Decameron*, trans. Waldman, 595.

32 Giovanni Boccaccio, *The Decameron*, trans. John Payne, with new illustrations by Steele Savage (New York: Blue Ribbon Books, 1931), 460.

33 Emma Grimaldi comments on this surprising carnal manifestation, which simply confirms the expectations some readers already have (and which in turn leads to other surprising developments, such as compar Pietro's instinctual interruption and his subsequent realization of what he has wrought by interrupting Donno Gianni). See Grimaldi, *Il privilegio di Dioneo: L'eccezione e la regola nel sistema 'Decameron'* (Naples: Edizioni Scientifiche Italiane, 1987), 344–5.

34 Bàrberi-Squarotti, *Il potere della parola*, 174–92 and Baratto, *Realtà e stile nel 'Decameron,'* 87–8 and 360–3.

35 Bàrberi-Squarotti, *Il potere della parola*, 178–9. The English translation is mine.

Chapter 7: Domestic Violence in the *Decameron*

1 The force of this misperception is widely acknowledged by scholars and researchers who study domestic violence; for one such critique, see Richard J. Gelles and Murray A. Straus, *Intimate Violence* (New York: Simon & Schuster, 1988), chap. 2, 'People Other Than Us: Public Perceptions of Family Violence.'

2 We might also include Arriguccio's beating of a woman he believes to be his wife in *Decameron* 7.8; but because the woman is a servant whom the wife has substituted for herself, readers seem not to register this episode as domestic violence.

3 Readers might well ask why I speak here of the scholar's cruelty toward the widow, and do not mention in the same breath the widow's cruelty toward the scholar, which, in his mind at least, justifies his cruel treatment of her. It is not insignificant to me that the novella of the scholar and the widow, which details cruelty on both their parts, has been widely considered the most misogynistic novella of the *Decameron*, garnering far more attention

than novellas in which women are openly beaten (*Decameron* 7.8, 8.3, 9.9). What is curious, and worthy of note here and elsewhere, is that women's violence against men proves not to have the same narratological and ideological weight as men's violence against women. I grant, however, that the issue of women's violence against men in the *Decameron* would merit a lengthier discussion.

4 See Nancy J. Vickers, 'Diana Described: Scattered Woman and Scattered Rhyme,' in Elizabeth Abel, ed., *Writing and Sexual Difference* (Chicago: University of Chicago Press, 1982), 94–109; Stephanie H Jed, *Chaste Thinking: The Rape of Lucretia and the Birth of Humanism* (Bloomington: Indiana University Press, 1989); Ann Rosalind Jones, 'New Songs for the Swallow: Ovid's Philomela in Tullia D'Aragona and Gaspara Stampa,' in Marilyn Migiel and Juliana Schiesari, eds, *Refiguring Woman: Perspectives on Gender and the Italian Renaissance* (Ithaca: Cornell University Press, 1991), 263–77; Barbara Zecchi, 'Rape,' in Rinaldina Russell, ed., *The Feminist Encyclopedia of Italian Literature* (Westport, Conn.: Greenwood Press, 1997), 280–3.

There is rather more attention to discourses of domestic violence in the study of medieval and Renaissance English texts, on account of the fact that in both Chaucer and Shakespeare we find frank references and representations of such violence (cf. Wife of Bath's Prologue and Tale, *The Taming of the Shrew, Othello*). But rape is the principal figure for violence against women in the study of medieval and early-modern French scholarship. See Carla Freccero, 'Rape's Disfiguring Figure: Marguerite de Navarre's *Heptameron*, Day 1: 10,' in Lynn A. Higgins and Brenda R. Silver, eds, *Rape and Representation* (New York: Columbia University Press, 1991), 227–47; Kathryn Gravdal, *Ravishing Maidens: Writing Rape in Medieval French Literature and Law* (Philadelphia: University of Pennsylvania Press, 1991); and Patricia Francis Cholakian, *Rape and Writing in the 'Heptaméron' of Marguerite de Navarre* (Carbondale: Southern Illinois University Press, 1991).

In general, sexual violence has been the filter through which we see violence against women in our study of the classical, medieval, and early-modern worlds. Tellingly, the 5-volume *A History of Women in the West*, under the general editorship of Georges Duby and Michelle Perrot (Cambridge, Mass.: Harvard University Press, 1992–4), treats rape throughout the centuries, but addresses the issue of domestic violence only in the final volume, *Toward a Cultural Identity in the Twentieth Century*, ed. Françoise Thébaud.

5 To be sure, Ser Cepparello dies in the very first story of the First Day, but his is an account of unexpected salvation: by means of a false confession, he gains sainthood. In the first story of Day 2, Martellino is beaten by the crowd, and threatened with torture on the rack, but he is soon liberated by a power-

ful lord. When people begin to die – an inevitability in storytelling that deals with fortune and misfortune – it tends to be only the minor characters and the villains who merit death. The highway robbers in *Decameron* 2.2 are hanged, but they are, after all, guilty of assault on the novella's hero, Rinaldo d'Asti; likewise, Ambrogiuolo, guilty of fraud perpetrated against the heroine Zinevra in *Decameron* 2.9, is sentenced to an ugly punishment and death. Various men fall victim to violence in 2.6 and 2.7 (the stories of Beritola and Alatiel), but like other men who have died violent deaths on Day 2, they are characters to whom we have relatively little attachment.

6 In *Decameron* 1.9, a woman of Gascony is raped as she travels to the Holy Land, but we are told nothing more about her rape experience; the story focuses not on her rape, but on her struggle to bring her predicament before the cowardly king of Cyprus. And when Zinevra is directly threatened with death in *Decameron* 2.9, the threat quickly dissolves; she pleas for mercy and is soon released because the servant 'was by no means eager to kill her' ('malvolientieri l'uccidea' [2.9.41; 147]).

7 I have explored this 'backlash' in Day 8 of the *Decameron* in my essay 'The Untidy Business of Gender Studies: Or, Why It's Almost Useless to Ask if the *Decameron* Is Feminist,' in F. Regina Psaki and Thomas C. Stillinger, eds, *Boccaccio and Feminist Criticism*, forthcoming in the Annali d'Italianistica book series, 'Studi e testi.'

8 Shirley Allen believes that the ending to this story is so unsatisfactory that Boccaccio must want us to read it ironically; see Shirley S. Allen, 'The Griselda Tale and the Portrayal of Women in the *Decameron*,' *Philological Quarterly* 56 (1977): 1–13, esp. 9. Allen, like Millicent Marcus, is of the camp that sees 'misogynists' as 'misreaders'; see Marcus's 'Misogyny as Misreading: A Gloss on *Decameron* VIII, 7,' *Stanford Italian Review* 4 (1984): 23–40. But this mode of reading has hardly lain the question of textual misogyny to rest. Mihoko Suzuki, for example, protests that readers of the *Decameron* have been far too blind to its misogyny, and that this misogyny continues to be reproduced on the grounds that it is 'merely' a literary trope; see 'Gender, Power, and the Female Reader: Boccaccio's *Decameron* and Marguerite de Navarre's *Heptameron*,' *Comparative Literature Studies* 30 (1993): 231–52. I am sympathetic to both of these intellectual positions: I think that misogyny can be exposed as misreading; but I also think it is a mistake to claim that misogynist discourse is so ironic (or so allegorical or so figurative or so textual) that it cancels itself out entirely. It does not exist within an exclusively textual context. To allow misogyny to exist as a narrative alongside any other, and of equal value to others, is a political mistake and ethically wrong.

9 See, e.g., the pages dedicated to Marie de France, 'The Man Who Had a

Quarrelsome Wife,' in *Fabliaux: Ribald Tales from the Old French*, trans. Robert Hellman and Richard O'Gorman (New York: Thomas Y. Crowell, 1965), 97–9.

10 Irene Eibenstein-Alvisi brought this to my attention.

11 See Susan S. Lanser, 'Toward a Feminist Narratology,' in Robin R. Warhol and Diane Price Herndl, eds, *Feminisms: An Anthology of Literary Theory and Criticism* (New Brunswick, NJ: Rutgers University Press, 1991), 610–29, esp. 617. Lanser's essay first appeared in *Style* 20:3 (1986): 341–63.

12 As Umberto Cosmo shows in his essay on *Paradiso* 13, Dante, in the Heaven of the Wise, lauds not only the love and the doctrinal wisdom of Saints Francis and Dominic, but also the prudent judgment of a king; see 'La prudenza regale,' in Bruno Maier, ed., *L'ultima ascesa: Introduzione alla lettura del 'Paradiso,'* 2nd ed. (1965; reprt. Florence: La Nuova Italia, 1968).

13 The Italian text is from Dante Alighieri, *The Divine Comedy*, trans., with commentary, Charles S. Singleton, 6 vols. (Princeton, NJ: Princeton University Press, 1977). The English translation is my own.

14 The Latin text (in a version closer to the one known by Dante and his contemporaries) is from Robert Weber et al., eds, *Biblia sacra iuxta vulgatam versionem*, 2 vols. (Stuttgart: Württembergische Bibelanstalt, 1969). The English translation is mine.

15 There can be no doubt that Boccaccio knew the biblical passage; and he would almost certainly have known the passage from Dante's *Paradiso*, which already links Solomon with practical wisdom (and Melissus with the lack of it). According to G.H. McWilliam, Boccaccio may have chosen Melisso's name in order to try to convey that the story took place in a distant past; I would say that Melisso's name is meant to trigger a memory of the Dantesque passage; see McWilliam's note to *Decameron* 9.9 in Giovanni Boccaccio, *The Decameron*, trans. G.H. McWilliam, 2nd rev. ed. (New York: Penguin Books, 1995).

16 By this I do not mean to suggest that it is permissible to beat animals. As Carol Adams has noted, 'In a patriarchy, animal victims, too, become feminized. A hierarchy in which men have power over women and humans have power over animals is actually more appropriately understood as a hierarchy in which men have power over women, (feminized) men, and (feminized) animals ... Recognizing harm to animals as interconnected to controlling behavior by violent men is one aspect of recognizing the interrelatedness of all violence in a gender hierarchical world.' See Carol J. Adams, 'Woman-battering and Harm to Animals,' in Carol J. Adams and Josephine Donovan, eds, *Animals and Women: Feminist Theoretical Explorations* (Durham: Duke University Press, 1995), 80.

17 I draw the terms 'offensive rhetoric' and 'defensive rhetoric' from Jonathan
    Potter, *Representing Reality: Discourse, Rhetoric and Social Construction* (London:
    Sage, 1996).
18 On the moral or tropological sense, see Henri de Lubac, *Exégèse médiévale*,
    3 vols. (1959; reprt. Paris: Aubier, 1993), vol. 2, chap. 9, 'La Tropologie
    mystique.'

Conclusion

1 My phrasing here is intended to recall the decisive contribution of Joan
   Wallach Scott, 'Gender: A Useful Category of Historical Analysis,' chap. 2 of
   Gender and the Politics of History (New York: Columbia University Press, 1988),
   28–50.
2 Franco Fido, *Il regime delle simmetrie imperfette: Studi sul 'Decameron'* (Milan:
   Franco Angeli, 1988), 16.
3 According to Franco Fido, all the modern scholars of Boccaccio's *Decameron*
   have confronted the problem of a unified reading of the work (*Il regime delle
   simmetrie imperfette*, 14 note).
4 All these difficulties, risks, and obstacles are, I would say – in chorus with
   Adriana Cavarero – the result of a reading response that is gendered female.
   Cavarero points out that the response gendered female has, however,
   immense advantages, since it is far less likely to collapse individual difference
   into a universal notion of 'Man.' See her *Tu che mi guardi, tu che mi racconti:
   Filosofia della narrazione*, 4th ed. (Milan: Feltrinelli, 2001), 78.
5 The schema is Vittore Branca's; see *Boccaccio medievale e nuovi studi sul
   'Decameron,'* 7th ed. (Florence: Sansoni, 1990), 18 and 96. It is taken up also
   by Thomas G. Bergin, who provides some qualifications: 'So it can be
   claimed that from the arrogant and unprincipled sinner we have moved up
   the Jacob's ladder of the hundred tales to the humble and saintly peasant
   girl, from the depiction of an utterly unprincipled man to a uniquely perfect
   woman. It is an appealing figure, although the intermediate rungs of the ladder are not immediately perceptible – and both sinner and saint are open to
   contradictory interpretations' (*Boccaccio* [New York: Viking Press, 1981],
   324–5).
6 For useful caveats about oppositional differences between male and female,
   see Joan Scott, 'Gender: A Useful Category of Historical Analysis,' in *Gender
   and the Politics of History*, 39–41. Careful to note that 'masculine and feminine
   are not inherent characteristics but subjective (or fictional) constructs' (39),
   Scott is particularly concerned to critique those thinkers who tend to conceive of the male/female binary opposition as fixed and ahistorical (39–41).

7 Giorgio Padoan, 'Mondo aristocratico e mondo comunale nell'ideologia e nell'arte di Giovanni Boccaccio,' in *Il Boccaccio: Le Muse, il Parnaso e l'Arno* (Florence: Olschki, 1978), 63: 'Il Boccaccio non ha idee politiche precise. Egli non elabora alcun principio proprio, ma piuttosto riflette condizioni che derivano da esperienze autobiografiche e, ancor più, dalla situazione sociale in cui vive' ('Boccaccio has no specific political ideas. He does not articulate any principles of his own; rather he reflects conditions that derive from autobiographical experiences and, even more, from the social situation in which he lives' [translation mine]). He goes on to assert that, to the extent one is able to talk about a 'message' of the author, it should be seen as a message regarding the exaltation of Love. As for woman, according to Padoan, she is able to affirm her being and her freedom within this love that often transgresses social conventions (72); and furthermore, as Padoan sees it, the author's favourable treatment of women who betray their consorts stands as proof of his openness toward the world of women (72).

8 David Wallace's *Giovanni Boccaccio: 'Decameron'* (Cambridge: Cambridge University Press, 1993) offers many such valuable insights; his book therefore stands as a noteworthy contribution, even though many of the readings in it remain somewhat sketchy.

9 The view of Decameronian storytelling as marginal had its heyday in the 1970s when readers, particularly in Anglo-American contexts, sought to emphasize textualist approaches to the *Decameron*; unfortunately, these readings had the drawback that they often divorced the rhetoric of the *Decameron* from any sustained consideration of social reality. One of the main voices in this trend was Giuseppe Mazzotta, *The World at Play in Boccaccio's 'Decameron'* (Princeton: Princeton University Press, 1986), particularly chap. 2, 'The Marginality of Literature.'

10 Giorgio Padoan, author of the seminal contribution on 'Mondo aristocratico e mondo comunale nell'ideologia e nell'arte di Giovanni Boccaccio,' implicitly points toward some of the complexities. According to Padoan, although Boccaccio's main allegiance is to the aristocratic world of two generations before – a world often described with the adjectives 'cortese,' 'cavalleresco,' 'liberale,' and 'onesto' (courteous, knightly, generous, and honourable) – he refuses to condemn the bourgeois and popular world that is characterized by trickery, adultery, and, above all, carnal love (see pp. 63–4). And yet, what one would want to understand more fully is this: How is allegiance to the aristocracy demonstrated? Is lack of condemnation on a par with allegiance? What place do condemnations of problematic behaviour – from representatives of various classes – have in this scheme of things?

11 Parts of my book – most notably my reading of the novellas of Madonna

Zinevra (2.9) in chapter 4 and of Madonna Filippa (6.7) in chapter 5 – bring this issue to light, but the topic of actual and possible worlds in the *Decameron* would merit a much more extensive study.

12 To echo Adriana Cavarero who echoes Hannah Arendt, 'the world is full of stories that await telling.' See Cavarero, *Tu che mi guardi, tu che mi racconti*, chap. 3, 'Il mondo è pieno di storie che aspettano solo di essere raccontate.'

Works Cited

Abraham, Nicolas, and Maria Torok. *The Wolf Man's Magic Word: A Cryptonomy.* Trans. Nicholas Rand. Foreword by Jacques Derrida. Minneapolis: University of Minnesota Press, 1986.

Adams, Carol J. 'Woman-battering and Harm to Animals.' In Carol J. Adams and Josephine Donovan, eds, *Animals and Women: Feminist Theoretical Explorations,* 55–84. Durham: Duke University Press, 1995.

Alighieri, Dante. *The Divine Comedy.* Trans., with commentary, Charles S. Singleton. 6 vols. Princeton: Princeton University Press, 1977.

Allen, Shirley S. 'The Griselda Tale and the Portrayal of Women in the *Decameron.*' *Philological Quarterly* 56 (1977): 1–13.

Almansi, Guido. *Il ciclo della scommessa: Dal 'Decameron' al 'Cymbeline' di Shakespeare.* Rome: Bulzoni, 1976.

– 'Lettura della novella di Bernabò e Zinevra.' *Studi sul Boccaccio* 7 (1973): 125–40.

– 'Lettura della quarta novella del *Decameron.*' *Strumenti critici* 4 (1970): 308–17. Republished in *L'estetica dell'osceno,* 131–42. Turin: Einaudi, 1974.

– *The Writer as Liar: Narrative Technique in the 'Decameron.*' London: Routledge and Kegan Paul, 1975.

Angelos, Mark. 'Urban Women, Investment, and the Commercial Revolution of the Middle Ages.' In Linda E. Mitchell, ed., *Women in Medieval Western European Culture,* 257–72. New York: Garland, 1999.

Austin, J.L. *How to Do Things with Words.* Ed. J.O. Urmson and Marina Sbisà. 2nd ed. 1975; reprt. Cambridge, Mass.: Harvard University Press, 1997.

Baratto, Mario. *Realtà e stile nel 'Decameron.*' 2nd ed. Rome: Editori Riuniti, 1993.

Bàrberi-Squarotti, Giorgio. *Il potere della parola: Studi sul 'Decameron.*' Naples: Federico & Ardia, 1989.

Bardi, Monica. 'Il volto enigmatico della fortuna: II Giornata.' In Giorgio Bàrberi-Squarotti, ed., *Prospettive sul 'Decameron,'* 25–38. Turin: Tirrenia, 1989.

Barolini, Teodolinda. '"Le parole son femmine e i fatti sono maschi": Toward a Sexual Poetics of the *Decameron* (*Decameron* II 10).' *Studi sul Boccaccio* 21 (1993): 175–97.

Bergin, Thomas G. *Boccaccio.* New York: Viking Press, 1981.

Bernardo, Aldo S. 'The Plague as Key to Meaning in Boccaccio's *Decameron.*' In Daniel Williman, ed., *The Black Death: The Impact of the Fourteenth-Century Plague*, 39–64. Binghamton, NY: Medieval and Renaissance Texts and Studies, 1982.

Bloch, R. Howard. *Medieval Misogyny and the Invention of Western Romantic Love.* Chicago: University of Chicago Press, 1991.

– *The Scandal of the Fabliaux.* Chicago: University of Chicago Press, 1986.

Boccaccio, Giovanni. *Corbaccio.* Ed. Giorgio Padoan. In Vittore Branca, ed., *Tutte le opere di Giovanni Boccaccio.* 10 vols. in 11. Milan: Mondadori, 1964–98. Vol. 5, tome 2.

– *The Corbaccio, or The Labyrinth of Love.* Trans. and ed. Anthony K. Cassell. Rev. ed. Binghamton, NY: Medieval and Renaissance Texts and Studies, 1993.

– *Decameron.* Ed. Vittore Branca. Milan: Mondadori, 1985.

– *The Decameron.* Trans. John Payne. With new illustrations by Steele Savage. New York: Blue Ribbon Books, 1931.

– *The Decameron.* Trans. Mark Musa and Peter Bondanella. New York: Mentor, 1982.

– *Decameron.* Trans. Guido Waldman. Oxford: Oxford University Press, 1993.

– *Decameron.* Trans. G.H. McWilliam. 2nd rev. ed. New York: Penguin Books, 1995.

– *Ninfale fiesolano.* Ed. Armando Balduino. In Vittore Branca, ed., *Tutte le opere di Giovanni Boccaccio.* 10 vols. in 11. Milan: Mondadori, 1964–98. Vol. 3.

– *The Nymphs of Fiesole.* Trans. Joseph Tusiani. Rutherford, NJ: Fairleigh Dickinson University Press, 1971.

Boccaccio, Giovanni, and Aldo Busi. *Decamerone da un italiano all'altro.* 2 vols. Milan: Rizzoli, 1990–1.

Boccaccio and Feminist Criticism. Ed. F. Regina Psaki and Thomas C. Stillinger. Forthcoming.

'Boivin de Provins.' In *The French Fabliau: B.N. MS. 837.* Ed. and trans. Raymond Eichmann and John DuVal. 2 vols. New York: Garland, 1984–5. Vol. 1: 62–79.

Booth, Wayne C. *The Rhetoric of Fiction.* Chicago: University of Chicago Press, 1961.

Brambilla Ageno, Franca. 'Errori d'autore nel *Decameron*?' *Studi sul Boccaccio* 8 (1974): 127–36.

Branca, Vittore. *Boccaccio medievale e nuovi studi sul 'Decameron.'* 7th ed. Florence: Sansoni, 1990.

– 'Isolate dal femminismo.' In *Il Sole – 24 ore,* 17 November 1996.

Brundage, James A. *Law, Sex, and Christian Society in Medieval Europe.* Chicago: University of Chicago Press, 1987.

Bruni, Francesco. *Boccaccio: L'invenzione della letteratura mezzana.* Bologna: Il Mulino, 1990.

Butler, Judith. *Exciteable Speech: A Politics of the Performative.* New York: Routledge, 1997.

Cavarero, Adriana. 'Per una teoria della differenza sessuale.' In *Diotima: Il pensiero della differenza sessuale,* 41–79. Milan: La Tartaruga, 1987.

– *Tu che mi guardi, tu che mi racconti: Filosofia della narrazione.* 4th ed. Milan: Feltrinelli, 2001.

Cerreta, Florindo. 'La novella di Andreuccio: Problemi di unità e d'interpretazione.' *Italica* 47 (1970): 255–64.

Cestaro, Gary. 'Rinaldo d'Asti: Drama of the Signifié.' *Carte italiane* 7 (1985–6): 14–27.

Cholakian, Patricia Francis. *Rape and Writing in the 'Heptaméron' of Marguerite de Navarre.* Carbondale: Southern Illinois University Press, 1991.

Cole, Howard C. 'Dramatic Interplay in the *Decameron*: Boccaccio, Neifile, and Giletta di Nerbona.' *MLN* 90 (1975): 38–57.

Concordanze del 'Decameron.' Ed. Alfredo Barbina. 2 vols. Florence: Giunti, 1969.

Cosmo, Umberto. *L'ultima ascesa: Introduzione alla lettura del 'Paradiso.'* 2nd ed. Ed. Bruno Maier. 1965; repr. Florence: La Nuova Italia, 1968.

Cottino-Jones, Marga. *An Anatomy of Boccaccio's Style.* Naples: Cymba, 1968.

– *Order from Chaos: Social and Aesthetic Harmonies in Boccaccio's 'Decameron.'* Washington: University Press of America, 1982.

David, Michel. 'Boccaccio pornoscopo?' In *Medioevo e Rinascimento veneto. Con altri studi in onore di Lino Lazzarini.* 2 vols. Padua: Antenore, 1979. Vol. 1: 215–42.

DeCoste, Mary-Michelle. '*Vano amore*: Representations of Women Desiring Women in Italian Renaissance Literature.' Unpub. PhD dissertation, Cornell University, 2000.

de Lauretis, Teresa. *Alice doesn't: Feminism, Semiotics, Cinema.* Bloomington: Indiana University Press, 1984.

– 'The Essence of the Triangle, or Taking the Risk of Essentialism Seriously: Feminist Theory in Italy, the U.S., and Britain.' *differences* 1 (1989): 3–58.

Deligiorgis, Stavros. *Narrative Intellection in the 'Decameron.'* Iowa City: University of Iowa Press, 1975.

de Lubac, Henri. *Exégèse médiévale: Les quatre sens de l'écriture.* 3 vols. 1959; reprt. Paris: Aubier, 1993.

De Michelis, Cesare. *Contraddizioni nel 'Decameron.'* Milan: Guanda, 1983.

Derrida, Jacques. *Eperons: Les styles de Nietzsche / Spurs: Nietzsche's Styles.* Trans. Barbara Harlow. Chicago: University of Chicago Press, 1979.

Di Francia, Letterio. 'La IV novella del *Decameron* e le sue fonti.' In *A Vittorio Cian, i suoi scolari dell'Università di Pisa,* 63–9. Pisa: Mariotti, 1909.

Donaggio, Monica. 'Il travestimento nel *Decameron*: Orizzonti e limiti di una rigenerazione.' *Studi sul Boccaccio* 17 (1988): 203–14.

Doob, Penelope. *Nebuchadnezzar's Children: Conventions of Madness in Middle English Literature.* New Haven: Yale University Press, 1974.

Encyclopedia Britannica. Available on the World Wide Web at www.britannica.com.

'L'evesque qui benei le con.' In Willem Noomen, ed., *Nouveau recueil complet des fabliaux (NRCF).* 10 vols. Assen: Van Gorcum, 1983–98. Vol. 6: 193–205.

Fabliaux: Ribald Tales from the Old French. Trans. Robert Hellman and Richard O'Gorman. New York: Thomas Y. Crowell, 1965.

Fedi, Roberto. 'Il "regno" di Filostrato: Natura e struttura della Giornata IV del *Decameron.*' *MLN* 102 (1987): 39–54.

Felman, Shoshana. *The Literary Speech Act: Don Juan with J.L. Austin, or Seduction in Two Languages.* Trans. Catherine Porter. Ithaca: Cornell University Press, 1983.

Felman, Shoshana, and Dori M. Laub, MD. *Testimony: Crises of Witnessing in Literature, Psychoanalysis, and History.* New York: Routledge, 1992.

Fido, Franco. 'Architettura.' In Pier Massimo Forni and Renzo Bragantini, eds, *Lessico critico decameroniano,* 13–33. Turin: Bollati Boringhieri, 1995.

– *Il regime delle simmetrie imperfette: Studi sul 'Decameron.'* Milan: Franco Angeli, 1988.

Fleming, Ray. 'Happy Endings? Resisting Woman and the Economy of Love in Day Five of Boccaccio's *Decameron.*' *Italica* 70 (1993): 30–45.

Fo, Dario. *Manuale minimo dell'attore.* Ed. Franca Rame. New ed. Turin: Einaudi, 1997 (1987).

– *The Tricks of the Trade.* Trans. Joe Farrell. Ed., with notes, Stuart Hood. London: Methuen, 1991.

Freccero, Carla. 'Rape's Disfiguring Figure: Marguerite de Navarre's *Heptameron,* Day 1: 10.' In Lynn A. Higgins and Brenda R. Silver, eds, *Rape and Representation,* 227–47. New York: Columbia University Press, 1991.

Freud, Sigmund. 'From the History of an Infantile Neurosis (1918 [1914]).' In *The Standard Edition of the Complete Psychological Works.* Trans. James Strachey. 24 vols. London: Hogarth Press, 1966–74. Vol. 17: 1–123.

Gallop, Jane. *Feminist Accused of Sexual Harassment.* Durham: Duke University Press, 1997.

Gelles, Richard J., and Murray A. Straus. *Intimate Violence.* New York: Simon & Schuster, 1988.

Gerbert de Montreuil. *Roman de la violette ou de Gerard de Nevers.* Paris: Champion, 1928.

Germano, Joseph E. 'La fonte letteraria della peste decameroniana: Per una storia della critica delle fonti.' *Italian Quarterly* 27 (1986): 21–30.

Getto, Giovanni. *Vita di forme e forme di vita nel 'Decameron.'* 4th rev. ed. Turin: Petrini, 1986.

Gianoli, Luigi. *Il cavallo e l'uomo. Il cavallo nella storia antica, nel medioevo e nel rinascimento. Le scuole, le Olimpiadi, la didattica, il galoppo, il trotto, il polo, la caccia, le razze.* Milan: Longanesi, 1967.

Gilligan, Carol. *In a Different Voice: Psychological Theory and Women's Development.* Cambridge, Mass.: Harvard University Press, 1982.

Gravdal, Kathryn. *Ravishing Maidens: Writing Rape in Medieval French Literature and Law.* Philadelphia: University of Pennsylvania Press, 1991.

Greene, Thomas M. 'Forms of Accommodation in the *Decameron.*' *Italica* 45 (1968): 297–312.

Grimaldi, Emma. *Il privilegio di Dioneo: L'eccezione e la regola nel sistema 'Decameron.'* Naples: Edizioni Scientifiche Italiane, 1987.

Grosz, Elizabeth. 'Voyeurism/Exhibitionism/The Gaze.' In Elizabeth Wright, ed., *Feminism and Psychoanalysis: A Critical Dictionary,* 447–50. Oxford: Basil Blackwell, 1992.

Güntert, Georges. *Tre premesse e una dichiarazione d'amore: Vademecum per il lettore del 'Decameron.'* Modena: Mucchi, 1997.

Hamilton, Mykol C. 'Using Masculine Generics: Does Generic "He" Increase Male Bias in the User's Imagery?' *Sex Roles* 19 (1988): 785–99.

Hamilton, M.C., Barbara Hunter, and Shannon Stuart-Smith. 'Jury Instructions Worded in the Masculine Generic: Can a Woman Claim Self-Defense When "He" is Threatened? (1992).' In Camille Roman, Suzanne Juhasz, and Cristanne Miller, eds, *The Women and Language Debate: A Sourcebook,* 340–7. New Brunswick, NJ: Rutgers University Press, 1994.

A History of Women in the West. General editors Georges Duby and Michelle Perrot. 5 vols. Cambridge, Mass.: Harvard University Press, 1992–4.

Hollander, Robert. *Boccaccio's Dante and the Shaping Force of Satire.* Ann Arbor: University of Michigan Press, 1997.

The Holy Bible: Douay Version. Trans. from Latin Vulgate (Douay, AD 1609; Rheims, AD 1582); preface by the Cardinal Archbishop of Westminster. 1956; reprt. London: Catholic Truth Society, 1963.

Irigaray, Luce. *Sexes and Genealogies*. Trans. Gillian C. Gill. New York: Columbia University Press, 1993.

Jed, Stephanie H. *Chaste Thinking: The Rape of Lucretia and the Birth of Humanism*. Bloomington: Indiana University Press, 1989.

Jones, Ann Rosalind. 'New Songs for the Swallow: Ovid's Philomela in Tullia D'Aragona and Gaspara Stampa.' In Marilyn Migiel and Juliana Schiesari, eds, *Refiguring Woman: Perspectives on Gender and the Italian Renaissance*, 263–77. Ithaca: Cornell University Press, 1991.

Kirkham, Victoria. *The Sign of Reason in Boccaccio's Fiction*. Florence: Olschki, 1993.

Klapisch-Zuber, Christiane. 'Zacharias, or the Ousted Father: Nuptial Rites in Tuscany between Giotto and the Council of Trent.' *In Women, Family, and Ritual in Renaissance Italy*, 178–212. Trans. Lydia G. Cochrane. Chicago: University of Chicago Press, 1985.

Kleinhenz, Christopher. 'Stylistic Gravity: Language and Prose Rhythms in the *Decameron* I, 4.' *The Humanities Association Review* 26 (1975): 289–99.

Kohlberg, Lawrence, Charles Levine, and Alexandra Hewer. *Moral Stages: A Current Formulation and a Response to Critics*. Basel: Karger, 1983.

Lanser, Susan S. 'Toward a Feminist Narratology.' In Robin R. Warhol and Diane Price Herndl, eds, *Feminisms: An Anthology of Literary Theory and Criticism*, 610–29. New Brunswick, NJ: Rutgers University Press, 1991.

Laufenberg, Lynn Marie. 'Women, Crime, and Criminal Law in Fourteenth-century Florence.' Unpub. PhD dissertation, Cornell University, 2000.

Lee, A.C. *The 'Decameron': Its Sources and Analogues*. London: David Nutt, 1909. Reprt. New York: Haskell House Publishers, 1972.

Lessico critico decameroniano. Ed. Pier Massimo Forni and Renzo Bragantini. Turin: Bollati Boringhieri, 1995.

Lombardi, Giancarlo. 'Boccaccio e Camus.' Unpub. graduate seminar paper, Cornell University, 1991.

Lucente, Gregory. 'The Fortunate Fall of Andreuccio da Perugia.' *Forum Italicum* 10 (1976): 323–44.

Marchese, Angelo. 'Strutture narrative della I giornata del *Decameron*.' In *Metodi e prove strutturali*, 248–53. Milan: Principato, 1974.

Marcus, Millicent J. *An Allegory of Form: Literary Self-consciousness in the 'Decameron*.' Saratoga, Calif.: Anma Libri, 1979.

– 'An Allegory of Two Gardens: The Tale of Madonna Dianora (*Decameron* X, 5).' *Forum Italicum* 14 (1980): 162–74.

– 'Faith's Fiction: A Gloss on the Tale of Melchisedech (*Decameron* I, 3).' *Canadian Journal of Italian Studies* 2 (1978–9): 40–55.

– 'Misogyny As Misreading: A Gloss on *Decameron* VIII, 7.' *Stanford Italian Review* 4 (1984): 23–40.

Mazzotta, Giuseppe. *The World at Play in Boccaccio's 'Decameron.'* Princeton: Princeton University Press, 1986.

Migiel, Marilyn. 'Beyond Seduction: A Reading of the Tale of Alibech and Rustico (*Decameron* III, 10).' *Italica* 75 (1997): 161–77.

– 'Giovanni Boccaccio (1313–1374).' In Rinaldina Russell, ed., *The Feminist Encyclopedia of Italian Literature*, 30–3. Westport, Conn.: Greenwood Press, 1997.

– 'How (thanks to a woman) Andreuccio da Perugia became such a loser, and how (also thanks to a woman) reading could have become a more complicated affair.' *Romance Languages Annual* 10 (1999): 302–7.

– 'The Untidy Business of Gender Studies: Or, Why It's Almost Useless to Ask if the *Decameron* is Feminist.' In F. Regina Psaki and Thomas C. Stillinger, eds, *Boccaccio and Feminist Criticism*. Forthcoming in the *Annali d'Italianistica* book series.

– 'Writing (Not Drawing) a Blank.' In Jonathan Monroe, ed., *Local Knowledges, Local Practices: Writing in the Disciplines at Cornell*. Pittsburgh: University of Pittsburgh Press, 2003.

Mineo, Nicolò Mineo. 'La sesta giornata del *Decameron* o del potere delle donne.' *Rivista europea di letteratura italiana* 3 (1994): 49–68.

Moi, Toril. *What Is a Woman? And Other Essays.* Oxford: Oxford University Press, 1999.

Muraro, Luisa. *L'ordine simbolico della madre.* Rome: Editori Riuniti, 1992.

Il Novellino: Testo critico, introduzione e note. Ed. Guido Favati. Genoa: Fratelli Bozzi, 1970.

Padoan, Giorgio. 'Mondo aristocratico e mondo communale nell'ideologia e nell'arte di Giovanni Boccaccio.' In *Il Boccaccio, le Muse, il Parnaso e l'Arno*, 1–91. Florence: Olschki, 1978.

Paris, Gaston. 'Le Cycle de la Gageure.' *Romania* 32 (1903): 481–551.

Partner, Nancy F. 'No Sex, No Gender.' In Nancy F. Partner, ed., *Studying Medieval Women*, 117–41. Cambridge, Mass.: Medieval Academy of America, 1993.

Paul, the Deacon (Paulus Diaconus). *History of the Langobards.* Trans. William Dudley Foulke. Philadelphia: University of Pennsylvania [Department of History], 1907.

– *Pauli Historia Langobardorum.* Hannover: Impensis Bibliopolii Hahniani, 1878.

Pennington, Kenneth. 'A Note to *Decameron* VI 7: The Wit of Madonna Filippa.' *Speculum* 52 (1977): 902–5.

Picone, Michelangelo. 'Lettura macrotestuale della prima giornata del *Decameron*.' In Tatiana Crivelli, ed., *'Feconde venner le carte': Studi in onore di Ottavio Besomi*. 2 vols. Bellinzona: Casagrande, 1997. Vol. 1: 107–22.

Potter, Jonathan. *Representing Reality: Discourse, Rhetoric and Social Construction.* London: Sage, 1996.

Potter, Joy Hambuechen. *Five Frames for the 'Decameron': Communication and Social Systems in the 'Cornice.'* Princeton: Princeton University Press, 1982.

– 'Woman in the *Decameron.*' In Gian Paolo Biasin, Albert N. Mancini, and Nicolas J. Perella, eds, *Studies in the Italian Renaissance: Essays in Memory of Arnolfo B. Ferruolo,* 87–103. Naples: Società Editrice Napoletana, 1985.

Prospettive sul 'Decameron.' Ed. Giorgio Bàrberi-Squarotti. Turin: Tirrenia, 1989.

Psaki, F. Regina. 'Women in the *Decameron.*' In James H. McGregor, ed., *Approaches to Teaching Boccaccio's 'Decameron,'* 79–86. New York: The Modern Language Association of America, 2000.

Pugliese, Guido. '*Decameron* II, 3: Un caso di contingenza causale.' *Esperienze letterarie* 5:4 (1980): 29–41.

Restaino, Franco, and Adriana Cavarero. *Le filosofie femministe.* Turin: Paravia Scriptorium, 1999.

Rizzo, James N. 'An Essay on Subjectivity and Trauma.' Unpub. A.B. thesis, Cornell University, 1995.

Robert's Rules of Order, Newly Revised (1990 edition). Glenview, Ill.: Scott, Foresman & Co., 1990.

Le Roman du Roi Flore et de la belle Jeanne. Due novelle antiche anteriori al 'Decameron' del Boccaccio che servirono d'argomento a due bellissime istorie contenute in esso in divin libro. Genoa: n.p., 1859.

Rossi, Luciano. 'L'evoluzione dell'intreccio: Bouvin e Andreuccio.' *Filologia e critica* 1 (1976): 5–14.

Sartre, Jean-Paul. *Being and Nothingness: An Essay on Phenomenological Ontology.* Trans. Hazel E. Barnes. London: Methuen, 1957.

Savelli, Giulio. 'Riso.' In Renzo Bragantini and Pier Massimo Forni, eds, *Lessico critico decameroniano,* 344–71. Turin: Bollati Boringhieri, 1995.

Scaglione, Aldo. *Nature and Love in the Middle Ages.* Berkeley: University of California Press, 1963.

Schilling, Bernard N. 'The Fat Abbot.' In *The Comic Spirit: Boccaccio to Thomas Mann,* 21–42. Detroit: Wayne State University Press, 1965.

Scott, Joan Wallach. *Gender and the Politics of History.* New York: Columbia University Press, 1988.

Sedgwick, Eve Kosofsky. *Epistemology of the Closet.* Berkeley: University of California Press, 1990.

Segre, Cesare. 'Functions, Oppositions, and Symmetries in Day VII of the *Decameron.*' In *Structures and Time: Narration, Poetry, Models,* 94–120. Trans. John Meddemmen. Chicago: University of Chicago Press, 1979.

- 'Funzioni, opposizioni e simmetrie nella Giornata VII del *Decameron.*' *Studi sul Boccaccio* (1971): 81–108.

Shippey, Thomas Alan. 'Listening to the Nightingale.' *Comparative Literature* 22 (1970): 46–60.

Silverla, Jeannette. 'Generic Masculine Words and Thinking.' In Cheris Kramarae, ed., *The Voices and Words of Women and Men*, 165–78. Oxford: Pergamon Press, 1980.

Smarr, Janet Levarie. *Boccaccio and Fiammetta: The Narrator as Lover.* Urbana: University of Illinois Press, 1986.

Spackman, Barbara. '*Inter musam e ursam moritur*: Folengo and the Gaping "Other" Mouth.' In Marilyn Migiel and Juliana Schiesari, eds, *Refiguring Woman: Perspectives on Gender and the Italian Renaissance*, 19–34. Ithaca: Cornell University Press, 1991.

Stassi, Maria Gabriella. 'Amore e "industria": III Giornata.' In Giorgio Bàrberi-Squarotti, ed., *Prospettive sul 'Decameron,'* 39–58. Turin: Tirrenia, 1989.

Stefani, Marchione di Coppo. *Cronaca fiorentina.* Vol. 30 of *Rerum Italicarum Scriptores.* Ed. Niccolò Rodolico. Città di Castello: S. Lapi, 1903.

Stefanini, Ruggero. 'La leggenda di Sant'Eugenia e la novella d'Alessandro (*Dec.* II, 3): L'esibizione apologetica del seno nella tradizione narrativa, con un "excursus" sulla "fortuna" nell'opera di Boccaccio.' *Romance Philology* 33 (1980): 338–410.

Stewart, Pamela D. 'La novella di Madonna Oretta e le due parti del *Decameron.*' *Yearbook of Italian Studies*, 1973–5: 27–40.

Suzuki, Mihoko. 'Gender, Power, and the Female Reader: Boccaccio's *Decameron* and Marguerite de Navarre's *Heptameron.*' *Comparative Literature Studies* 30 (1993): 231–52.

Tannen, Deborah. 'The Relativity of Linguistic Strategies: Rethinking Power and Solidarity in Gender and Dominance.' In *Gender and Discourse*, 19–52. Oxford: Oxford University Press, 1994.

Van der Woort, Cok. 'Convergenze e divaricazioni tra la Prima e la Sesta Giornata del *Decameron.*' *Studi sul Boccaccio* 11 (1979): 207–41.

Vasvari, Louise O. '*L'usignuolo in gabbia*: Popular Tradition and Pornographic Parody in the *Decameron.*' *Forum Italicum* 28:2 (Fall 1994): 224–51.

Veneziano, Gian Mario. 'La cornice a teatro: VI Giornata.' In Giorgio Bàrberi-Squarotti, ed., *Prospettive sul 'Decameron,'* 97–111. Turin: Tirrenia, 1989.

Vickers, Nancy J. 'Diana Described: Scattered Woman and Scattered Rhyme.' In Elizabeth Abel, ed., *Writing and Sexual Difference*, 94–109. Chicago: University of Chicago Press, 1982.

Wallace, David. *Giovanni Boccaccio: 'Decameron.'* Cambridge: Cambridge University Press, 1993.

Wofford, Susanne L. 'The Social Aesthetics of Rape: Closural Violence in Boccaccio and Botticelli.' In David Quint, Margaret W. Ferguson, G.W. Pigman III, and Wayne Rebhorn, eds, *Creative Imitation: New Essays on Renaissance Literature in Honor of Thomas M. Greene*, 189–238. Binghamton: State University of New York Press, 1992.

Woman Defamed and Woman Defended: An Anthology of Medieval Texts. Ed. Alcuin Blamires with Karen Pratt and C.W. Marx. Oxford: Clarendon Press, 1992.

Woolf, Virginia. *A Room of One's Own*. New York: Harcourt, Brace and World, 1929.

Zandrino, Barbara. 'La luna per lo sole (VII Giornata).' In Giorgio Bàrberi-Squarotti, ed., *Prospettive sul 'Decameron,'* 113–30. Turin: Tirrenia, 1989.

Zecchi, Barbara. 'Rape.' In Rinaldina Russell, ed., *The Feminist Encyclopedia of Italian Literature*, 280–3. Westport, Conn.: Greenwood Press, 1997.

Zingarelli, Nicola. *Lo Zingarelli 2003: Vocabolario della lingua italiana*. 12th ed. Bologna: Zanichelli, 2002.

Index